African Union
Pan African Analytical
Foundations

Published by
Adonis & Abbey Publishers Ltd
P.O. Box 43418
London
SE11 4XZ
http://www.adonis-abbey.com

First Edition January 2006

British Library Cataloguing-in-Publication Data
A catalogue record for this book is available from the British Library

ISBN   0-905068-16-6 (paperback)
          0-905068-17-4 (Cloth)

Cover Design: MegaGraphix

Printed and bound in Great Britain by Lightning Source UK Ltd.

African Union
Pan African Analytical
Foundations

By Kofi Kissi Dompere

Adonis & Abbey
Publishers Ltd

Dedication

To the children of Africa whose future
Rests firmly in the hands of African thinkers
And practirioners of true African thinking system;

To Mother Africa whose
Past, present and future glory
Lies in the uniting forces of her children
In mind, body and sprit and
In AfricanTrinity of
Creative Force, Spirit Force and Light Force.

To the Pan-Africanists whose struggle against
Imperial oppression, injustice and racism
Is a constant reminder of
Africa's golden tomorrow.

To the Casssablanca group whose
Vision of continental African government
As a strategy of full spectrum resistance,
Against full spectreum imperial dominance must
Sustain Africa's strength, courage, hope and wisdom;

To Kwame Nkrumah whose
Vision and wisdom were misunderstood
By African intellectuals and political elite.

And to the courageous Africans who perished in the Atlantic Crossing,;
and to the Africans and their descendants whose forced Free labor went to
enrich other lands and emporvirished Africa.
You are gunue branches and fruits of our Ancestral Tree.

To Africa Must Unite and Afican Union!!!

ACKNOWLEDGEMENTS

I wish to express my thanks to all my friends who one way or the other have given me encouragements and emotional support as I tried to clear some logical haze surrounding global politics and African difficulties. My special thanks go to my mother Adwo Fosua and father Kwasi Kissi who gave encouragements during my primary school days. I give my gratitude to Professor Akwasi Osei of Delaware State University, Professor Mbaye Cham of Howard University and Professor Kwame Botwe-Asamoa of Pittsburg University for their encouragements and interests in my work on cognitive foundations of Africa's philosophy and unity as they relate to Africa's emancipation; and their constant insistence that my work be presented and shared with academic organizations of African Studies, Africana studies, Black Studies, Pan-African Studies and Afrcan-American studies. I am especially grateful to Professor Molife Kete Asante of Temple University for inviting me to present part of the monograph at Diop Conference in Philadelphia. I am also grateful to my graduate and undergraduate students whose energy flows have been the sources of encouragements for my remaining at Howard University with a deep sense of fulfillment. Great thanks to Ms Modupe Fadope for editorial suggestions on the first draft. I also thank Ms Mary McCalop for secretarial support.

Controversial ideas and terminologies are intentional and intentionally directed to restructure the paradigm of contemporary African individual and collective thinking that has become problematic in decision-choice space whose outcomes invariably define the path of peoples' progress and history. I accept responsibility for any error that may arise in the arguments.

TABLE OF CONTENTS

PREAMBLE

THE AFRICAN

Just as I am!
Just as I am –
Counted with those who breathe,
You cannot break my bone
Just as you can
Not scan the sun;
Let watching witches watch
And leave my brook to bark!
Just as I am!
Just as I am –
In eyes of those who see,
You cannot grade my grain
Just as you can
Not catch the wind;
So let fighting flies fight
And leave my land to lie!
Just as I am!

Just as I am –
Counted with those with limbs,
You cannot catch my cow
Just as you can
Not arrest clouds;
Let singing lizards sing,
And let my grass to green
Just as I am!
Just as I am –
To touch of those who feel,
You cannot sing my song
Just as you can

Not hold the air;
So let standing stones stand
And leave my cooks to crow!
Just as I am!

Just as I am –
To noses of those who smell,
You cannot sail my sea
Just as you can
Not reach the sky;
Let falling fairies fall
And leave my fish to float!

Just as I am!
Just as I am –
Counted with those who walk,
You cannot shake my spear
Just as you can
Not count the stars;
So let crawling cows crawl
And leave my mind to move!
Just as I am!

Just as I am –
Counted with those with tongue,
You cannot face my foe
Just as you can
Not drink the dam;
Let wailing wizard wail
And leave my waves to break!
Just as I am!
Just as I am –
In ears of those who hear,
You cannot burn my bush
Just as you can
Not count the ants?
So let swimming sheep swim
And leave my stars to shine!
Just as I am!

Just as I am –
Counted with those with hearts,
You cannot know my woe
Just as you can
Not drink the dam;
Let fading flowers fade
And leave my seed to sink!
Just as I am!
Just as I am –
To minds of men who think,
You cannot cut my corn
Just as you can
Not count the sand;
So let talking trees talk
And leave my goats to graze!

JOHN OKAI. (From Okyeame, *Ghana's Literary Magazine*, Vol. 4, No. 1, 1968, pp 30 – 31.)

PREFACE

I have always had the tendency toward writing long prefaces to my books. This tendency stems from my cognitive orientation as to the role that a preface can and must play in the communicational process between the author and his or her audience. The preface, by making explicit the motivation of the book, historic evolution and the intentions of the author, provides the necessary unity of cognitive purpose that establishes among other things the preconceptions and objectives of the author. The preface of this book, therefore, will not be exception.

After an intensive and extensive study of the literature on Pan-Africanism, examination of its policy practice and critical analysis of contemporary African problems, I became convinced that the monumental flood of discussions on questions. On African unity through the Pan-African ideology and Africentric conceptual system the African political practitioners, educators and clergy have not fully and seriously appreciated the accumulated output of the African-centered intellectuals. This unfortunate state has made me very much aware that the task of practicing Pan-Africanism has been made much more difficult without the philosophical understanding of the African essence and the African unity that it commands. Here the real difficulty lies in the philosophical understanding of Africa's social formation from Africentric position and how such an understanding will help to illuminate the nature and behavior of internal and external constraints on application of the Pan-African thinking system.

I am of the opinion that the organizational mindset that fosters a new and important ethnicity and tribalism has become important imprints of African political mind and personality of decision making. Such a mindset that sees Africa in terms of governments of colonial territories and the artificial boundaries that these predators have established needs to be dislodged at the level of cognition. This level of cognition must lead to the development of an Africentric thinking system that will confront the held views of African nationalism that is cast as territory-specific and demolish them at the level of philosophical thinking and politico-economic theory.

This Africentric thinking system in terms of politics, law and economics must redefine African nationalism that is unity-supportive, and assert the vision of the all encompassing Pan-African nationalism where its relationships to the state-specific nationalism, ethnic affinity and tribal communities are explicitly amplified for political and economic understanding. The task, then, is to construct an Africentric position at the level of philosophical reasoning that will dislodge this colonial mindset, set free the forces of unity and at the same time provides guidance to the most, important and difficult phase of Africa's complete emancipation which is Africa or the African Union.

We must understand that the long dependence on Eurocentric thinking system that has been created to assert European dominance has prevented and continued to prevent the independent growth and refinement of philosophical skills essential in reconstituting African social formation on the basis of African traditions that can be modernized in accordance with Africa's needs, progress , humanism and moral codes in order to deal with true sustainable socioeconomic development and the threats of imperial predation.

This does not deny our right, to utilize certain tools that belong to the general intellectual history of humanity to which Africa's foundation is as monumental as her historic landmarks. These tools of common intellectual heritage of humanity must be reshaped by a process of creative thinking in order to allow them to be of effective service to Africa's emancipation, unity and social and institutional reconstruction for Africa's progress.

The fact remains that the solutions to African problems can only be found in Africa and only in African unity. This book makes a philosophical case for it. By appealing to Pan-African nationalism the analytical construct accepts the essential fact that we are all Africans and have common interests in making Africa as great as she was. And not only that, but we are responsible for ourselves and all other Africans irrespective of place of birth and residence and in accordance with the African tradition of *each for all and all for each* under one Creative Force, Spirit Force and Light Force but not *each for himself and God for us all*. The former statement takes the community as the primary category of reality and the individuals as derived category of reality. The latter involves a situation where the individual is viewed as the primary category of reality and the community as derived.

The current trend of political instabilities in Africa, economic globalization and formation of mega groups teaches us some important lessons. One of the lessons is simply each African state in the current separatist form is surrounded by plethora of windows of woundarability that endangers her economic development and growth in this global trend of capitalism to which I have provided extensive discussions [44a]. Another important lesson is that most of these windows of woundurability can only be closed for protection of each African state only when African states accept the traditional African wisdom of each for all and all for each, and work together as a team and in an inseparable unity.

At this point in African history the fear and predictions of Nkrumah [105][107] and Diop [40] have been realized in that Africa is not only Balkanized but South-Americanized where Africa would be made up of a proliferation of litter dictator-ridden countries without organic ties one to another, ephemeral, afflicted with chronic weakness, governed by terror with the help of outsized police forces, but under economic domination by foreign countries, pulling strings through the mere presence of an embassy. It is these Balkanization, South-Americanization and the lack of political will to reconstitute Africa in unity along the Pan-African ideals that have exacerbated poverty, famine, useless wars and untold suffering of the African masses who are appealing to the African political elite for relief. Thus all things considered, Pan-African nationalism emerges as the dialectical moment that would induce Africa's progressive transformation while at the same time guarantee peace, stability and security for individual states and the federation without which economic and spiritual prosperity will always be wanting.

Pan-African nationalism imposes on us race consciousness. It demands African unity and Pan-African-centered ideological consciousness. African unity is not a simple vision of Africa's tomorrow but a map of emancipation. Its visionary map is a potential. It is a living essence of Africa's golden path to the land of true emancipation. As a potential it must, therefore, be actualized in practice in the sense of categorial conversion from categories of potentialities to elements of reality. This actualization must stem from the yearning need of Africans to forge ahead the building of Greater Africa. Here the Pan-African intellectuals must stand firm, sharpen their cognitive tools and fine-tune them to wither the intellectual storm by first philosophically re-Africanized our minds and collective personality to truly excavate the required transformational path that our history and contemporary problems impose on our cognition.

This book, *African Union,* is a companion volume to *Polyrhythmicity: Foundations of African Philosophy.* Both of them arise as an extensive and improved exposition of certain critical issues that space and time did not allow me to discuss in my book Africentricity. Polyrhythmicity establishes an Africentric philosophical essence on the basis of which the theoretical arguments in the book on African Union are constructed. The objective here is to make a case that at the core of African complete emancipation, independence and development is African unity, which is engendered by Pan-African nationalism.

This book is, therefore, organized in a manner where Chapter 1 introduces the subject of interest. Chapter 2 discusses other views of African Nationalism. Chapter 3 deals with the Africentric concept of African nationalism that establishes the basic conceptual foundation of Pan-African nationalism. African nationalism and state-specific nationalism are compared and contrasted in Chapter 4. Chapter 5 is devoted to explicit analytics of differences among state-specific nationalism, ethnic affinity and tribalism and the positive and negative roles that they can play in establishing the Pan-African nationalism and the transformation path toward Africa's complete emancipation.

The organizational constraints on the unity process, from within and without, are treated under the title of the Theory of Crony Imperialism in Chapter 6. Here we bring into light the working mechanism of the global imperial system and the constraints that it places upon the Africa's path to freedom, justice and complete emancipation. The roles of the political leaders, intelligentsia and clergy are examined in relation to the neocolonial destructive-constructive process of predation. This allows us to discuss the concept of *negrosis,* negative role that political, intellectual and religions askari and zombies play in impoverishing and bringing suffering to the African masses in disunited Africa. Chapter 7 is devoted to the African nationalist agenda where the basic structure for the Nkrmaist model of Africa's complete emancipation through African unity is presented as a solution to current African difficulties as well as a struggle against crony imperialism. The book is concluded with Chapter 8 that deals with reflections, comments and conclusions.

The book, thus, makes a case for African unity and African nationalism that is all encompassing without which, I am convinced beyond any reasonable doubt, that the African people will wonder in the barren lands of pure spiritual, cognitive and material emptiness. All controversial ideas in this book are intentional, which I hope will motivate other intellectual works in line with Africentric scholarship. Here we must keep at the forefront of Africentric thinking: "Africa must unite.' We have before us not only an opportunity but also a historic duty to actualize its potential. We must understand that the imperial predators will work against African Unity and for Africa's disunity while they unite their forces for intensive and extensive predation in the global resource space of which Africa is an excellent contributor. They will continue to present Africa socio-economic policies as irrational that lead to lack of development. They will not mention and discuss their role in creating poverty and underdevelopment in this resource-rich continent of ours. They will present themselves as missionaries of socio-economic development, technical assistence and philantropy in bringing relief to the suffering Africa.

1

GENERAL INTRODUCTION

All human emancipations of social significance that are of lasting nature begin with the emancipation of the mind. In so far as the mind, the regulator of action and behavior, is in bondage so also is everything that is connected to it such as the spiritual and physical selves. Emancipation of the subjugated is about something fundamental and critical. That something is the mind. True emancipation begins with freeing the mind from ignorance and forces that hold it in servitude. Africa's complete emancipation thus must begin with the development of a relevant thinking system that will unleash cognitively progressive forces to combat dependency syndrome and slave mentality. This relevant thinking system defines a philosophical system, which we shall refer to as polyrhythmicity in Chapter 2, with its support Africentricity, both of which are discussed fully in chapter 3 of a companion volume [44b].

In this book, we wish to present a particular conceptual position of African nationalism and relate it to the concept of Africentricity, African personality and African unity on the basis of which the African Union must be structured and nurtured for growth and development. It is a position that we believe does not only satisfy a number of conditions external to the subject matter of Africa's complete emancipation and applications that may be required for success of revolutionary positive actions, but also elucidates the psychological forces of inner and external selves that must be enlisted and mobilized to set free all Africans and their descendants around the globe. Even though the book looks at the past, present and the future, the main analytical and conceptual focus is Africa's tomorrow.

We will argue that African nationalism and African unity are inseparable in concept and practice within the Nkrumaist decision scheme to emancipate Africa and her children. African nationalism and African unity are viewed as mirror images of one another where one is a complete reflection of the other. To demonstrate this, the notions of African Unity and African nationalism must be clear and sharp. Their relationships to Pan-Africanism must be easily seen and logically structured relative to contemporary unfolding history of global conflicts, resource flows and imperial predation. The personality that functions in the choice-decision space to propel Africa forward must be sharply defined. The supporting thinking system must be African-centered. Education and institutions of learning must reflect African values, African unity and the problems and solutions of integration of the members of the African Union. A critical examination, however, of the extensive literature on Pan-Africanism, reveals the concept of African nationalism to be amorphous. It lacks a clear content that should give guidance to positive action and practice. The concept of African unity is also vague except the one advanced by Kwame Nkrumah [105] [114]. The works done by Duchein [50], Olugboji [123] and Diop [40] are important contributions to the concept of African unity while the works of Padmore [126], DuBois [42] and Garvey [59] provide foundations for Pan-African unity and African nationalism.

African nationalism as a concept that must instruct action and practice, therefore, needs to be restructured and made succinct if the practice of African unity, Pan-Africanism and African Union are to succeed and if the concepts of African unity and African nationalism are to be understood by the current and future generations of Africans, and to help those Africans that want to devote their lives to the struggle for their realization as well as bring about the complete emancipation of Africa and all her children around the globe. We shall examine the concept and meaning of African nationalism. Unlike other writers on African nationalism, we would like to examine the concept and meaning of African nationalism within the framework of Nkrumaism, African unity, the African Union and the Pan-African agenda that would lead to a complete integration and emancipation on political, economic, scientific and cultural fronts in terms of the success of the African Union.

The first task is to lay down the philosophical foundation of African nationalism. The second task is to relate this philosophical foundation to Africa's past and present political and economic realities as well as to future possibilities. In this respect, we shall examine the socio-political constraints, economic difficulties and external factors affecting the practice of African nationalism and how to overcome them. The process of overcoming these constraints and difficulties requires the development of tactics and strategies for action. These tactics and strategies must find residence in the African collective mind, African nationalism and African unity. In all these discussions, we will only mention or make reference to other writers in so far as their ideas are complementary to the development of the concept and meaning of African nationalism that we wish to advance. The intellectual tools that are fashioned here for implementing African nationalism and thus African Unity are abstracted from Africentricity and the philosophical polyrhythmicity guided by the logic of polyrhythmics whose rules of reasoning are found in relational dynamics.

Our goal is to provide extra and logically consistent ammunitions for the Nkrumaist and Pan-Africanist with the proper understanding of the concept and meaning of African nationalism that is relevant to overthrow the existing bankrupt order and dependency psychology and at the same time arm him or her with the required ideological consciousness that must guide the African unity movement and the struggle for complete African emancipation. Our objective is not to re-educate the Westerner, the European and the like, nor is it to pick ideological bones with them. We consider this as a useless expenditure of time, and a task not worthy of Africa's intellectual labor at the current point in time where the suffering, in all its forms, of all the dead African generations weighs heavily like Kilimanjaro on our thoughts and the thoughts of truly enlightened living Africans whose goals and objectives are to rescue Africa from the global madness of the constructed system of Africa's exploitation and demise.

We are convinced beyond all doubt that in order for African nationalism to guide action and thought in restructuring the African world and its relationships with others, it must constitute an unshakable principle backed by collective passion and commitment to Africa's tomorrow. Those Africans whose lives and practices must be guided by Africentric thinking should truly understand the meaning of the concept of African nationalism and how this must be related to the protracted and painful struggle to liberate Africa and its children from foreign domination, material poverty, cultural dilutions and technological backwardness. As the winds of Africa's ancient and modern past blow to the shores of Africa, they carry with them factually painful realities in that history is for the people and created by the people. Through the peoples' sweat and decisions the path of history is excavated not under the conditions that they choose but under those conditions that they are experiencing and have painfully experienced in the past through the outcomes of internal and external decision-information-interactive processes.

History is an output of change as well as an input of change. As an output it shows the efficiency of collective decisions of the society; as an input it reveals the limitations and possibilities of new collective endeavors. In both cases, history teaches us some important things about the state of our collective knowledge and ignorance, conditions of success and failure, our perceptive understanding and our actions toward the actual and potential. History, therefore, is a tool to wage wars against or in favor of oneself depending on the collective cognition and interpretation of historical facts. In the case of the task at hand these historic facts of Africa's past and social currents must be related to African nationalism and African Union. But what is African nationalism and what conceptual system holds it together? Let us turn our attention to African nationalism as the central principle of African union, keeping in mind that national history is nothing more than an enveloping of success-failure process in the choice-decision space with information entering as input from the actual-potential process.

2

OTHER VIEWS ON AFRICAN NATIONALISM

To get into the substance of our task, there are a few words that we would like to say about some views that have appeared on the concept of African nationalism. There are currently a number of literary works with "African nationalism" in the title [51a] [84b] [89] [94] [129b] [132]. Most of these works seems to be historical accounts of the African drive to dismantle colonialism and the imperial machine of exploitation, oppression and anti-democratic practices in Africa and to prepare the way to completely reclaim Africa for Africans. In other words, the anti-colonial movements on the Continent of Africa are considered as synonymous with African nationalism by these accounts and views. On the other hand, there are also some accounts and analyses that have come to view the anti-racist struggle against European racism and terrorism and the supporting racist satellite system as African nationalism. Even here, the struggle for human rights as we have outlined in a companion volume [43b] is viewed in terms of African nationalism instead of in terms of natural rights and human dignity.

2.1 Historical Reflections on the Rise of African Nationalism

On the question of history, much of these accounts is devoted to the analysis of the origins of African nationalism without explicitly defining the concept of African nationalism. In these accounts, the historical origins of African nationalism are drawn from the sociology of European racism which derives its epistemics from the philosophy of each against all and all against each and the theory of race superiority of the European people, as we have pointed out in the preface a companion book [43b] (see also [13]). Of course, the proponents of this theory of race superiority came to be known in the realms of struggle and under the eyes of egalitarians as imperialist anthropologists whose research work is to find some scientific documentation to justify the existence of racial inequality and false conception of God where Mary and Jesus are Europeanized contrary to the known historic accounts.

We must point out that even under the current conditions of so-called racial enlightenment there are constant efforts on the part of certain European scholars searching for a new logical system for presenting the same theory of racial superiority in a manner that would be palatable even to an enlightened African. In other words there is constant intellectual camouflage in support of racism and racial propaganda. The search continues on the part of certain European scholars and political practitioners not so much so as to find the scientific truth of racial differences but to find an acceptable logic for presenting the same foulest intellectual rubbish of racial superiority of the European as the global conditions alter. In this way, they can maintain the same age old racial propaganda against the African both at home and abroad. Ironically, however, other racial groups from Asia and Latin America have bought into this intellectual stupidity, and in fact have become collaborators in the propagation of this racial myth and propaganda. The success of such logical presentation will even arm some educated Africans not only to argue against themselves as a group but also to prepare the platforms for their own executions, as well as assisting the Europeans to execute other members of the African people as sacrifices to the satisfaction of the gods of Europeans and at the altar of racial superiority of Europeans. This is easily achieved by shaping the African mind to adopt epistemic paradigms of Europeans. The case in point is the new propaganda offensive taken by Western scientists against Africa. This new offensive stems from the abstracted origin of Acquired Immune Deficiency Syndrome (AIDS) which is attributed to Africa. Ironically, some African scientists have bought into and supported this propaganda offensive against Africans. They fail to point out that Africa is a victim to biological and germ warfare. This scientific propaganda on race research is particularly prevalent in the United States of America where every disease seems to originate from somewhere except America. So we have the "Russian flu", "Asian flu" and many more. On the other hand, democracy and civilized world are associated with the Western countries contrary to the accumulated facts of global history.

The fact of the matter is that the struggle against European racism, bigotry, injustice, slavery, racial violence and terrorism is not African nationalism. It is simply a human rights struggle. It was because the practices of racism, the orgy of genocide, oppression and slavery by Europeans were race-specific that they defined the historic origins of the African anti-European struggle so that it seems to other writers as though anti-colonialist struggle is African nationalism. On the contrary, the drive to demolish racism, unjust treatment and human exploitation is not African nationalism but simply the rise of collective consciousness of an oppressed people searching for freedom, justice and democracy in the way out of European imperial dictatorship and its epicenter of global injustice and oppression. Still, it is important to note that the presence and practice of European racism, directed particularly against Africa, and the vehicles of slavery and colonialism as instruments to effect the practice of such an orgy of racial brutalities, along with the use of Christianity and a false conception of God to promote the intellectual rubbish of racism are important historical contributing factors to the rise of an "unorganized" African collective consciousness. Such collective consciousness came as a spontaneous and localized response against European oppression, racial injustice and undemocratic practices in governance. Keep in mind that the Europeans entered Africa with violence and ruled with terror at all levels of institutions. To reduce Africa's resistance to occupation they destroyed all effective traditional institutions of governance and established rules of democracy and governance. In their place they imposed dictatorship and orgy of terror through violence. Furthermore, the struggle to democratize institutions of dictatorship left over from the colonial order has nothing to do with the value system of Western Nations. It is simply a struggle to reactivate the African traditional values of governance, statecraft and social management.

The lines of territorial partition of Africa following the Berlin Conference affected the demographic distribution of the Africans into the present African countries; they also affected the structure of distribution of European powers over that demographic distribution and the new African countries formed. Socioeconomic relations of a master-slave type were established between the two distributions where the Africans were on the slave end and the Europeans were on the master end of human exploitation. In terms of histography and logical sequence of events the socioeconomic relationships between the demographic distribution of Africans and the power distribution of the European governmental systems affected the nature and degree of human right abuses, colonial practices and the treatments of Africans. Such a nature and degree of human right abuses which took the form of slavery, coerced labor, execution of people, mistreatment, severing of limbs and legs, disruption of social order, distortions of history and many more over a period of time led to the rise of collective consciousness among African people irrespective of where they were, albeit at different junctures.

African people who lived under British colonialism, imperialism, racial bigotry and human rights abuses and authoritarianism rose against Britain as a matter of course. They could not have risen against the Soviets since the Africans have no history that relates to Soviet colonialism and slavery. Those Africans who, as a result of the created lines of demarcation, lived under the French, Portuguese and Belgium colonialism, imperialism, orgy of violence, and human-right abuses and undemocratic governance rose up against France, Portugal and Belgium. They could not have risen against the Chinese for the same reason as given above. Those Africans and their descendants who lived under the oppression, racial genocide, and human rights abuses in United States of America rose up against the United States of America as a matter of course. They could not have risen against the Vietnamese. All these Europeans participated in crimes against humanity. Our knowledge of the known history of human struggle does not reveal a single record where people rise against unfavorable conditions they have not experienced.

People rise up against conditions of suffering, but they do so under the confines of their experience and under conditions not chosen by them but rather under conditions that are encountered directly from the past and present, and projected into the future. The African struggle against imperialism and colonialism cannot be said to be free from the struggle against injustice of capitalism, racism and crimes against humanity. There is no historic basis for struggling against communism or socialism. Racism, slavery, colonialism and orgy of brutality as practiced against Africans did not take place under the conditions of communism or socialism. Africa does not have such a record of history.

We want to make this stated point clear. We want to emphasize it. There are times that we find ourselves disturbed about the type of

African intellectuals that we have so far produced. A number of them spend precious African hours to argue against communism without even understanding the simple historic relations between Africa's present state and the growth and development of capitalism, particularly that of Western Europe and North America. Neither have they understood the simple historic conditions among colonialism, slavery, and the European capitalist order and the current wealth of North America and Europe [150]. Africa's present state and current realities were not produced by socialism or communism; on the contrary, they were produced by the practices of the European capitalist and competitive imperial order. At that period of European imperial subjugation the traditional African sociopolitical and economic order was completely dislocated, millions of her children removed forcefully, packed like cargo into filthy ships destined to the Americas, and were then enslaved in the Americas to forced labor to produce wealth for Europeans in Europe and America through the triangular Atlantic Slave Trade. The resulting inhumanity and colonial forceful and brutal exploitation imposed on those left on the African continent paralyzed major African creative activities in all fronts of self-determination. It further diverted Africa from her natural path of socioeconomic development while her traditional democratic institutions were ravaged or destroyed with complete mode of governance destroyed. In place were erected alien non-democratic colonial institutions for exploitation and thievery. It is stupidity of the intellect and mockery of rationality to entertain the idea that the Europeans brought civilization and Christianity to Africa and Africans. This is a bankrupt ideological position that is not supported by history as we know it. How can one enslave and kill people in order to bring them to civilization and Christianity? Can we, with intellectual integrity and reasonable cognitive reflection on known global history, associate the rise of Christianity with Europe? What are the relationships among Judiasm, Christianity and theological and philosophical foundations of Pharaonic priesthood system (see [43d])? The situation is the same for today's argument where some imperial nations claim the divine righteousness to use weapons of mass killing on other peoples of different nationalities in order to bring them to the divine altar of democracy and development.

When people are under conditions of suffering and pain they gravitate toward anything except those that they are experiencing and those conditions of suffering that the past has revealed to them. Africa has no historic records of pain or pleasure under the conditions of communism; neither does she have records of such with other parts of the world except with Europe and her people. The African collective consciousness does not have roots in Russia; neither does it have roots in communism. The struggle was against injustice, racism, oppression and human-right abuses as perpetrated by Europeans through the apparatus of state terrorism. On the account of modern African history terrorism was a European invention as a method and technique against African resistance. The victimized were Africa and her children. The perpetrators and the victimizers were Europe and her people; particularly, Britain, France, Portugal, Belgium, Germany and the United States of America whose population was drawn from the imperial Great Britain, France, Portugal, Belgium, Germany and other parts of Europe under the self-appointed promoters of civilization and Christianity. The struggles of the Africans were against Europeans not because they originated from Europe or had different skin pigmentation but because they were the perpetrators of crimes against Africa, her children and humanity. The point of emphasis is that a wrong historiography and problem identification have built-in tendencies to draw African intellectual energies toward searching for solutions that have no relevance to Africa's current problem. This is because the African mind is controlled externally by Eurocentric system of thinking.

2.2 Africentric Thinking and the Analysis of African Nationalism

In terms of Africentric cosmology, the search for relevant solutions to Africa's problems in a complete field of ideological deception is a typical foolish person's paradox where the fool is surprised at not finding dung at a place where the cow never browsed. The African must be unshakably clear that the resistance to Africa's complete emancipation does not lie with communism or socialism; neither does it lie with Cuba, Russia or China. The resistance lies at the doorsteps of Europe, North America and their capitalist order which together created and produced the nutrients for Africa's current economic and social conditions. The manners in which these conditions are maintained with the model of Africa's effective resistance are discussed in the later chapters of this book.

The resistance aimed at creating a non-racial world economic and social order in the United States of America, in Great Britain, in Brazil, in Germany, in France, and many more countries does not lie at the doorsteps of Russia, China, communism, or socialism. The resistance lies at the doorsteps of the Europeans and the institutions of economic, social and intellectual control that they have temporarily managed to create as assets of subjugation and total control. The African must be clear about this portion of Africa's modern history. We are not arguing in support of communism or socialism. We are neither arguing in support of what was the socialist USSR and her governmental system. We do not have such luxury of time. These are trivial ideas discussed by the ideologues. I am an African whose main effort in theory and practice must be directed to handling the complexities of the African struggle toward Africa's complete emancipation. This task is not simple since the people we need to convince are the intellectually and culturally confused Africans but not Europeans. A similar trivial suggestion that we are against democracy is drawn by the same ideologues whenever and wherever we present the idea that there is no theoretical and empirical relationship between development and democracy as we have been made to believe. There is no nation or country - not Great Britain, not the United States of America, not France and the list continues - that can take claim to have developed through democracy. The factors that affect development do not include democracy. They however include ideology of good governance, political stability, dedication to nation building and other qualities on the part of the leadership and the collectivity of the populace. Democracy is not synonymous with capitalism or private property ownership. It is not a Western idea as popular discussion seems to suggest.

Within the African struggle against British, French, Portuguese and Belgium colonialism, and human rights abuses, as well as the oppression against Africans in the United States of America, the Caribbean and South America, the struggles were waged within the confines of a colonial system and the partition of Africa. Thus those Africans who happened by accident of history to live in the British colony of Gold Coast could not struggle together with their African brothers in Nigeria, Sierra Leone, and Gambia. Neither could these

Africans in the West Africa coordinate their struggle against British inhumanities, oppression and occupation with their brothers in Kenya, Northern and Southern Rhodesia, South Africa, Nyasaland, Bechuanaland, and others.

This unpleasant situation of African struggle was also true of the waves of French, Portuguese and Belgium colonialism and inhumanity. Ironically, the struggle to free all Africans from European oppression, racism and direct abuses of human rights could not be coordinated with Africans in the United States of America whose direct suffering stands unique in the history of the African world as well as the global history of human genocide. Neither could it be coordinated with the African people of the West Indies and South America, particularly those in Brazil. The Africans were terrorized, massacred and dehumanized. This is the European way of life wherever they have gone to in the globe. Even in these modern times of general global enlightenment of diplomacy, civility, human dignity and moral sensibility some Europeans and their descendents speak of democracy and still hold colonies and indulge in brutalities of overthrowing constitutionally elected governments in other parts of the world under lies, false accusations and demonizations.

The lines of imperial partition of Africa artificially imposed demographic lines of colonial and occupying partition on the African people. This led to the lines of partitions of African nationalism into state-specific forms in the process of the drive to decolonize Africa, reclaim her lands and free her citizens from the imperial grip. Thus we hear of Nigerian nationalism, Tanzanian nationalism, Angolan nationalism, Algerian nationalism, Egyptian nationalism, and others. These so-called independent countries did not exist in their currently defined forms until the European predators artificially made them up to suit their predatory interest in other to territorially establish European imperial colonial equilibrium. The "nationalisms" are simple sectionalisms that emerged from the rise of uncoordinated African collective consciousness against European colonialism, imperial order, terrorism, land seizures and crimes against humanity that produced Africa's disorder. These forms of nationalism cannot be considered as African nationalism in the true sense of Africa's emancipation where the Europeans brought barbarism instead of civilization and the worship of material things instead of the true worship of God.

It must be noted, in addition, that the conditions under which Africans struggled against colonialism and are still struggling against racism, exploitation and vestiges of colonialism are not of their own choosing; rather they are conditions that are encountered directly by the Africans through history. This must be understood clearly by every African at the present or in the future. We cannot neglect the footprints of facts as revealed by history. The redesigning of a new set of conditions required to favor victory in the African struggle over the imperial order and lack of meaningful development is a painful experience that must be shaped by a well structured program, as well as development of a clear understanding of the conditions that have molded the current historic state of Africa and her people and the Western resistance against anything that pulls Africa away from the Western sphere of influence, because the Europeans by tradition operate by four principles of ownership, exploitation, control or destruction (OECD).

2.3   The Rise of all Encompassing African Nationalism

Historically, across the Atlantic Ocean, in the hearts of the Americas, the interrelated institutional play of forces of European oppressions, terrorism, human-right abuses, execution of Africans, lynching, racism, and barbaric treatment of Africans entrenched in the economic, political, judicial and social life of the Europeans in the United States of America and the surrounding areas of the Americas and Europe itself gave rise to the germination of an important and powerful seed of all encompassing African nationalism [3b] [41b] [72b]. In passing, we must point out that the full colonization of Africa and its people by Europeans was not completed until after the end of the nineteenth century. Recall, for example, that the last war between the British and Ashantis led by Nana Yaa Asantewa ended in 1900 and that modern Ethiopia was not colonized.

It was not by accident that the seed of African collective consciousness encapsulated in pan-Africanism was sown by African descendants in the Caribbean and the United States of America. By their experience and painful suffering, lynching and brutalities at the hands of the entrenched Europeans, some enlightened ones yearned to be back to Africa to build it great from the ashes of her great history as they recalled. It was therefore not by any accident of history that the organic African nationalism was born in the soils of United States of

13

America and Caribbean. The rise of African nationalism and the agitation to stop European brutality, terror campaigns and orgy of genocide were unitary in their approach. It could not have been otherwise; the conditions were not chosen by them, but were chose by experiences encountered by them, imposed on them, transmitted from the past and seen by them through the eyes of the present day. In those areas of USA, Caribbean and South America where the African people and their descendants found themselves, they were always classified into the same group and called different names, the "Negroes". They were treated under the same harsh conditions of inhumanity in the mist of human existence by the Europeans. These conditions of inhumanity were conducted through the institutions of terror that the Europeans have established. The conditions were codified into their laws and back with order of violence through state power as well as given divine justifications through Christianity. These Africans saw some of their fellow Africans lynched, their feet severed, their women raped, their men castrated; they were considered not as humans but as possessions belonging to some European who claimed divine and economic mastership of their lives and labor. Slavery with violence and subjugation was given divine sanction.

The Africans were remanufactured and stamped "made in the Americas" with a special product name, slave. Classified into the same group, Africans and renamed Negroes, by a yardstick of skin pigmentation, by the place of origin and by the ships of their Trans-Atlantic journey, they were brutally treated as a group with barbarity with most uncivilized code of conduct. All their rights of human beings were denied to them, irrespective of whether their fathers, mothers and parents came from the Coast of Gold, the Coast of Slaves, the Coast of Ivory, the Basin of Congo, the Upper Nile or the Heart of the Sahara. This is not to argue that they should have been treated differently one group from the other, but rather to make the point that to the European the territorial origins of these Africans had no relevance to decision and treatment. Their background, African names, distinct cultures if any, or religious practices mattered not. What mattered to the Europeans was that they were Africans (Negroes) and, therefore, fit for dehumanization, humiliation, human rights abuses, and deprivation of all opportunities of freedom, justice, wealth formation and pursuit of happiness so that the European could profit from the African labor through slavery that was maintained by unjust laws, violence and fear.

To the eyes of their oppressors and predators they were all Negroes who came from Africa, had no names and spoke the language *"gambo-gambo"*. They had not made any contribution to human history; neither did they have civilization of their own. They had no culture. They were sub-humans whose energies must go to enrich the Europeans, the God-chosen people. This was constantly reinforced with the help of the Bible as the document that presents God's words and wishes through divine inspiration as it is claimed. Their human essence was completely stripped away, in ways justified by the Bible and enforced by the state power through the principle of law and order without justice, without fairness, and without compassion. For examples of these atrocities and crimes against humanity in America and Africa see [3b] [71a]. Naturally, the same harsh and brutal conditions were taking place under the same cruel hands of the Europeans in Africa itself. We will return to this point, but we want to remind the Africans and their descendents that all these Africans were and are the same people separated by historic conditions not of their choosing.

To this group of Africans, named by Europeans as "Negroes" in the Americas and adjoining islands, they saw themselves as sufferers, terrorized, oppressed and faced individual and collective annihilation at the hands of European inhumanities and barbarism, not because they had done anything against anyone, and not because they came from a particular place in Africa, but simply because they were all the same people, of the same race, "Negroes", from Africa as they were perceived (see for example [64b] [68b] [72b]). As Africans, they were, therefore, unilaterally judged to be guilty at the shrines of European terror and barbarism and condemned to slavery with hard labor by the Europeans who constituted the police, the prosecutors, the judges, jury, jailers and executioners. The crimes of the Africans were that they were endowed by their Creator with labor power that the Europeans needed to build wealth for themselves and their offsprings.

The Africans were condemned to a world of slavery and prison of human abuse for life without relief so that they would supply free and uninterrupted hard labor to enrich the Europeans and build the Western nations as divinely projected (see the preface of this book). Their charges were unknown to them and yet they were condemned to perpetual suffering at the altar of European supremacy by the laws of the European fabricated Holy Book, the Bible, and enforced by the political, legal and institutional system of the social order. Their crime, as it was to be understood by them latter, was and is still not of their own making. It was the crime of being African, and dark in their skin pigmentation, a creation of nature which has been demonized by a false conception of God, a conception that was forged from the true African theology. They did not see other people outside their group condemned to suffer at the same altar.

To these Africans outside Africa, the lines of demarcation were clear. They were Africans and must act together to liberate themselves as Africans. This was the driving force of the true African collective consciousness, a collective consciousness that had a unitary goal. The unitary goal was, however, very limiting with the general objective being merely the better and humane treatment of the Africans in the Americas. Even under these conditions some Africans thought of localized liberation. There were some that were more visionary and thought in terms of global African emancipation. The philosophical and theoretical basis of the unitary approach in terms of global African emancipation is what has come to be embraced as Pan-Africanism. It is a view that embraces the totality of the principle of African nationalism. Its supporting social thinking system we have shown to be Africentricity [43d].

This view and concept of African nationalism are all encompassing, revolutionary and destructive to the principle of divide and rule as practiced on continental Africa by the European colonialist, human rights abusers, mass murderers and diabolical tricksters. This all-encompassing concept of African nationalism and approach to Africa's emancipation were born in the fire of suffering at the altar of European racism, molded and shaped by the gods of "European race supremacy". There were important social exigencies that produced the fuel of quicker and correct analysis of the racial situation by the Africans in the Americas. These social exigencies included observable and non-observable conditions of the Africans operating within the same legal-political space with their oppressors in United States of America and other parts of the Americas. The exigencies included the conditions where the Africans had the empirical basis of comparative differential treatment of Africans and the people of European descent. The very nature of the situation with observable and non-observable conditions of Africans and sharing the same political space with their oppressors in the USA and other parts of the Americas, and having the empirical basis of comparative differential treatments of Africans and Europeans, produced the fuel for quicker analysis of the effectiveness of collective will of these Africans and their descendants toward collective African emancipation. This, we are afraid, the Africans at home have not come to understand with foundational appreciation. Neither do they have the knowledge and appreciation of the European brutalities and genocide against the Africans and their descendants in the Americas, for lack of information.

2.4 The Rise of Territory-specific Nationalism

When we turn our attention to Africa itself, a different picture of the rise of African collective consciousness emerges. The revolt against unjust treatment of and undemocratic governance over the Africans was territory-specific and confined within the colonial set-up and limited by the experience of the people. The original aims and goals of the collective consciousness on the mainland Africa, however, were broader.

They were not directed toward better and humane treatment of the Africans. They were directed toward reclaiming Africa - to reclaim the land, its people, its culture, and its destiny without which freedom has no meaning. Hence there were agitations for self rule but within the confines of the lines of partition. The philosophical and logical foundation of this type of the rise of African collective consciousness was "separational", limited to specific colonial territories and induced by the conditions encountered, but not of conditions of Africa's own choosing. The approach to African nationalism which was born in the fire of suffering from the orgy of cruelty of Europeans and their descendants in the metropoles of England, France, Portugal, Belgium, the United States of America and their satellite system of racial genocide and oppression of the Africans was not possible on the African continent. The social, political and economic conditions on the African continent at that time could not give rise to the development of African collective consciousness that is unitary in nature. This, the Africans brought to the Americas and Caribbean have not come to understand and appreciate, owing to lack of knowledge. Neither did they come to appreciate the suffering of their brothers and sisters at the same wicked hands of the Europeans on the continental Africa.

There were, therefore, two types of concept and meaning of African nationalism that were born from the womb of European oppression against Africans both at home and abroad. The sets of conditions that gave rise to them were socially, politically and materially the same in the final analysis. They, however, varied territorially in intensity and approach. These conditions are rooted in intensive and extensive exploitation of human and nonhuman resources for wealth creation at a minimum cost to the European predators. One type of African nationalism was born outside the continent of Africa and had a reformist attitude but a unitary approach. The other type of African nationalism, born inside Africa, had a revolutionary attitude where the Africans wanted control over their destiny through the establishment of their own governmental mechanisms; it, however, had a separatist approach that was territorially specific, imposed by the colonial lines of exploitation, predation and resource exploitation.

It may be pointed out that each type of the African nationalism had important and good characteristics. The one born on the continent had a revolutionary goal of Africans reclaiming their lands and sovereignties with the hope of controlling their destiny. The one born outside the continent, that is, in the Diaspora, had a revolutionary method of approach toward the whole question of Africa through a united front to realize the goal of complete African emancipation. In the historic process, therefore, and out of the separatist approach of African nationalism emerged some important conceptual and applied cross-fertilizations. Such cross-fertilizations made it possible to bring the two types of African nationalism together by combining the revolutionary goal of complete African emancipation with the revolutionary method of "unity" for the achievement of the goal.

Without the doctrine of European race supremacy as practiced in Europe, Americas and Africa, and without the colonial oppression in Africa and slavery which put African people at a disadvantage in World history, we are almost certain that the rise of modern African nationalism, particularly that which is of an all-encompassing nature in a unitary sense, would have been substantially delayed. People do not rise up in anger under conditions they have not encountered, rather revolution emerges out of conditions that the people do experience, and these conditions usually are not of their own making. Throughout the treatise, our central concern remains the concepts and practices of African nationalism and African unity within the historical context of colonialism and post-colonialism and the advancement of a thinking system (Africentricity) that must guide their successful execution.

What has been outlined so far, therefore, is merely the precondition for the establishment of the morphology of African nationalism. By means of logical development, we would like to again identify and expand on the two types of African nationalism within the context of Africa's complete emancipation. First, there is African nationalism in the historic context of decolonization. This type of African nationalism is territorially specific and arose under many different names depending on the region and territory in question. We have already cited examples of this type of African nationalism such as Zambian nationalism, Congolese nationalism, and others. The term "pre-independence African nationalism" is reserved for these types of African nationalism which are colonial-territory specific.

The structure and form of the pre-independence African nationalism are not clear. Its political and philosophical foundation seem to lack content and substance as we look forward to the future; its usefulness toward Africa's complete emancipation seems either doubtful, or at the very best misunderstood in the current context of Africa's modern history and experience; its future historical significance is questionable and its liberating force is almost nonexistent. Pre-independence African nationalism acquires content and significance only in reference to the decolonization movement which is the first step toward Africa's complete emancipation.

One can narrate and interpret the conditions that gave rise to pre-independence African nationalism. One may even invest time and effort to study the facts of this recent African history. And after all of these are done one will still face the question, what is African nationalism and of what use is it? What is African nationalism if African states can fly their flags without capacity to feed, protect and defend the Africans as well as provide even the basic necessities of life and do little about the continent turning into a land of beggars and useless wars, some may even ask?

In the pages to follow we shall attempt to answer the question: What is African nationalism and of what use is it? A more general concept of African nationalism relevant to Africa's contemporary conditions will be advanced within a framework of Nkrumaism and Africa's complete emancipation. Our task is to chart intellectually the conditions and requirements for post-independence African nationalism that is relevant to Africa's integration, unity and development. In so doing, we will lay down the theoretical framework

19

of African nationalism and its philosophical and ideological foundations. We will, therefore, show how the theoretical framework and the philosophical foundations translate into the basic principles of post-independence African nationalism required for Africa's complete emancipation. We will then illustrate the differences in the concept, content and historical significance of pre-independence African nationalism and post-independence African nationalism. Finally, connections are made among these principles of African nationalism and the practices of Nkrumaism, African Unity, Pan-Africanism and the African Diaspora.

The main objective here is to specify the basic principles of post-independence African collective consciousness that must guide the practices of Nkrumaists and Pan-Africanists toward a complete emancipation of Africa and her children all over the world. Therefore we will combine the best of the past, present and the future potential of the rise of African nationalism.

We shall then demonstrate that the post-independence African nationalism must be completely revolutionary by combining the revolutionary goals and objectives of destiny control with the revolutionary methods of goal achievement through unitary principles. This concept of African nationalism is advanced to integrate the state-specific nationalisms without replacing them but using them in defining the requisite ideological conditions for Africa's integration and unity. In the foregoing discussions, the term African nationalism will be reserved strictly for post-independence African nationalism except otherwise stated or specified. An explicit definition of post-independence African nationalism is provided based on the general discussion on the content and form of the principle of African personality that is presented in [43d]. Let us turn our attention to African nationalism that is relevant for Africa's emancipation, integration toward an effective African Union and sustainable development of the African Union. The required African Nationalism has a Pan-African foundations and world view to which we turn our attention.

3

AFRICAN NATIONALISM
A PAN-AFRICAN VIEW

Theory is about something and so also are philosophy and ideology. This something is always about social existence or about nature itself and how social existence is dependent on, as well as influences nature. The knowledge about this something is always buried among the natural order of things, arranged in accord with certain laws and hidden from the naked eye in such a way that the general human mind has no immediate understanding and awareness. The truth is always buried under what usually seems disorder in the eyes of humans. The nature of discovery of truth and verification of such truth, therefore, compel us to always study critically other theories to see how the order of things in nature and society is arranged as mental pictures by others and how the understanding may be translated from inertia to action for either evolution or revolution.

All successful and lasting revolutions are born out of, and based on firm theoretical principles. These theoretical principles, providing the rational basis for action, are grounded on solid logical foundations, and are unshakable by opposing ones until such foundations are broken. Revolutions without firm theoretical, philosophical and ideological principles are shortlived as well as usually producing disorder and unintended consequences. For African nationalism, therefore, to have a revolutionary character and guide action toward Africa's freedom, it must be grounded unquestionably on firm theoretical principles as well as on a solid logical foundation that is relevant to Africa's modern history and current experiences within the global system of power distribution, resource flows, production and trade. Such theoretical principles and logical foundation must be thoughtful as well as providing guidance for action. They must also be practical and useful in accomplishing the objective of Africa's complete emancipation. Nationalism, generally, may take many forms but not all these forms are either liberating or progressive. For nationalism to be liberating as well as progressive it must be anchored in the conditions encountered and experienced by the people. Nationalism must be experiential and logically directed. In other words, African nationalism must derive its nutrients from African history, Africa's experiences and African culture, and in addition must be developed by certain logical principles. African nationalism must be the African ideology for decision, action and practice.

The concept of African nationalism that we want to advance is that which is both liberating and progressive within the confines of Africa's experience and history. It is a nationalism that takes its roots from the unitary approach of Pan-Africanism, but has the goals and objectives of independence, sovereignty and national self-aspiration of Africa as a whole. The concept of African nationalism must be viewed by Africans and their descendants not only as a solid principle but also as a vision and belief that must be actualized through Africa's internal organization toward the goal of complete emancipation. The information supporting such a vision and belief is rooted in Africa's past as well as being grounded in Africa's modern history, current experiences and history of future possibilities.

African nationalism as viewed within Nkrumaism, African Unity and emancipation is a composite of four basic characteristics in unity. It connotes firmly African collective consciousness regarding the past, present and future. The collective consciousness reflects the ideology of unitarism in politics, economics and culture. As an ideology of unitarism, African nationalism holds the principle that a federation of all African states is the ideal form of political and economic organization with a full federal sovereignty, with some type of state autonomy that must be worked out. It is an ideal sociopolitical organization as measured against the task of complete African emancipation within the system of global power distribution over various nations and imperial predatory activities in the global resource space. It also affirms the principle of diversity in unity of Africa's historic past, as well as the great and rich cultural tapestry of her people as naturally valid. African nationalism is, therefore, a sum total of Africa's collective consciousness, political unity, economic unity and cultural unity with a clearly defined state autonomy and individual and collective freedom in theory and practice. It recognizes the beauty and strength in diversity as the foundation stones of unity. In diversity is unity and in unity is diversity. This is unity-diversity duality where each one is a precondition for their mutual existence. African nationalism is a great revolution; and like all great revolutions, it must be the work of unshakable principles, rather than fantasy. It must be first achieved in thought and then in material arena. When it is first achieved in thought, it will be brought into practice by assembling together the will and courage of the African masses, irrespective of place of residence, into a unified force for common action. The conceptual and ideological foundations of African nationalism must be spread among the African masses through programs of education and actions.

3.1   African Nationalism as African Collective Consciousness

One thing stands out clearly in our mind as we try to establish the morphology of African nationalism. This one thing is the relationship between African nationalism and African collective consciousness. The establishment of the relationship requires that the content of African collective consciousness must be defined and grounded in the truth of African history and current experience in the world political-economic order as seen from the African point of view. Special attention and emphasis should be placed on the modern history of Africa while at the same time making references to the past and present so as to devise the correct awakening of the collective consciousness toward the construct of Africa's future. Modern African history is simple to explain to a layman. It is a history of European occupation of the African continent. Along with the occupation came domination, oppression, slavery, brutality, orgy of genocide, human exploitation, land confiscation, intellectual darkness and undemocratic governance.

It is a history where the Africans were denied the credit of their own past through the Europeans' aggressive dis-information campaign and thievery of historic facts and events whereby Africa's monumental works were whitewashed. It is also a history full of European deception, propaganda against Africa, misinformation and disinformation merely to discredit, humiliate, inferiorize, dehumanize and demoralize the Africans. It is a history of European psychological warfare against the African in order to support the Europeans' claim to racial superiority and Caucasianization of Africa's achievements. It is simply a history of

European terrorism against the Africans in the theater of colonial oppression and imperial subjugation. These are techniques and methods of occupiers throughout history. In Africa, these practices were done through a simple but powerful mechanism of psychological torture, of racial inferiority, deceptive religious practices of Christianity, preaching of a false conception of God and the propagation of the bankrupt goal of the so called "African salvation as the white man's burden". Here the Africans were massacred in cold blood in order to bring civilization and Christendom to them in the graveyard. The same process is taking place now under the cover of democracy, good governance, debt forgiveness and development. The conceptual and ideological tools to jestify oppression and subjucation are constantly being revised to meet the changing global conditions and circumstances.

How does one explain, under conditions of rationality and logical thinking, except under primitive ideology, the notion of bringing civilization and democracy to the dead? Civilization cannot be brought to a people. Civilization is of the people; it is a process that evolves by the sweat, experiences and hard work of the people. "Civilization and democracy" can neither be given nor bestowed on a people. In fact, the period of relevance is a history of Europe against Africa when African history was reinterpreted and rewritten by Europeans to suit their propaganda machinery whereby Africa and Africans were discovered and Livingstone could be made to discover some waterfalls when in fact the falls were shown to him. The waterfalls, the African lakes and pyramids are known to the Africans from antiquity. The mere idea that some European discovered Africa and Africans is not only travesty of rational thinking but stupidity of historical recording. It is just like Africans claiming to discover Europe and Europeans without which the Europeans were non-existent.

We should emphasize that amidst all these African sufferings and historic darkness, there is something glorifying that should rekindle the personality that is truly African in the sense of being rooted in the all-encompassing fearlessness of the African in an unknown environment of struggle to achieve the ultimate of the African vision, and that is, in every living thing, there is a yearning to be free and to democratically pursue liberty and happiness. These are concepts that Europeans promote among themselves but deny their true practices with violence when the practices do not conform to their interest. Such a yearning, in this period of African history, is the African resistance against the European physical, mental and psychological warfare both at home and abroad. This history must constitute an integral part but not the totality and not the whole general foundation of African collective consciousness on the rebirth of the African mind. From the rebirth of the African mind the African yearning for a complete emancipation must involve full-spectrum resistance against full-spectrum dominance that the imperial predators want to impose.

The true African mind is one that stops to teach the African child the ideological lies such as that Africa was discovered in 1471 and that Livingstone discovered "Victoria Falls" whose African name is *Mosioatunya* (The Smoke that Thunders). These are all intellectual rubbish that has no roots in factual correctness of human history. Africa was not discovered by any European. It is a stupidity of human intellect to speak of some human been discovered by other human beings. We, therefore, speak of a new African mind, a collective consciousness, that rejects European intellectual falsehood, a false concept of God and racial misconceptions about Africa and its history. We are not calling for nither vengeance nor even animosity. This would be inconsistent with the nature of African personality whose true structure rejects vengeance and abhors anti-humanism. We are simply calling for a new rethinking by Africans on Africa's current and past conditions that have created Africans' current dilemma, poverty in the midst of richness, and starvation in the midst of plenty; and have shaped the current environment on the basis of which social decisions are taken to affect Africa's destiny.

Another part of the history from which the African collective consciousness must be drawn is the post-decolonization history of Africa. It is a history of material poverty, technological and scientific backwardness, international racism, mental slavery, psychological torture, social disruption and confusion, political blindness, military intimidation, neo-colonialism, Western economic sabotage and socioeconomic destabilization through wars that are sometimes artificially manufactured by the imperialist predators. It is a history mixed with the practice of "one-step-forward-and-two-steps-backwards" social movements complicated by imperialist and neo-colonialist tricks based on the principles of divide and rule with lip service to development assistance and technical aid without substance. It is a history with numerous accounts of Western countries' support for reactionary governments, military coups d'état against progressive African governments and their replacement with puppet ones who always dance to the tunes of the imperialists and serve the interest of neocolonial machinery but never the interest of the people they govern. In other words, it is a history of servitude upgraded from the previous colonial one, where the puppet governments in the hands of their Wesrern protectors restrain and constrain Africa's freedom, progress and development. This is true, without exception, of all decolonized African states. It is also a history of reformed slavery where colonialism, resource exploitation, racism, oppression, human rights abuses and intellectual deceptions are packaged in pleasant-tasting capsules, for Africa to swallow. The capsule comes in many different and disguised forms such as democracy, good governance, civil society, human rights, anti-terrorism and many fancy brand names.

The post-decolonization history of Africa is again a history of repackaged Europe against Africa. It is a history of the West against Africa where the West is the same Europeans, now enjoying the fruits of their imperial and colonial predatory activities. It is the current order characterized by imperialism hidden under the promotion of democracy, good governance and much more. In this current order the characteristics of the previous order are present. The only things that are different from the previous order are the methods and techniques of the European practices. The packaging of the characteristics of oppression and subjugation has also changed where slavery, humiliation, brutalities, resource exploitation, racism, and above all intellectual bankruptcy are packaged in the capsules of democracy, good governance, and humanitarianism and development aid. Here, the Africans are treated like school pupils where they are instructed to follow externally prescribed rules for the practice of democracy, good governance and decent conduct of international behavior with outlined civilized codes. They are not supposed to operate outside the parameters defined by these rules as imposed by the imperial predators. They must follow the law and order without questions or thinking on fairness and justice.

Ironically, some Africans, particularly the so-called educated ones, sit in glory of this kind of democracy and development. They have become useful intellectual instruments for European propaganda in the theater of intellectual and psychological war against Africa. They join in with their neocolonial masters and abstract by force from the mouth of the poor African children the simple basic life's substance without shame and without glory either. They prepare their own burial grounds and the platforms for their own execution without a single thought about their children. They live in moral filth without recognition. Their only great reward is condemnation by their masters after they have ceased to be useful and serviceable to them. They forget that African nationalism and not any other nationalism is their road to glory. The major countries of the so-called developed world did not accumulate wealth through democracy or civil codes of human decent behavior as our known history reveals. Democracy is good when it evolves as part of the cultural process of the people in accordance with the needs of their social formation and values as imposed by the evolving individual-community duality. Democracy has no roots in the culture of the people when it is imposed by force or otherwise. There is no one brand or path to democracy which simply involves individual-community duality in collective behavior in the social decision space.

The African leaders fly the flags of independence, speak of freedom, and beg for food. They celebrate independence days and beg for water. They recite national anthems and beg for arms instead of knowledge; talk about democracy and turn their arms on their citizens to the benefit of the imperial predators. They condemn communism and lick the feet of their capitalist oppressors. This is the current history of Africa. There is nothing glorious about this history; neither is there anything meaningful about these conditions of Africa. It must be clear that Africans, as human beings, are in these degrading conditions because they are Africans or African descendants. It is not because they are Nigerians, Libyans, Tanzanians or Gambians. Whether they attain their independence through protracted armed struggle or through negotiation or on a silver platter, they are all in the same neocolonial boat as the current African history reveals. This current history of Africa must constitute an essential part of the general foundation of the African collective consciousness that must characterize the content of African nationalism.

The completing part of the foundation of African collective consciousness must be abstracted from the future history, the history that must be a vision of new Africa whose strength is drawn from her past and whose sense of purpose is her new foundations drawn from the current African realities. This future history, Africa's potential, must not be left to the blind social forces while Africans accept whatever the outcome may be. We must not allow Africa's potential and future realities to be controlled by forces of imperial predators who elevated slavery and racism to the height of terror and social absurdity, and who continue to drain Africa of her resources. Africa is the cradle of history of man and his civilization. Africa is the center of germination of the seed of the so-called Western civilization, so that in fact, there is nothing Western about that civilization except the adjustments that have been made to it in terms of the common intellectual heritage of humanity [8b] [10c] [13] [36] [39]. Obviously, the Europeans have added to and shaped what they copied to suit their conditions. We however must note that the major religions of our contemporary world have their foundations rooted in African philosophy.

There is no question about the fact that Africa produced the guiding rules of decent behavior and the code of conduct of civility of people through the creation of the foundations of some dominant religions of the modern world (see [13] [14] [25] [36] [39] [93a-d]). The Ten Commandments attributed to the Hebrews, for example, were not God-given; they were copied verbatim by a Hebrew leader or at the very best abstracted from his understanding of the legal order of the Nile Valley civilization through his study of legal documents when he was in the Pharaoh's Palace (see also [13]). This is past. But this glorious past and its ashes must cement the new African vision toward the creation of the future history and a new African social order. We must accept unconditionally the foundational work of Anta Diop regarding African cultural unity and Africans as one people [37] [38] on the basis of which African Nationalism must stand. We must speak of Africans but not Egyptians, Nigerians, Somalis and others. We must not divide ourselves in cultural schizophrenia and socioeconomic extinction that will destroy Africans.

This future history, therefore, must be created with a well-designed program of thought and actions based on the vision of a prosperous, glorious and integrated Africa. We are Africans and must work our destiny together as Africans to make Africa great and peaceful to be able to defend her children. In other words, we must create a new Africa that was once there but brought to modernity, an Africa that is at the center of world history as it should be, just as geographically Africa is placed in and occupies the center of the world.

A new Africa should be an Africa for all Africans both at home and abroad; an Africa whose material and spiritual relationship with her children that are geographically not residing on the continental Africa is just as strong and inseparable as with her children who reside on the continent in terms of the usual African symbolic representation of the icon of the mother and child. It must likewise be free from neocolonialism, foreign domination, human rights abuse sufferers, puppet governments, technological backwardness, material poverty, mental sterility, mass intellectual backwardness and one whose character would be a symbol of shining hope for the human race. It is an Africa whose world leadership in the glorious past is upgraded, improved and brought into the modern age. Africa was the center of world civilization in the beginning; and Africa must be the center of the world civilization in the end to complete the natural circle of order. This has to be the vision on the basis of which the African collective consciousness must be abstracted, formed and shaped. Africans have nothing to lose by a united front but the chains of poverty. We have everything to gain from unity at a minimal cost as her philosophical foundation points to [43d], but everything to gain. The future of Africa must motivate the formation of African collective consciousness, a mind in unity, which is tolerant to and appreciative of Africa's tapestry of diversity. Those who want to lead Africa and shape her destiny must accept this as a first principle which is unity of diversity and diversity in unity as our strength that must enhance our glory.

Social consciousness that is territorially limiting by the boundaries of the colonial set up cannot generate the collective consciousness required to create the new Africa. Collective consciousness that is state-specific is, in itself, self-defeating. We want to project not Sudanese collective consciousness or any consciousness that is state-specific. We simply want to project African collective consciousness, and African nationalism that implies cohesiveness, a sense of African unity that identifies individually liberated states within the African Union (AU) or the potentially existing Continental Union Government of Africa (CUGA). Here we are calling for an African nationalism whose foundation is rooted in the common elements of our African history, intellectual traditions and culture; an African nationalism that glues together the various state-specific consciousness through certain common affinities; an African nationalism whose thought foundation and practices are directed toward goals and objectives of common political and economic creeds of Africa, a common federal government linked together by a well designed system of communication channels, a common military system under a central command in defense of state and federal sovereignties within the union, and with a common continent-wide socioeconomic development policy on the basis of collective self-reliance, economic and political integration where Africa's resources are utilized to satisfy primarily the needs and wants of peoples of Africa whether born at home or abroad. This collective consciousness must be translated into the African ideology that must guide perception formation, fact interpretation, reason and practice by Africans toward other Africans both at home and abroad and toward Africa itself. African nationalism, therefore, must constitute the correct African ideology, and the correct African ideology must be derived from Africentricity which must be nourished from African culture and past and current social exigencies with a philosophical foundation of polyrhythmicity and rules of reasoning of polyrhythmics (see [43d]).

3.2   African Nationalism and Correct African Ideology

The correct ideological foundation of African nationalism must be based on the following:

(1) The principle of independence of the African states within a federated state where a Continental Union Government of Africa does not mean a loss of sovereignties of the individual states but rather a strengthening of the state sovereignties within the federated nation where the African Union is the beginning;

(2) The principle of national progress on economic, scientific, technological and cultural fronts for all of Africa;

(3) The principle of the national mission of Africa as the center of world history where Africa interacts with other member nations of the world community, friends and adversaries alike, on equal footing, where Africa is no longer the battleground of imperialists, neocolonial forces, global justice and peace through terror and where the African people are no longer the beggars of dough that they have produced and the Europeans and other imperial predators are suppliers of dough that they never produced;

(4) The principle of patriotism based on supreme and uncompromising loyalty to the federated state of Africa with allowance and tolerance for state-specific affinities; and

(5) The principle of freedom, justice and peace that reflects traditional Africa's humanistic sense of life where the concept of each for all and all for each operates but not each against all and all against each.

The principle of a federated African state requires a complete and uncompromising devotion on the part of all Africans both at home and abroad to the idea of achieving independence for all African territories and their people as well as grand devotion to achieving the ultimate, the united Africa under one central, political and military command for Africa's defense against imperially self-imposed righteousness and ideology of preemption on all fronts. Africa cannot be redeemed by the West or foreigners. Africa can only be redeemed by Africans. This redemption must take place from a united front. The united front presents a high cost to the predators while increasing the strength of Africa's global resistance to predation that can easily be practiced over individual states. This principle of federated African states calls for the slogan "People of Africa Unite! You have nothing to lose but your chains! You have a continent to regain! You have freedom and human dignity to attain!" [114, p. 134].

Additionally, it calls for an uncompromising belief in preserving the sovereignty of the federated nation to be created and sovereignties of member states within the confines and rules of the federation, as well as freedom and pursuit of happiness for all citizens and residence in the federation.

The possibility of such a federated state is based on the belief that:

…the forces that unite us (Africans) are intrinsic and greater than the superimposed influences that keep us apart. These are the forces that we must enlist and cement for the sake of the trusting millions who look to us, their leaders, to take them out of the poverty, ignorance and disorder left by colonialism into an ordered unity in which freedom and amity can flourish amidst plenty [105, p. 221]

Similarly, it must also be understood, within the struggle for Africans to be free, that the principle of a federated nation embraces completely the idea that "African unity gives an indispensable continental dimension to the concept of African nation" [112, p.27] without which the goal of freedom for Africans cannot be accomplished.

The principle of national progress on economic, technological, scientific and cultural fronts dictates the following objectives:

(a) Economic progress for every member state and the federation in an integrated and complementary manner;

(b) Technological progress for all member states in a uniform setting as well as for the federation;

(c) Political progress on all fronts for all the state, federal, and social organizations with common theoretical denominator of law and general rules of behavior;

(d) Cultural progress regarding the age-old genius of African art, music, dance forms, the totality of African ways of life and values, within each member state as well as within the federation where our diversity is our strength and beauty of our unity;

(e) Freedom, justice and pursuit of happiness for all Africans under peace, tranquility and one common destiny; and

(f) Solutions of African problems are sought by Africans within Africa rather than from without.

The principle of national progress, while acknowledging the existence of other cultures, holds the African culture to be the best for the African people because it is of our own creation and gives us our identity and the African essence.

Additionally, the principle of national progress holds that Africa is endowed with excellent human resources and that the African people are the only ones capable of organizing themselves and their resources to improve their quality of life, to create the comfort that all human beings desire and to develop fully the culture that has always been a fascination to an outsider. The principle of national progress, therefore, translates into African economic and cultural self-determination in all fronts of human endeavors. It must, therefore, assert itself in the work ethics of the Africans. The demand is simple, that Africa must turn her attention and efforts inward and rededicate her energies and strengths to the development of her resources for the benefit of her people. Africa must not turn her attention and effort outward by carrying a beggar's basket in shame and humiliation just to be forced through all kinds of global institutional conditionalities to carry water in a basket with the hope of enriching the African lands.

Supplementing the principle of national progress is the principle of state progress based on internal self-reliance. The two move in the same direction at all times. They are duality in complementary relation.

The principle of a national mission of Africa from within demands that we the African people commit ourselves to accept the continental-wide government and collective endeavor to engineer Africa's progress and her history through our efforts. It acknowledges the existence of material poverty, technological backwardness, and ignorance locked in mis-education and illiteracy, famine, degradation, and enslavement as continental phenomena. The national mission is the creation of a new Africa, and a new Africa that is completely free from colonialism, imperialism, colonial proxy governments and all the multitude of ills of a dominated and suffering society. The principle translates into a slogan: out of the ashes of Africa's glorious past must arise the new Africa and Africans to reconstruct Africa on the basis of Africa's effort, hard work and ingenuity on the basis of African cognitive tradition. This slogan is part of the ideology of African Nationalism.

The mission calls for political, economic and cultural emancipation with maximum development for the continent. This maximum development must be based on collective efforts of all Africans where material and human resources are efficiently utilized along the lines of an integrated continental economy, where complementary sectors are developed in such a way as to eliminate duplication and waste; and where the African people are united in soul and efforts to create compatible institutions that serve African needs as well as opposing external adversaries and eliminating internal strife. The creation of such conditions requires collective African efforts in order to overcome internal and external detractions and impediments that prevent Africa's complete emancipation. Let us keep in mind that socioeconomic development is a labor process on the basis of hard work, commitment and dedication. Such a labor process comes from within but not without being conditional on the premise that external and internal slavery is unacceptable. A premise, whose violation is an indictment of Europe and the Americas.

Committed to the ideal and to the contemporary realities that Africa's emancipation is by definition a collective phenomenon that demands every African talent and effort, the mission calls on the current and possible future leaders of various states of the continent to accept unconditionally the mission of African nationalism and work diligently toward its realization. Since this mission is a collective phenomenon, it imposes a restriction on the acceptable and operational boundaries of sovereignty of individual states in Africa as conceived within the emancipation process. It also imposes a strict code of conduct implied by its principles as to how other Africans are treated across state boundaries. An African is an African whether he or she is in Kenya and from Liberia or otherwise. He or she is governed by the principle of freedom, justice and pursuit of happiness as required by Africa's own self-survival.

All serious research and studies about Africa's modern history including colonial, post-colonial and independence history point to one cardinal reality of African conditions. This cardinal reality is that no African state can succeed within the current international order, global system of finance, international resource game, global power distribution, trading systems, system of military aggressions, production and future ones to come, to emancipate itself culturally, economically, technologically, scientifically and politically by going alone without other African states. This is an impossibility unless one wants to live in a state of delusion, self-denial and suicidal tendencies. We have, at every opportune time, insisted on this African reality so that it has become an immutable social theorem in our thought process.

We, therefore, reiterate that the first important thing required by the mission of Africa's emancipation is for every current and future African nationalist to initialize the intellectual and operational position that no African state can succeed in being free from imperial domination, economic exploitation and external predatory activities by struggling alone without her sister African states. The internal sentiments must then be reinforced by the positive belief that Africa must be freed by whatever means possible. This yearning need and will to free Africa and her people must magnetize the African states to one another to form a unified force to break the chains of slavery, to throw away the yoke of servitude and to fight against oppression, racism, exploitation and humiliation as practiced by the so-called "civilized" Western nations and for that matter any other nation that would dare to follow the route of the Western nations. "Africa must unite!" must always be our slogan and the social gospel if the African children are to be freed and if the African interests are to be preserved and protected.

As long as the leaders of individual African countries do not see their countries as having national interests to protect, their countries and people will not only be continually preyed upon by the imperial predator but will be moving through the globe with a beggar's mentality by begging for trivialities of life. Similarly as long as the leaders of African countries hold the view of vain and meaningless sovereignties that they think will protect their national interests without collective African effort and collaborative action their countries and the African people will remain in the imperial zone of predation, terror and torture. There is no free lunch in the imperialist world of operations. Every give- away or all technical assistance and other aid is a trap into the zone of predation and intense exploitation. We must keep in mind that there are no free lunches in the jungle of capitalist creed and competition for resources. The imperialist give-away acts just like a piece of food on the fisherman's hook for the fish to trap it for a catch.

If the mission of African nationalism is not followed diligently with the souls and minds of the Africans, the current conditions of Africa will worsen and swiftly degenerate into a situation where Africa would be swept completely into the orbit of a new and deeply entrenched servitude that is more punishing, more genocidal and more exploitative than the past and current ones. The neo-servitude will be more devastating with uncontrollable destructive force. Furthermore, it will become not only chronic but an acceptable part of African people's way of life. The African leaders will constitute, if they have not already constituted, a powerful buffer class that will be used by the Western imperial powers and neocolonialists to absorb the shocks that may result from legitimate revolts of African masses against injustice and oppression resulting from international capitalist, racists and the imperial order composed of sheep and wolves. The African leaders and their business elite, manipulated by their neocolonial masters through perks and personal favors, will use the armed forces at their disposal and munitions supplied to them at cutthroat prices by their masters in the service of the imperial powers and at the expense of the lives and bread of the people they are supposed to serve. The position is affirmed by Cheikh Anta Diop who recognized the process and the trickery of the West as slowly guiding the African independence movement from the state of Balkanization to a new state of South Americanization.[40] He states:

> [Africa] would be made up of a proliferation of little dictator-ridden countries without organic ties one to another, ephemeral, afflicted with chronic weakness, governed by terror with the help of oversize police forces, but under economic

domination by foreign countries, pulling strings through the mere presence of an embassy.[40, p.15]

From the viewpoint of the African unity imperative this situation is already present in most African countries and is in the making in others. Nkrumah puts the same analytical idea as:

> If we do not formulate plans for unity and take active steps to form political union, we will soon be fighting and warring among ourselves with imperialists and colonialists standing behind the screen and pulling vicious wires, to make us cut each other's throats for the sake of their diabolical purposes in Africa. [110, p. 9]

All these are already happening on the continent of Africa and in varying degrees in various African states.

In this framework of African nationalist thought the African states must not only be responsible to themselves alone. But also the African states must be responsible to one another as brothers and sisters in the struggle to capture the gold, the gold of Africa's emancipation. This should be the mental frame of every African nationalist. The mission of Africa's emancipation, therefore, translates into the mission of African unity. African unity and Africa's emancipation must then be conceptualized together as the national mission of every African nationalist. In this respect, the "Black man's burden" and the "Black woman's burden" are seen by the African nationalist as Africa's emancipation through African unity. It is a principle that opposes completely the bankrupt racist principle of the "White man's burden" to civilize the African by Christianizing him or her. The African nationalist must first embrace this mission of African emancipation through the vehicle of African unity, internalize it and then accept the responsibility to act and spread the faith and the gospel to every African in Africa and its Diaspora. Here we preach the gospel of African nationalism, African unity and emancipation.

It must be made clear, and uncompromisingly so, that the current African leaders and the so-called educated Africans must stop fooling the African masses and at the same time making fools of themselves. They cannot go on running with the hare and hunting with the hounds. It is a stupidity of the first kind where the African masses always watch the foxes to be selected by the imperial predators under some amorphous concept of democracy to head the henhouses. What sense does it make to always bring the wild dogs as door-keepers of the meat house? Within the cognitive system of African nationalism, there is no wisdom, neither is there any credibility in a series of flimsy institutional patchworks of Africa's associations with fake international institutional structures that work to maintain the imperialist predators and their activities in Africa.

It must be clearly understood by the true African leaders and their supporting intelligentsia that these international institutions like the World Bank, International Monetary Fund, Department for International Development, United States Agency for International Development, the United Nations and many others are instruments of exploitation at the disposal of the world's imperial and neocolonial systems to enforce and maintain full spectrum dominance by the imperial club. These institutions are not for development even though ideological propaganda and sales techniques project them to be so. They do not promote democracy even though they claim to hold its master key. These international institutions have become creators of tricks to destabilize African states and other weak states through a system of deceptions and propaganda. They support violence and terror under just wars to bring civilization, Christendom and democracy. The earlier the African leaders and their supporting intelligentsia come to acknowledge and accept the realities of these institutions and bring about the ultimate break or restructuring of Africa's relationships with them, the better position will Africa be in to find correct path and solutions to her development problems (see Chapter 6 of this volume).

The correct solutions lie in African unity, the federated nation to be and African nationalism, and African nationalism as the ideology of the people, and not with the people who had long exploited the human and non-human resources of Africa for their development and wealth creation. Their advice and consultant services have no moral authority. They constantly preach how poor Africa is and that they are working to bring development just like in the previous era of colonization, slavery and exploitation they preached on the moral principle of bringing civilization and God to Africa while they plundered Africa's precious resource and condemned her people to slavery for their wealth creation. History is a teacher but for only those who have ears to hear and listen, and minds to correctly process and digest its teachings into a knowledge base that must become an input to current and future decisions.

The African leaders must clearly understand the law of the wilderness. It is an illusion on the part of a wild dog to think it can hunt in the midst of lions with the hope that the lions will make some big catches and so leave some unwanted or juicy leftovers for its hunger and appetite. The reality is that the wild dog will be the first on the line of the catch for the lions' insatiable appetite. The law of the wilderness and self-preservation requires the wild dog to seek association and unity with its kind for protection, growth and development and in fact, against the lions and related predators. Protection, growth and development of Africa are not possible within the current international institutional setup and the types of African association with these institutions, with the current organizational form of Africa and the type of leadership that is imposed. This must be understood clearly by the African nationalists. And this must become almost a theorem in the thought process of the true African nationalists. The current framework of international institutional configuration is a mere wilderness where lions are at liberty to prey on the weak and meek; where individually the weak has no protection except either in servitude or in unity with its kind and where international institutional racism is such that the first to fall as preys to the lions are Africa and her children. The case for African unity is strong and the events taking place on the continent of Africa and in the rest of the world make it unquestionable and even stronger. We have before us, as Africans, a choice to make for self-preservation, liberty and development. The choice is between unity or slavery, and between Pan-Africanism or neocolonialism and between African collectivity or poverty. Slavery, neocolonialism and poverty are not options for an African nationalist. By logical extension we must choose unity, Pan-Africanism and African collectivity as vehicles to achieve self-preservation, liberty and development.

The African nationalist must, therefore, accept unquestionably the principle of African emancipation through African unity. He or she must then not compromise on this major principle either in theory or in practice. He or she must also accept the responsibility of helping to develop and refine the strategies for executing positive action for Africa's development in accord with this principle. He or she must understand that African unity must be the primary basis of a nationalist policy of Africa's complete emancipation that encompasses political freedom, economic freedom, cultural freedom and sovereignty of statehood of all decolonized areas within the confines of the federated African nation. To the true African nationalist, the vision is clear and the goal is attainable. This is the African nationalist optimism. We should not spend the time to argue on the feasibility of the goal of African unity. Europe is uniting to defend European interests.

The African leaders must accept the unity goal as imperative on the principle of hope on behave of the African masses. The only thing that remains now is the development of right strategies, tactics and positive action program for its realization under the principles of courage, perseverance and hard work. Part of these strategies and tactics, and directions to them have been advanced in [40] [50] [97] [105] [123], but they need refinements and organizational updating in terms of institutional restructuring, tactics and strategies as time moves along and global resources and power conditions alter. These refinements and organizational restructuring must flow from African nationalism and Africentricity as its supporting thinking system. We cannot say less than this. African unity makes sense. It is Africa's salvation. African nationalism makes sense. It is Africa's ideological light. Both African unity and nationalism make sociological and anthropological sense. They define a strategic path to Africa's glorious tomorrow.

3.3   African Nationalism as the African Ideology

African nationalism is projected here as the African ideology. The manner in which it is conceived arises not simply from cognitive abstraction that is independent of global production relations but also from the material life, the history of African societies and the way in which this material life has been affected by global forces of material exploitation and European imperial subjugation and terror. Hence the causes impelling the conceptual and content development of African nationalism are to be abstracted from Africa's history of colonial exploitation, slavery, orgy of genocide committed by Europe, and global racism, while the causes impelling the direction of such development are to be found in Africa's current material life and interconnected system of global exploitation conditional on Africa's rich resources that continually attract external predation.

As the African ideology, African nationalism must be developed to serve the interest and needs of all Africans and Mother Africa. It is simply an intellectual tool fashioned to correspond first and foremost to the material, mental and spiritual needs of Africa's current historical position. Its content and development must reflect not only Africa's conception of good life and happiness, and the role that external forces play to restrict such life, but her vision of tomorrow regarding the conditions of her children as united under one system of organization of production, distribution and defense. African nationalism is an ideology of African unity, emancipation and progress.

To serve the objectives of unity and complete emancipation of Africa, African nationalism must constitute a coherent system of ideas that are corroborated by facts as experienced, ascertained and interpreted by Africans as of yesterday's events, today's events and projected events of tomorrow. As viewed, the aim of African nationalism is to unite the different African social thinking, cultural tapestry and choice-decision actions of Africans toward the goal of Africa's complete emancipation. It seeks to establish an order in the collective consciousness and social practices of either all or at least majority of Africans. As such it defines the permissible range of acceptable behavior for the individual and the collective. Furthermore, it seeks to establish conditions of conformity without which the unity of behavior and its maintenance cannot come about. It instructs us that the strategic path to Africa's emancipation and redemption lies in unity, self-determination, collective work and responsibility, socioeconomic cooperation, the defined purpose of our existence, our genius and creativity and faith in ourselves to engineer Africa's tomorrow.

On the conceptual level, African nationalism constitutes an apparatus of the mind, a system of thinking which will help Africans to be ideologically correct in the sense that their point of reference in decisions and choices is always Africa. On the level of social practice African nationalism requires a sort of Cultural Revolution, a new synthesis that will replace the schizophrenic cultural conditions handed over to us by the European intruders, predators, and destroyers. It is a synthesis that is African centered. It is also a synthesis that Africa cannot afford not to undertake. It is Africa's vision (Afrivision).

Basically, the view is that Africa is one and African nationalism requires all Africans and their descendents to believe in this basic principle of oneness, defend it and act in accordance. The arguments about differences as barriers to unity must cease. They serve no useful purpose to our emancipation process. They just intensify our division while serving the interests of our adversaries. The behavior and actions of Africans must conform to the process required to bring about African unity, emancipation and self-reliance that are implied and directed by African nationalism, whose principle of oneness and complete emancipation would prevent Africans from acting as if we are different and are each other's adversaries as is occurring on the African continent now between states and within states. Our cognition must accept the need for African unity and our arguments must center on strategies, tactics, policies and programs of action that will bring about unity toward our emancipation and redemption.

African nationalism is the totality of African collective and individual consciousness. It thus encompasses the whole life of African diversity, people and culture. As such it must manifest itself in African traditions of all forms, as well as taking cognizance of African ethnic differences, global racism and other forms of global relations that are either favorable or antagonistic to Africa's freedom, peace, happiness and survival. As a guide to Africa's behavior in the global competitive space, it rejects all connotations that Africa and Africans were discovered by some Europeans as well as all the malicious myths crafted by European thinkers that Africa was impelled into history by these European intruders, predators and destroyers. It also rejects any division of Africa into either Black Africa and non-Black Africa, or Africa South and North of the Sahara. Africa is one and Africa must be one and indivisible. In fact the rest of the world views Africa in oneness. This principle of oneness suggests to us that these divisions and names of Africa are strategies of the European predators to destroy the unitary fabric of Africa so as to carry on their rent-seeking activities without any important African resistance while they work to unite their people by overlooking their deep differences by harmonizing them into a set of commonness. The European leaders are working for European unity and simultaneously working against African unity. One must ask the question why and find an answer to it.

The principle of oneness is the foundational stone of African nationalism and its development. The cultural unity of Africa enforces this principle. On the level of organization, African nationalism is integrative in the sense of bringing together possible and rich diverse elements of African states, people and culture in addition to the common elements from the North, South, East and West into a unity of thinking and action so that we can confront Africa's challenges and opportunities and the rest of the world with a unified voice, the voice of Africa, in order to mobilize the resources of the continent to ensure full and rational development of various parts of the states in unity, self-reliance and progress for the benefit of Africans first.

Rational development and resources utilization involve decisions and choices at various levels of social practice that must be directed collectively in an ideological sense. As such African nationalism as the ideology in general does not only project what must be done but also what must not be done in the choice-decision space by Africans and their descendants. In this respect, certain contemporary actions by African leaders and elite, business people, academics, industrialists or otherwise would be incompatible with the basic principles of African nationalism where the objective is emancipation, self-reliance and development. For example, the simple decision to hold huge legitimate or illegitimate personal accounts outside Africa, particularly in the homelands of Africa's predators, or the acceptance of foreign bases on African soil by some African States would be inconsistent with the vision of building Greater Africa and creating the corresponding sovereignty. Why should other countries have military and propaganda bases in Africa but Africa not have bases outside Africa? Additionally, these foreign bases would undermine the struggle for the complete emancipation of Africa and the goal of rational reconstruction through self-reliance. We must keep I mind that the strategy of the wolf is to befriend the sheep through a disguise by dressing in the sheep's clothing with the hope of satisfying its appetite and stomach needs.

The ideology of African nationalism compels us as Africans and African descendants to place the interest of Africa first, and secondly to work with other nations whose interest are complimentary to those of Africa. Additionally, it compels us, as Africans, to believe that it is only through unity that Africa hopes to break the chains of subservience and exploitation. This unity can only come about by good thinking, proper knowledge utilization and sensible decision-choice rationality, all of which must be directed toward Africa's interest through the practice of the ideology of African nationalism.

3.4   African Nationalism, Knowledge and Decision-choice Rationality

Understanding the emphasis placed on African nationalism as the African ideology in the overall African struggle is extremely important if we, Africans, are to rally together the internal forces of Africa to rescue Africa and her children from the imperial predators and to propel her and her children to the land of ancestral freedom in this twenty-first century. Ideology, as we have pointed out in many places, projects a general order that defines boundaries of acceptable collective and individual decision-choice behavior which is guided by a particular concept of rationality [42] without physical cohesion. Rationality is imbedded in ideology as well as taking its meaning and validity in decision-choice space. This decision-choice behavior and the corresponding rationality take place within the ambit of a given social environment whose countenance is ideologically induced.

The decision-choice behavior and the corresponding rationality are affected by the perceptive activities regarding information, knowledge and reality within the framework of the ruling ideology. The decision-choice behavior and rationality are also affected by preferences that are shaped by collective consciousness regarding social goals and objectives and the rank order that they may take. In this way perceptions and preferences affect the individual and collective choice-decision events (that is, the manner in which reality is perceived, goals and objectives are formed, choices are made and actions are implemented) whose outcomes define the path of national destiny and history. Here national history is simply an enveloping of success-failure processes in the choice-decision space whose outcomes are governed by rationality that is ideologically controlled.

Perceptions and preferences are formed individually and collectively within behaviorally acceptable social boundaries that are defined and set by the ruling ideology. In this way, ideology shapes directly both perceptions and preferences of the nation while simultaneously the perceptions and preferences mold the structure and form of the ideology. For example, if a slave is indoctrinated by terror or otherwise with and believes in the ideology of his or her master that he or she is created divinely to be a slave and that the master is a master over him or her by Divine Providence (as we have pointed out in the preface of this book), his or her perceptions and preferences will lead him or her to decide and choose activities of servile behavior, in the sense that freedom and servitude are the same in the eyes of the slave. His or her very nature demands him to act as such (see also the analysis of Carter G. Woodson [152]). The servile mode is blessed and elevated divinely to the same status as freedom and given permanency. We must not forget that some aspects of certain theological teachings and literature of some of the major religions have been designed craftily to justify slavery and the exploitative relationship between slaves and masters. Sometimes we wonder about human cognitive rationality that leads people to believe the claim that such documents portray the words of God and written with His inspiration. This is not different from the claim that some wars are just and hence killings are divinely blessed.

Similarly colonialism, racism, imperialism, ethnic superiority and orgy of genocide against Africans were divinely sanctified by Europeans to the point that some races claimed to be children of God while others were inferior to them. Dangerously, this ideological teaching and the supporting literature have been handed over to Africans to ensure a continuous justification of the greatest atrocities committed by the Western nations against Africa as well as to maintain the existing master-servant relationship established by the colonial order. Ironically, this anti-African ideology is being promoted actively by some Africans in their pulpits to Africans and their descendants.

In this context of divine setting and ideology of oppression, the slave will not go away from the master even if he or she is set free by the master and told to leave. The slave is held in physical servitude not by the force of the master but simply by the ideology that has become engrained in his or her mind and continues to shape his or her perceptions and preferences in the world of events. It may be pointed out that this is not different from the ideology of socioeconomic dependency on aid, technical assistance and foreign consultancy. In his or her mind he or she is a slave and his oppressor is a master by divine creation and nothing whatsoever can alter this God's craft. His or her conditions of existence and his or her relationship with the oppressor are ideologically set in the mind to be divinely permanent as well as enshrined in a stone of immutable nature. These descriptions seem to define the general conditions in Africa today where the African leaders emerging from conditions of direct colonialism and European indoctrination believe that they can only develop their societies with the help of their former slave masters from Europe and America. This is simply false.

The African is not educated to conceptualize the Africentric philosophical idea that creation and and evolution, through transformation-substitution duality, are never-ending processes enshrined in marbles of change and that social relations are the works and crafts of humans but not divine creations. Like nature itself the structure of social relations is subject to the laws of change. With complete enslavement by the mindset that has been nurtured carefully by the master through slavery and colonialism, force is not needed to maintain the subservient and exploitative relationship. Any problem and difficulty arising on the continent forces them to run back to their former oppressors to seek a solution instead of seeking a solution from the ingenuity of the continent. The content of the mind of the slave is his or her problem. It is inimical to his or her struggle for freedom, justice and independence. It has to be emptied if the slave is to be freed and enjoyed the fruits of liberty that are natural gifts of the Creator. The African must empty the anti-African ideology that continues to enslave us. We must take lesson from the pages of history of the Chinese revolution. The enemy of Africa in bringing effective solutions to problems of underdevelopment, poverty reduction, peace and prosperity in Africa is our current Afrcan collective mind that has become inimical to our progress and hence needs radical restructuring if such solutions are to be found.

Most African independent states are locked in the house of this slave-master mode with the Western nations, which they believe directly or indirectly to be permanent and divinely established. This has been made possible by the collective African mindset and its content, which are anti-African in nature. This African mindset and its content have been shaped by anti-African ideology which has been developed by the colonialists, imperialists and neocolonialists to create a cognitive environment where racism, servility, oppression, inferiority complex, bigotry and imperialist predatory activities can flourish with minimal African resistance. There is minimal African resistance because African perceptions, preferences and actions defined over the decision-choice space are dictated not by the African interests but by anti-African ideology that has cognitively transformed Africa's true costs into illusions of Africa's interest and benefit and vice versa. In fact, we are proud to use what we do not produce and happily produce what we use not. Some Africans even argue that colonialism and neocolonialism are good for Africa. Africa and Africans cannot continue in this mode and hope to be emancipated on all fronts of human endeavor. The anti-African ideology acting as a powerful narcotic on the African cognition places Africans at a subservient relationship with the predators and destroyers. This allows the predators to undertake active predatory and exploitative activities without Africa's cognition because Africans have come to accept this as a Divine ordinance. Again, the collective mind of contemporary Africa is Africa's greatest enemy. The fight against this enemy is within us. It requires restructuring of our cultural values and our institutions of learning that will bring about the true African personality to operate with correct ideology to effect correct outcomes in the decision-choice space.

The colonialists, neocolonialists, imperialists, Western predators and destroyers are not the problem of Africa. We should make this clear. It is the content of the collective mind of Africa that is the major problem of Africans in the process of working toward Africa's complete emancipation. The African leaders, educators, and elites have failed miserably to grasp the powerful relationship between the content of Africa's collective mind on the one hand and African perceptions, preferences and goal formation that are shaping our national life, and rational use of information and knowledge, on the other hand. Thus even our education systems have become captive of this anti-African ideology where education is not viewed as an instrument of national liberation but rather to train Africans to service the thievery system and the corresponding institutions that the predators and destroyers have set up. We brag about the importance of working for international organizations which are under the control of the predators rather than being proud of working for our domestic institutions. This type of African mindset must go through ideological restructuring through a destructive-constructive process that is African-centered.

There are a number of Africans that we must exclude from those that I have indicted. Among them is Kwame Nkrumah, the first President of Ghana, whose incisive understanding of the role of ideology in shaping national consciousness, social choices and national history led him to establish the Kwame Nkrumah Ideological Institute at Winneba in Ghana. Nkrumah's objective in this regard was to provide a medium for creating a correct ideology that would serve the

African people as well as combat the neocolonialist and imperialist propaganda through the established anti-African ideology and put a stop to the subservient role that Africans have being playing with pride through the colonial mindset of anti-African ideology in the global system of exploitation to the demise of Africa and her children. Nkrumah adopted from the beginning the ideology of African nationalism. Similarly, we must excluded from those accused Cheikh Anta Diop whose monumental works stand as important intellectual combatants against anti-African ideology [36-40]. There are some few other African leaders and elite that we have not mentioned that may also be excused [6a] [8b] [10c] [13] [88][153a].

Blinded by the mental servitude, lack of understanding of the powerful role that ideology plays in shaping national life, destiny and history, the ignorance about the need for the correct African ideology and the detrimental role of anti-African ideology that the imperial predators have planted in the minds of our people, the February 1966 traitors of Africa in Ghana, who with the support of the Western imperial predators dislodged violently Nkrumah and the legitimate democratic government of Ghana, also dismantled, to the happiness of Africa's predators and destroyers, the Ideological Institute, the Young Pioneer Movement and the Workers Brigade [60b] [138c]. Ironically, the African traitors in Ghana operating in the zone of cognitive imbecility praised the Western youth organizations such as the Boys and Girls Scouts but violently condemned the home-grown youth organization, The Young Pioneer Organization. By so doing these African traitors in collaboration with the imperialist predators strengthened the anti-African ideology that some of the founding leaders were trying to dislodge, weakened the ideology of African nationalism and set Africa on the course of poverty generation, state and ethnic conflicts that Africa has been experiencing.

Africa and the African leaders being guided by anti-African ideology, but not the ideology of African nationalism, with a leadership vacuum of true African nationalism created and the voice of Africa dismantled by the removal of Kwame Nkrumah from the super political leadership and scene, the remaining leaders quickly lost sight of the Great Vision and the history of Africa's modern relationship with the imperial West. Thus the imperial predators and destroyers were able to manipulate the divided Africa and set the divisions against each other in intra-state and inter-state wars. In this way it was easy for the imperial predators to foster different conflicts among the Africans such as Southern Sudan against Northern Sudan, Eritrea against Ethiopia, internal conflicts in Sierra Leone, Somalia, Liberia, Rwanda, Angola, Mozambique, Algeria, Egypt, Morocco, the Democratic Republic of Congo and the whole of the "Great Lakes Region" and many more. These conflicts have common elements, and that is that they are to destroy Africa and set Africa backward into Stone Age and slavery because the Africans collectively hold anti-African ideology that devours any meaningful progress except the sort that goes to support the imperialist system of exploitation.

The anti-African ideology compels African leaders in different states, acting not in concert with other African states, to mortgage the African resources and her future to create conditions for Africa's destruction. In this way Africa pays for her own destruction while Africans pay for their enslavement. What an awkward position Africa finds herself in! The anti-African ideology is a cognitive cancer devouring voraciously everything African in its way. Instead of the African leaders fighting to emancipate and unite Africa they fight to disunite Africa, and to protect the interest of the imperial West and Africa's predators. What bizarre behavior!

This bizarre behavior is maintained by a dangerous concept of education, which is held by the members of the political, academic and religious elite of Africa. To them education of the nation is setting up institutions of learning to show the Africans what the Europeans have done and so the Africans can come into these institutions and find out the great mystery of Europe, learn it and go and mimic it in the African world. These institutions of learning teach no critical thinking. They also teach practically nothing about what Africans have done, and how best to improve and practice it in Africa, so that the mindset that emerges would be African-centered as it should be with African ideology. With African-centered education on the principles of African interest, this anti-African mindset that is attached to the collective and individual cognition of the Africans will be removed and Africans will be cognitively moved to a perceptive environment, where the Africans believe that "the ancestral greatness, the unimpaired genius, and the recuperative power of the race, and its irrepressibility which assures its permanence, constitute Africa's greatest source of inspiration" [130d, p. 265] but not the European gimmickry of democracy, good governance, and development.

The nature of the anti-African ideology places the African way of life in a semi-paralyzed mode where the African collective cognitive machinery is in dislocation with the result that Africans have become a subservient people irrespective of where you find then in this world. We must shake loose this cognitive constraint that limits our horizon, blinds our vision and constrains our rhythmic motion through external controls of our knowledge diameter that defines the circumference of our creative possibilities. This cannot be done with the current African institutions of learning and policy transmission. The current African institutions of learning have dangerous levels of accumulation of combustible materials of anti-African ideology and imperialist propaganda that have turned them into instruments of miseducation for mass destruction of African culture, personality and essence. When these combustible materials of anti-African ideology and imperialist propaganda ignite, they will bust into unquenchable flames that will incinerate the African mind into non-salvageable ashes as a final destruction of the African personality leading to an external imposition of neo-servitude.

African nationalism, as an African collective consciousness, stands in opposition to Africans killing Africans for nothing beneficial to Africa but mainly to assist the success of the predatory activities of Africa's imperial destroyers. As the African organic ideology, African nationalism calls upon us to think African and continentally. It compels us to remember that even in the ancient times Europe looked to Africa for new and exciting ideas: ideas that inspired the cognitive apparatus of Europe in such a manner that they became engrained in the European way of life through the expression *ex Africa semper aliquid novi* (out of Africa always comes something new). We would like to suggest that there is a missing link that must connect the forces of independence to those of complete emancipation. This missing link is the African nationalism that must be instilled in the collective mind of Africans, the belief that African existence is a mere parody unless it is engraved with the ideology of African nationalism, African unity and a thinking system that is African centered.

Let us recall that African nationalism, as the ideology, is to unite Africa first at the level of cognition where unity of thinking and action as directed to the improvement of Africa are the norms of collective thinking of Africans. It seeks to create conditions where Africa's perceptions and preferences defined over the choice-decision space are molded by cognitive apparatus that is not dislocated from its African roots and conditions of existence. At the level of practice African nationalism and the corresponding thinking system will guide us to decide, choose and act in a manner that benefits Africa and her children. The thinking here is that without correct African ideology and the corresponding thinking system Africans will in most cases decide, choose and act to the detriment of Africa's future because of the thinking framework left by Africa's imperial predators. We are Africans first before we belong to any state, and that any African belongs to a particular territorial area called a state is a result of accidents of demographic evolutions of the African people and the historical accident of slavery and colonialism. Let us not forget that the current African states and territorial boundaries are the craft of the greedy Western imperial predators. Our task is to reconstitute them into viable unity and our challenge is to establish African nationalism.

We are the same people with a common struggle and one destiny before our Creator. Therefore African nationalism instructs us all that:

> Never before were the signs of the times clearer than the present as to the coming together of Africans throughout the world. Instinctively it is being felt that in race solidarity is the coming strength of a people who have once again in the cycle of the ages to contribute substantially to the new civilization that is about dawning…. It is but asserting the common place when we say that the expatriation of some of our people to America and to the West Indies in times past was, in order of Providence, to hasten a national consciousness; and to-day our brethren there are turning with longing eyes to the fatherland [137, pp.402-403].

This national consciousness is African nationalism that looks forward to the poetic statement of P. Isaka Seme that:

> *O Africa!*
> *Like some great century-plant, that shall but bloom*
> *In ages hence, we watch thee; in our dream*
> *See in thy swamps the Prospero of our stream;*
> *Thy doors unlocked, where knowledge in her tomb*
> *Has lain innumerable years in gloom.*
> *Then shalt thou, waking with that morning gleam*
> *Shine as thy sister lands with equal beam.* [130d, p. 265]

This morning gleam is the sudden birth of African unity and the equal beam is Africa's permanent and sustainable prosperity. Here lies African nationalism as the African ideology that must shape African perceptions and preferences over the choice-decision space. If African nationalism is to succeed in bringing about unity and prosperity to Africa, it must rest on the will of the African people where such a will is anchored on African-centered mind and correct ideology but not on anti-African ideology and imitation of trivialities of other lands. Here the African nationalist intellectuals have no choice. They must face the intellectual storm and take the bull by its horns to shake loose the Euro-centric anti-African ideology and institutions of learning in Africa that maintain and promote it. In place of this we must construct a true African ideology, the corresponding thinking system and institutions of learning that draw their nourishments from African history as well as their fire from the perpetual flame of African culture, the same flame that the imperial predators could not extinguish. This construct is forced on us by African history, ancestry and the Greater Africa that is. In an important characteristic way, Diop puts it thus:

> Historical circumstances now demand of our generation that it solves in a felicitous manner the vital problems that face Africa, most especially the cultural problem. If we do not succeed in this, we will appear in the history of the development of our people as the watershed generation that was unable to insure the unified cultural survival of the African continent; the generation which, out of political and intellectual blindness, committed the error fatal to our national future. We will have been the unworthy generation par excellence [40, p. 14].

To accomplish this, African-centered ideological education is required. We think that these ideas are reflected in the thinking that led to the establishment of the Ideological Institute in Ghana by Kwame Nkrumah. Let us reflect on the institute and how it fits into the process of establishing organic African nationalism as well as structuring a set of strategies to reclaim Africa's past, understand the forces that are shaping current conditions and thus select an appropriate path to Africa's future.

3.5   A Reflection on the Kwame Nkrumah Ideological Institute at Winneba

When a people has been subjugated and indoctrinated by false conception of totality of life, even including God and their history over a long period, and has emerged from oppression, terror, slavery, colonialism and imperial system of exploitation or predatory activities, it has a particular mindset that flows from an ideology that is inimical to its own survival and progress through a program of conditioning and indoctrination. This is the case of Africans and the ideology is anti-African one. This is historically true of the Americas, Caribbean and Africa itself. The indoctrination of Africans with anti-African ideology was orchestrated through the use of institutions of information media and education systems that were controlled by the colonialists and imperialists. (The reader may consult Chapter One of a companion volume [43d]). Additionally, all the institutions that they have built and transferred them to the Africans are infested with this anti-African ideology, in the sense that the content of the subject of instruction, particularly social sciences, speaks not to the interest of the African but to his or her destruction. Thus in an important respect the Africans and the colonial institutions operate to the detriment of Africa and Africans. The result is that this ideological campaign based on aggressive disinformation and misinformation has produced a collective African mindset where in fact God is presented in the image of the predators and racial superiority of European people is given divine preeminence.

When an African state emerges out of these conditions of servitude and oppression with an anti-African mindset, the people and the inherited institutions of religion, politics, law and economics are held in hostage by the regime of anti-African ideology and foreign domination. National progress is practically impossible until the African state breaks itself from this cognitive chain of oppression, subservience and racism. Nkrumah understood that this anti-African ideology must be dismantled and be replaced with an Africentric ideology that satisfies the conditions required for Africa's complete emancipation as well as the needs of Africa's sustained development and progress through internal self-motion and self-reliance.

The colonial way of doing things and the anti-African mindset were nurtured to service the colonial machinery of territorial exploitation and hence produced a personality that was not and is not favorable to Africa's emancipation and progress. In order to establish and promote African nationalism and correct African ideology that would shape our history and mold our actions toward a complete emancipation after decolonization, Africa needed institutions of thinking and not imitation, where the concepts and contents of African nationalism and African ideology could be developed and disseminated among Africans. The degree of success of "re-ideologization" of Africans would determine the path of progress toward Africa's complete emancipation and sustained progress. We are sure that Nkrumah was aware of this ideological problem when he pointed out how the imperialist predators used distorted African history, anthropology, malicious myths and intellectual deceptions as instruments of European oppressive ideology. In the same spirit, it is useful to consult the monumental works of Anta Diop [36] [37], a number of African thinkers [88], Ben-Jochannan [13] [14] [15], Williams [150b], Woodson [152], Asa Hillard [70b] among others [8b].

The members of the African academic elite, carbon copies of their imperial educators, who inherited the African institutions of learning from the imperialist predators, were hostile to the idea of integrating the teachings of African nationalism and African ideology into the existing curriculum structure. And not only that, they were hostile to the idea of developing an independent African academy with its own autonomy and identity. In this connection the analysis of an American educator, Eicher may be referenced [155, pp. 27-34]. As his thesis he states:

> African education is intimately linked with the international aid and education industry, and that the donor/client dependency relationship has inhibited the development of African institutions and the capacity of Africans to develop educational policies which are socially relevant and financially feasible, for the last quarter of this (Twentieth) century.

This viewpoint has long been recognized and analyzed by Woodson who points out the problems of Black education [152]. The same indictment can be levied against approaches to African socioeconomic development where donor/client dependency relationship has been created under dependency and donor ridden ideology. The integration of the African ideology into the existing curriculum structure that is infested with the anti-African ideological virus will require either an overhaul or radical restructuring of the educational system.

The creation of an independent African academy will require that the African academic elite trained in colonial traditions become African-centered educated, separate from their masters and develop a new and alternative paradigm of education based on African culture, needs, sensibility and historical facts rather than on European fictions of anthropology, archeology and racism about Africa. Either the radical curriculum restructuring or the development of an independent African academy requires critical and creative thinking that must relate education to Africa's needs but not imitation of the foolishness of other people. Since education of the African academic elite has been primarily imitative and has resulted in cognitive enslavement the members could not embark upon the role that history demanded of them. Blinded, therefore, by their colonial education, they went to school to simply find out what the Europeans have done, imitate it and practice it in Africa even if it is to their own detriment. Sociologically European historic facts, material life and cultural behavior are given universal status in the same way as facts of scientific life. They are then practiced in Africa like one shoe fits all with due disregard of African traditions and institutions that holds the Africans together.

The members of the African elite thus failed to appreciate the power of correct African ideology in changing the course of African history simply by providing the capacity to alter Africa's perceptions and preferences over the choice-decision space. It is here that national aspiration and Africa's vision come in conflict with academic freedom. When the academy abandons its historic mission as a liberating force, and separates itself from the culture that provides its existence, it loses its social legitimacy and hence its claim of support in terms of finance and society's obligation (see Chapter 6 of this volume for further analysis).

In this respect, new and independent institutions of higher caliber of creative thinking and friendly to the concept and development of African ideology are required to resolve the internal conflict. The inherited colonial institutions of higher learning were not appropriate because they were seriously infested with colonial propaganda and anti-African ideological virus, particularly in the areas of social sciences where interpretations of social truth are affected by the ideology of the imperial predators. Kwame Nkrumah was convincingly aware of this as he remarked that "in order to provide a steady flow of ideologically sound cadres to carry on the work of politicization of the masses it became necessary to establish an institution where training and instruction could be given" [114, p. 161](see also [60b].

On the basis of this critical observation, the Kwame Nkrumah Ideological Institute at Winneba in Ghana was born in February 1961. The original name of the institute is Kwame Nkrumah Institute of Economics and Political Science. What a vision and what a creative thinking! At this juncture and on this ideological question one can quickly refer to Nsanze, the former ambassador of Burundi to the United Nations [117]. It was a vision and thinking that other African leaders did not have and did not emulate. A vision and thinking that some members of the African academic elite sought to destroy by calling it communistic, anti-West and many silly characterizations on the basis of false conceptions and bankrupt interpretations of historic facts. This vision of creating correct African ideology and promoting Pan-African ideas was destroyed by the imperialist predators working through their Ghanaian collaborators in February1966.

The Ghanaian traitors were produced by the colonial education with a subservient mindset. They and their elite supporters believed that the West is the best and Africa is darkness that needs to be whitened by the light from Europe as they had learned primitively and imitationally from the anti-African ideology orchestrated through institutions set up by the parasitically imperial predators. Contrary to the Pan-African great intellectuals such as Nkrumah, Diop, DuBois, Padmore, Garvey, Duchein, Ben Bella, Ben-Jochannan and many more, these traitors and their elite supporters failed to understand that they are Africans and that the world is seen through many windows each of which provides a different view that is reflected in perception and in accordance with the ideology that governs the collective sight and perceptions. Each ideology allows the society and its individual members to see the world's events through different windows. And even through the same window different views and perceptions are projected by different ideologies. The European sees slavery in terms of its benefit to his wealth creation. The African on the other hand sees slavery in terms of cost and devastation of his or her homeland.

However these traitors and their supporting elite failed to understand that finding the windows with the corresponding ideology that meets the factual correctness of Africa's experiences as well as satisfying the cognitive requirements for complete Africa's emancipation was a challenge that could be met not by the inherited colonial institutions but by the establishment of institutions that would develop and disseminate African-centered ideas among Africans on the basis of Pan-African ideology and African nationalism.

The objective of the Winneba Institute was to disconnect the African from his or her acquired colonial mindset, re-Africanize him or her to the African roots imbued in him or her, the African personality, energize him or her to the ideology of African Nationalism so as to set free the African creative essence for complete emancipation. Remember the effective role of ideology in shaping perceptions and preferences which affect social decision making. In national history, it is the collective perception that shapes the path and direction but not what reality connotes. By restructuring the social ideology we alter the environment of social decision and hence national life and the history that follows. It is within this context that the contribution of the Kwame Nkrumah Ideological Institute must be analyzed and understood. It is also within this context that the contributing spirit of the Ghana Young Pioneers and the Workers Brigade must have decision reference point for analysis. Accordingly, the analysis and conclusions in the document entitled "Nkrumah's Subversion in Africa", supposed to have been authored from Ghana Ministry of Information and Broadcasting, are not only intellectually bankrupt but subversive to Africa's emancipation and progress [60b]. Such an analysis and the like are the works of those Africans operating in the zone of cognitive imbecility.

As analyzed, we cannot emphasize it enough that the major problem of Africa in bringing about unity and complete emancipation is not the imperialists and neocolonialists for they will work to undermine the process of African unity as well as maintain Africa's disunity that facilitates their predatory activities. The major problem is simply that the African institutions of learning were set up to destroy the traditional creativity and to produce education that is imitative of what Europeans have done in order to service the institutions of Africa's oppression under the conditions of illusions of belonging. This Eurocentric education destroyed traditional learning institutions, craftiness, inventiveness and teaching methodology. The imitation has always been of the wrong kind that has resulted in the cognitive enslavement and anti-African ideology that hold Africa's progress in check, creativity in a dormant state, her achievements in the museum of foreign lands, her people in bondage and her modern history as an appendage to the history of European imperial order that tries to obliterate the history of her intellectual and technical gifts to the rest of the world.

The trained Africans with no African-centeredness generally know very little as to what African people have done in the past, and even much of the little that they know is what the Europeans have written distortedly and projected through institutions of learning to be the truth and they believe and teach the fiction. Africa's past is presented in disconnected mode and every achievement is claimed to be European, and where it is difficult to claim, it is credited to some alien beings.

Every independent and creative attempt by enlightened African scholarship to reconnect the current Africa with Africa's creative past is obstructed by the African intellectual *askari* and rent seekers supported by the imperial predators. The African intellectual *askari* hiding imitatively behind false conceptions of democracy, governance, development, divinity, academic freedom and much more become destructive forces on the path to Africa's social truth. They do not know and do not seriously teach what Africans have done, so they cannot imitate their own people while the Europeans claim achievements of Africans and improve upon them as their own. The Europeans discovered Africa and her people, and if it is possible they will even claim that they created the Africans. In fact, they have indirectly claimed so by simply representing God and His or Her lieutenants in their images. Thus by logical extension and fundamental absurdity they created the African through divination.

All these conditions of anti-African ideology were clear to Nkrumah in that to achieve Africa's independence, emancipation, unity and social progress, an ideology of African nationalism was not only essential but required by decision imperatives that are needed (and still needed) to counterbalance and discredit the malicious myths, propaganda and anti-African ideology as promoted (and still being promoted) by Europeans and certain miseducated and misguided members of the African elite. In fact we are comfortable to state that the rise of the Nation of Islam in the United States of America was a direct response to these European vicious myths and anti-African ideology. This ideology of African nationalism must be developed, promoted and disseminated among the African masses by new institutions of learning that are African-centered and free from the ills and infections of the

European malicious myths and propaganda against Africa and her children. Nkrumah saw the new institutions as ideological institutes devoted primarily to satisfy Africa's needs and the internal and external relationships that are required for Africa's search for true independence and social progress without once again becoming a victim to imperial predatory activities. Let us summarize the ideological content of African nationalism.

3.6 Summary of the Ideological Contents of African Nationalism

Let me now turn my attention to an important dimension of African nationalism and the correct African ideology that must guide African integration and union. The dimension is the ideological content of African nationalism. The understanding of the content of a particular ideology is very crucial to its correct practice. Hence a clear specification of the content is a demand on theory and the demand by practice. The ideological content, as a system of ideas and conceptual ideals geared toward Africa's emancipation, is what we are referring to as the ideological system of African Nationalism. The ideological system as a foundation of belief places priority on loyalty to the formation of the African Union and the corresponding Continental Union Government of Africa. In the content of African nationalism is defined a clear position that true emancipation of Africa rests on the principle of African unity, not simply some form of loose associations, in all fronts of human endeavor. The principle of African unity is viewed as an instrument by means of which cultural, technological, scientific and socioeconomic development can be forged from the current contradictions leading to the building of the good life to the benefit of all, regardless of tribe, creed, color or stage in life. In other words, the practice of African unity supported by the ideology of African nationalism must lead to the improvement of the general welfare of the African people under conditions of peace, justice and political stability irrespective of the state of one's residence.

African unity is a concept plan in the ideological system of African Nationalism. It is derived from conditions encountered as well as needs of modern Africa. It also embraces the glorious history and cultural unity of African civilization to which Western and Eastern civilizations and their derivatives are heavily indebted [10c] [10d] [10e] [13] [14] [36]

[39]. As an instrument for developing the social infrastructure and institutions through which the collective resources of Africans can be organized on a continental scale, African unity satisfies all the necessary conditions for an accelerated technological and economic development that Africa needs without external dependency [40]. In order for the potential inherent in African unity to be actualized through the application of a system of positive actions, its supporting ideological system of African nationalism must hold certain basic ideas as self-evident truths that constitute its general and specific contents. These ideas that are set out below, therefore, constitute the general and specific content of African nationalism.

(1) Africa cannot be emancipated if each state views its territorial boundaries as defining a sovereign nation that has nothing in common with other African states except the usual international relations.

(2) The sovereignty of each liberated African state can neither be secured nor guaranteed; and racism, and racial injustice against African people all over the world will not stop unless African leaders realize beyond all conceivable doubts that Africa's salvation and progress rest securely on unity and not on external dependency such as aid or begging from here or from there, and not from patchworks of relationships with international institutions that have become vehicles of neocolonialism and imperialism.

(3) Colonialists and imperialists will continually reenter Africa and show their ugly heads through new forms by the method and techniques of divide and rule through the international institutions that they have set up to promote propaganda of development help, democracy, good governance, human rights, population control, poverty reduction and others. They will encourage fighting and warring in and among the African states in such a divided Africa leading to retardation of technological, scientific and economic emancipation thus rendering African independence meaningless if not useless. This will provide other intellectual munitions for the mis-educated African to even argue that judging from contemporary facts colonialism was better than independence. The neocolonialists and imperialists with their supporting global infrastructure (seeChapter6) will encourage the annihilation of the most important and revolutionary core of the African intelligentsia, thus retarding the natural development of African modern thought. In this respect, the history of Africa will be recorded as showing that independence has

been nothing but a failure for the Africans. This will be a self-fulfilling prophecy for the laughing enjoyment of the West. The imperialists' objective here is not only creating the conditions where new forms of exploitation and racism are acceptable to the African masses but also to create a structure that justifies the old intellectual nonsense of the European concept of race superiority.

(4) The idea of re-exploitation is supported by the fact that current territorial divisions of Africa, if maintained, place African economic, technological and cultural institutions at the mercy of foreign interest rather than to the service of African people. Fragmentation has no place in Africa's struggle for complete emancipation. The maintenance of the current territorial divisions with the supporting sovereignties will lead to the weakening of the defense mechanism of the individually decolonized states and hence to further weakening of the emancipation and defense of Africa as a whole.

(5) The completion of the historic task of complete emancipation of Africa and her people irrespective of their places of dwelling from the chains of slavery, abuses and oppression by the Europeans; the subsequent survival of decolonized Africa; and the maintenance of Africa's freedom and the effective development of her human and non-human resources toward the bright future on which Africa's hope and endeavors are pinned, rest on the reconstitution of much divided Africa into a political, military and economic union. Without this, no African state, and no African irrespective of the place of birth, will be free and can sensibly claim to be a free person. This must be a theorem in the revolutionary thinking and practice of every African and African nationalist on whom the construction of new African world order rests, and with whom the responsibility in moving Africa through the twenty first century and the new millennium firmly resides.

(6) The lack of political, legal, economic and military unity for common development and defense forces the decolonized individual African states, out of sheer desperation and out of sense of insecurity and hopelessness, to enter into defense pacts with foreign powers to protect them against other African countries and internal strife, seek useless and meaningless loans and economic aid, sometimes with and from the same colonial predators and oppressors. Furthermore, economic, political and military insecurities drive these disoriented African states to undertake a constant patchwork of faked and exploitative relationships with international institutional structures

which racially dislike and reject them, instead of making a bold break from these hostile international institutions and redirecting their energies to collectively create the needed institutions that will serve Africa and her children. Africa must enter into international institutions with one voice, The Voice of Africa. Undoubtedly this constant patchwork of faked and exploitative relationships with the established international institutions where the Voice of Africa is silenced endangers the economic and military security of all decolonized African states as well as all Africans both at home and abroad, and at the same time makes it difficult to complete the independence movement as well as Africa's emancipation.

(7) No African state, irrespective of the size, big or small, or where it is situated on the continent, can afford to live in isolation from other African states and hope to preserve its sovereignty and independence; and at the same time hope to make a headway into technological, scientific and economic development in the present international circumstances, and in the world that is completely hostile to Africa except when her human and non-human resources are allowed to be exploited freely without Africa's resistance. This is a historic reality that must sink deeply into the stubborn minds of Africans who are always trying to be something else besides African. The sovereignty of African states and the freedom of Africans stand completely open to danger as long as the African states remain apart from one another and blinded to the true colors of the international institutional configuration and its exploitative tendencies.

(8) Looking at history and the stigma that has been attached to Africa and the African, irrespective of where he or she resides, or his or her position in social order as laid down by the imperialist predators, particularly in the Eurocentric world, the political, economic and military weight of each African state is insignificant in international negotiations. The combined political, economic and military weight of united Africa, in addition to mobilizing the support of her children outside Africa to speak with one voice, the Voice of Africa, where Africa speaks for herself and is not spoken for, can however generate an effort and force that can soften imperialist and neocolonialist predatory activities, the stubborn challenges of technology, science, and economic development, and at the same time break its way through the obstinate obstacles of the predators' obstructions and sabotage that impede the general African development and complete emancipation.

(9) There are no free lunches, give-aways and philanthropies in the global capitalist system, not in Europe, not in the Americas and not in Asia either. Aids, grants, loans and benevolent activities are deceptive instruments developed by neocolonialists to create dependency syndrome and an environment of debt traps that fix the countries in revolving doors of illusions of development and international inclusion. In this way conditions are manufactured in the African countries for foreign rent-seeking and imperialist predatory activities under the camouflage of democracy which is ideologically equated to privatization and then to Christendom.

(10) Self-reliance is the golden principle for emancipation and social development under conditions of freedom, justice and true democracy. Thus, the first-best approach is to stay away from these deceptive traps of the neocolonialist gimmicks and deceptions of of the imperialist predators. Loans, aid, grants, technical assistance and all other benevolence are welcomed to the extent to which they fit in the overall plan of Africa's emancipation that is Africa's creation.

These are just some of the basic ideas and beliefs that must cement the ideological foundation of African nationalism. In this respect, any African nationalist must understand that there are battles to be fought on the continent and outside the continent of Africa, as much as there are obstacles and impediments to overcome. The task is a completely radical restructuring of Africa's social, political, military and economic order and her relationships with other parts of the world. The job is not easy. The enemies are many. However, there is African dignity to be won; there is a continent to be reclaimed; there are Africans to be saved; there is a glorious history to be redeemed and there are prosperity and power to be regained in order to place Africa in its proper place in history for the defense of her children and interest. "Africa must be free and Africa must unite" is the slogan. Africa and Africans all over the world have nothing to loose by uniting. The African nationalist, therefore, must understand that ideologically African unity is the first uncompromising requisite for the total emancipation of Africa and Africans. Primary and basic for Africa's needed technological and economic development leading to the improvement of the welfare of the Africans is the long-awaiting formation of the Continental Union Government of Africa, as Nkrumah had reflected [105].

The true African nationalist must also understand that African nationalism with the ideology of African unity and the subsequent

Continental Union Government of Africa is a revolution; it is a program. Such a program, to be effective as a guide to action, must be derived from a new, general, positive and organic principle of totality of Africa's historic past as well as the holistic experience of her modern history, current difficulties and recent problems. Such a new, general, positive and holistic principle is African nationalism that must lead to African unity. To the African nationalist, therefore, the first and most important thing is to accept unconditionally the principle of African unity. Having accepted this principle he or she must make sure that the development of the concept of Africa unity, the ideological content of African nationalism and strategies for the attainment of Africa's emancipation and unity is confined to the people who believe in the principle of African unity. Such people must, therefore, be liberated from every tie and connection opposed to Africa's emancipation and African unity. These statements and the corresponding logical structure flow from foundations of African philosophy and its self-contained logic of reason.

In this line of reason the Organization of African Unity (OAU) failed in that there were many people who were not believers in the unity objective but work there just for a living without the ideological consciousness, the African nationalism and African personality that African unity and emancipation require. We are not sure if these problems of African collective consciousness and personality may be overcome with the new African Union (AU) without substantial Pan-African institutional building as well as institutional and ideological restructuring of the individual African states. This will require the development of intellectual African-centeredness with strong African personality, and African nationalism with complete redefinition of Africa's relationship with herself and the rest of the world.

One may ask, and rightly so, what are the opposing principles to African unity. We can dwell extensively on this question which we do not want to do at this time. We will rather provide you with examples and ideas so that one can complete the trend. Examples among the class of opposing ideas are the concept of national sovereignties of the decolonized territories or loyalty to a specific state at the expense of loyalty to either African unity or the federated state to be. Another example is to hold a position that one decolonized territory is superior to others in one way or the other. The African nationalist must pursue the line of reasoning that all Africans states have more in common than they have in differences. He or she must take a position that the development of the concept of African unity must emphasize the common grounds of African people and design strategies to reduce their actual or perceived differences. The African cultural unity that has been impressively demonstrated by Anta Diop [37] must be accepted unconditionally as a fact of African life, refined and aggressively promoted among the Africans both at home and abroad as is also being done by Van Sertima [143a-b][144a-b]. This requires the rise of a leadership which believes in the value of African nationalism with Africentric consciousness, in addition to the development of marketing strategies and institutions through which the strategies may be refined and implemented.

It also must be kept in mind that central to the reasoning system of African nationalism is that African unity gives a substance to African independence as well as content to the concept of African nation. At the core of the concept of the African nation is political, economic, monetary, legal and military union. Its substance is derived from the formation of a continental defense network, common economic development with well planned complementary sectors, and communication and intelligence gathering machinery linking together all institutional, territorial and functional sectors of African societies while monitoring all forces opposed to Africa's emancipation and progress and interest.

The ideological content of African nationalism calls for African unity; African nationalism calls for African self-determination; African nationalism calls for collective responsibility and hard work; African nationalism calls for collective development on all fronts of economics, science, technology and culture; African nationalism calls for purposefulness where the sweat of the African brow is directed carefully toward Africa's emancipation as well as improving the welfare of the Africans both at home and abroad; African nationalism calls for creative thinking to design new and improved ways of emancipating the African, to break loose the chains of physical, spiritual and mental slavery and to set free the creative energies of the Africans; African nationalism calls for unshakable faith in African unity, the African people and all their descendants, and above all the African creative energies to set free the life that is frozen.

In this respect, African nationalism prescribes a code of conduct for Africans in the way we view each other and our states; the way we view the position in history of our states and Africa; and the way we must act toward one another and toward Africa. And lastly, a question must be asked, what are you? Are you an African nationalist or not, and if you are not, are you willing to be an African nationalist? If your answer is yes, then the first and most immediate act is to examine critically yourself, your mind, your previous behavior toward yourself and other Africans and their descendants, and then answer to yourself whether your actions reveal you as a disgrace to your race, or as a promoter of Africa's compete emancipation agenda or as a liberator of your people.

In this process of critical examination, we would like to suggest to you that if you would confess with your lips to yourself and the African world that African unity is the vehicle for complete emancipation, and would immutably believe in your heart that true African personality and spirit of freedom have risen from the ashes of Africa's glorious past, from the tombs of her great Kings, Queens, Pharaohs and members of High Priesthood, and from her recent suffering to emancipate her children, you would unquestionably be saved, liberated and at peace. You are then an African nationalist. In the framework of Africa's complete emancipation, the concept of African unity strikes a burning chord through the world imperial system of exploitation. The unity between true African leaders and enlightened African American leaders projects fire through the soul of United States of America (see for example Zbigniew Brzezinski's secret Presidential Review Memorandum/NSC-46 on the subject of Black Africa and the U.S. Black Movement, date March 17, 1978, declassified). African unity and Pan-Africanism are prime targets for destruction by Africa's adversaries because they define the correct path to the complete emancipation of Africa and her children. Let us turn our attention to the concept of state-specific nationalism and its relationship to African nationalism in terms of enhancement and destruction.

4

AFRICAN NATIONALISM AND STATE-SPECIFIC NATIONALISM

So far we have laid down the basic reasoning and ideological system of thinking and operational basis of African nationalism. African nationalism is projected as African collective consciousness that implies a political, economic, monetary and military cohesiveness, an African unity where the individual decolonized states are identified with and glued to one another to constitute the federated state to be formed. It is a collective consciousness where the individual African is a citizen of the African nation that is continental in nature; where everybody, man, female, child, old, irrespective of his or her level of education can travel over the continent without the hassles of document fillings and re-fillings that disadvantage the illiterate. It is a collective consciousness where there is a complete mobility of resources and goods within the confines of the continent without unnecessary and artificial interruptions and impediments; and where every African can enjoy the beauty and bounty that the continent is generously endowed with. It is collective consciousness that instructs us that every state and every African has equal rights within the bounds of the established federation and within the established rules of economic, judicial and political engagements, where freedom and justice are rules and there is a foundation of democratic social cohesion; this implies freedom to worship as one chooses, since the African philosophical and theological tradition holds God to be one and declares that there is not only one way but many avenues of communication with the Creator, and access to the Creator is democratically established for all individuals and the collective.

A number of important and perhaps disturbing questions arise within the concept of African nationalism that we have advanced. The obvious and immediate one is the question of the relationship between state-specific nationalism (for example Nigerian, Kenyan, Egyptian, Ghanaian and other forms of nationalism) and African nationalism. In most of the existing literature the forms of state-specific nationalism, as we prefer to call it, are classified as African nationalism, particularly by Western writers. Of course, some African writers, lacking intellectual independence, have also followed in the footsteps of their intellectual colonizers from the West to use the term without redefinition or examination of it against the background of Africa's historic experiences. These writers have confused themselves and their readers through their inability to distinguish between the drive to repossess the African lands by the Africans through the decolonization of specific territories that acquired pseudo-nationhood within the boundaries of the imperial system of exploitative relationships, and the drive to create an African nation that is continental in nature. We would like, now, to state clearly and crisply the complete position of the African nationalist.

4.1 Conditions of State-specific Nationalism

The rise of state-specific nationalism as in the Kenyan or Angolan form was derived from the will on the part of the Africans to reclaim the lands that were confiscated by force and occupied by Europeans and to free themselves from European oppression an exploitation, just like any other territory that was to be decolonized. The will to be free from European oppression, violence, terror and racism is all African and rooted in the very soul of the African. However, the nature and structure of the distribution of European power over African continent required specific methods of operations that were territorially specific in nature. The strategy was to arouse and motivate the African masses that fell under a particular European colonial sphere to rise up against such an imperial political power that is completely foreign to Africa. One must refer to the All African People's Congress held in Accra in December 1958 as one example where strategies of decolonization were mapped out, coordinated and put into practice [114]. The collective consciousness of the Africans of these specific territories aimed at overthrowing the European governing systems which were notoriously known for racism, terrorism, brutality and oppressive exploitation of human and non-human resources, and making a way to unity, is what has been referred to as African nationalism by other writers.

This is not our conceptual position. This particular notion of African nationalism arose as a result of operational necessity and political feasibility. In fact, the gains of the decolonized territories and the speed with which such gains and victories came would not have been possible under the direct application of the concept of African nationalism that we have advanced here. The only strategy that would have been available under the direct application of the concept of African nationalism advanced here would have been direct and collective military operations by the people of the colonies against the European political powers with their notorious practices of terrorism, racism and hypocrisy. This approach was politically not feasible and organizationally daunting. Even if it were possible it would have unified the European colonizers to approach the problem of decolonization with a common military policy and operations since they all belonged and still belong to the same military union, the North Atlantic Treaty Organization (NATO). The assessment is that Africa would have lost the decolonization battle but not necessarily the war of freedom, given the number of trained soldiers and technical levels of military operation of both Africa and Europe. In view of this, the optimal strategy was that which was chosen which was to offer indirect support for territory-specific decolonization movements while at the same time maintaining the division of the European powers.

The above strategy for decolonization toward the road of Africa's complete emancipation had a number of advantages. It also had a number of drawbacks. Such drawbacks are basically futuristic ones that are reflected in limited current cooperation among the Africans, mounting contemporary problems and increasing difficulties in the correct understanding of the concepts of African nationalism and African nation within the framework of the Nkrumaist program of Africa's emancipation. For one thing, most of the states with territorially specific collective consciousness as a strategy for territorial decolonization either lost their proper relationship to the general African collective consciousness that must form the basis of complete Africa's emancipation, or the leadership in these territories failed to either understand or make the right connection, or they were bought by their colonial masters. This failure on the part of African political leadership to make the right connection has become an important source of ethnic conflicts in post-decolonization Africa. The regrettable drawback which Nkrumah also observed at very early stages of mass decolonization is that the territorially specific collective consciousness for the territorial decolonization has become cemented as the permanent notion of African nationalism, where all-encompassing African nationalism is replaced by state-specific African nationalism and where closer political, military and economic ties were formed between the decolonized African states and their former colonizers and predators rather than among the decolonized African states.

It must be understood clearly that decolonization is part of the process to attain independence. It is not independence. That decolonization is not independence is seen in the idea that independence implies control of a nation's destiny in all fronts of human endeavor. The fact is, there are direct and indirect types of colonialism. Political colonialism is that which is direct and obvious. There are other forms that are indirect; they include mental, cultural and economic colonialism. These indirect forms are the most stubborn to decolonize. Hence a nation can be politically decolonized and yet have no control over her destiny. This should not surprise the true revolutionist. Political decolonization is simply a necessary condition but not sufficient for national independence and preservation of her sovereignty. This is because other latent forms of colonialism will still operate to make the country completely dependent on other powers, as it is the situation with current African states. All African states are still connected to their former colonizers through the institutions that they operate. Political decolonization is a first step toward sovereignty, just as the right to vote and social ability to exercise this right are firsts toward a true democratic tradition. Sovereignty is a step toward political power. Political power is a step toward independence. Independence is a step toward national freedom and justice with peace that will lead to democratic practices in all aspects of national life.

When a nation is born out of decolonization, it is still under the sphere of influence of the colonial power because all the formal institutions were created to serve the colonial machine and thus maintain a continual dependency relationship for the decolonized state. Steps, therefore, must be taken to create the conditions required to attain independence. These conditions are those that are hostile to indirect colonialism. The conditions require a radical restructuring of the inherited institutions and sometimes the demolition of some of the institutions and new ones created in their place (see for example some aspects of Nkrumah's program of positive action as crudely and distortedly presented in [60b]. In this respect, while African states have been politically decolonized from direct occupation by various

Europeans, we think they have no claims to independence and I hope they do not claim so. We are personally convinced beyond any conceivable doubt that while territory-specific collective consciousness has brought about perceived political decolonization or an end to direct colonization it has failed to bring about independence in the true sense of the word. Rather, it has intensified indirect colonialism and brought about illusions of sovereignty and power that the African states do not have. These are stubborn facts of contemporary Africa that we must face. Given the regime of current territorial boundaries, let us examine the positive and negative characteristics of state-specific nationalism and the role it can play to enhance or present problems for African nationalism through the thinking and actions of the African separatists.

4.2   State-specific Nationalism and the African Separatists

The concept of African nationalism interpreted and understood from the viewpoint of the process of decolonization of Africa is territory-specific and strategy-induced. It is, therefore, considered as state-specific nationalism whose content is limiting and lacking continental dimension and substance of the concept of an African nation. In view, therefore, of the holistic concept of African nationalism that we have advanced here, state-specific nationalism would be considered "tribalistic" if it is held and/or practiced at the expense of complete African emancipation. The position held within Nkrumaism is that the concept of state-specific nationalism was and is merely an operational and tactical necessity in order to decolonize the African territories. As such it is a stage in the organic process toward Africa's complete emancipation. If properly conceived and practiced, the concepts of state-specific nationalism and African nationalism are complementary and inter-supportive in the holistic framework of Africans' quest for complete emancipation of Africa and her children where Africa's development path is internally induced but not externally dictated and imposed as appendage to imperial interest.

Generally and uncompromisingly, any principle of state-specific nationalism that is opposed to the concept and practice of African unity must be viewed as subversive to the principle of African nationalism as well as disloyal to the charted course of complete African emancipation and hence against the African masses, the fatherland and Mother Africa. Any person that either follows or practices or spreads or advocates the principles of state-specific nationalism that opposes the concept and practice of African unity is a separatist who can contribute nothing to African nationalism, African unity and the process of complete Africa's emancipation. Such a person is his or her own enemy as well as an enemy of his or her state and Africa. The character of the African separatists is thus clear. In general discussions about African unity, the African separatists are always observed to have cognitive fixity on perception of the impossible goal of African unity and look for reasons to justify their hostile position against African unity and African emancipation.Their engrained personality with a trademark "made in the West" demands of them this anti-African position. Their very nature and personality are such that they will go out of the temple of Africa's struggle through the back door of the temple; and if there is no door, their intellectual essence operating in the zone of cognitive imbecility will force them to create one for their convenience. There are two most important elements about the intellectual personality of the African separatists that fascinate us. The African separatists do not condemn the concept and vision of African unity. Politically, they cannot and dare not to condemn it. They accept either indirectly or directly the concept of African unity to be a good thing and in fact they embrace the goal. They, however, argue against its practice by simply advocating the principle of do-nothingness because they contend that African unity is an operational impossibility. Usually, discussions with them are energy-draining and hope-damping. Intellectually, they are bankrupt and useless for the African course, and from the viewpoint of African holistic history, they are malnourished. Intellectually colonized and mentally enslaved, these African separatists cannot make any meaningful contribution to the development of tactics and strategies for the actualization of African unity unless they revolutionize themselves and acquire a personality that is trademarked "made in Africa". At this point, we owe all Africans some additional explanation.

The African separatists have developed in them an intellectual sterility. Such an intellectual sterility has created blind spots on their cognitive eyes, impairing their ability to clearly see and correctly analyze Africa's current problems in the light of African experiences and conditions that Africans have encountered within the international system of economic, political and military relations. They fail to see that the future history of any people is a potential inherent in the nature. There are many and different potential elements. These potential elements in nature can be ranked in accordance with the degree of social desirability. Each one of them can be actualized with varying cost-benefit relations. However, without a properly charted course and program of action to guide the process of history the least desirable element can be actualized simply by blind social forces. To avoid this, the Africans born at home and abroad like you and we must act with a sense of purpose (Nia). This purpose is African emancipation through African unity. Separatism has no place in this process; neither does it have any place in Africa's collective social life.

The African separatists are caught in a web of contradictions and completely paralyzed by such a set of contradictions that seems to act as destructive force on their cognitive processes. They do not have any logical way out of this web. If they argue against the concept of African unity they know that they do not have the intellectual munitions, while at the same time they will be chastised by African social environment. And yet, the acceptance of African unity is a bitter pill for the separatists to swallow. There are many reasons for this. It may be noted that any leader of an African state cannot and dare not argue against the concept of African unity and enjoy a good political ride even with the African separatists. What then are the problems? We will explain them in Chapter 6 that will help us to understand the operational difficulties of African nationalism.

Only intellectually blinded Africans will be surprised to find out that most of the current so-called African leaders are essentially African separatists in the last analysis. They will, of course, deny it if the question is put to them, "Are you an African separatist?" They will say amen, if you ask them whether they support African unity. And yet if you have a follow-up question as to what plans have they made toward actualizing it you will be left in a blur. Those who will attempt to answer will provide you with the separatist argument. They will provide you with reasons why unity is difficult instead of providing strategies to overcome these problems of institutional organization. The problem of bringing into being of African unity, in the sense that is being advanced here, is simply a problem of organizational will to sacrifice, courage to act and strength to change the current regime of costly international relationships. Similarly, the problem of putting Africa on the path of sustainable progress is not the lack of resources or money. The problem is simply an organizational one at all levels of human endeavors in the use of Africa's rich resources.

Let us, therefore, point out to the African separatist and all African leaders, separatists and unitarist alike, that African unity is a revolutionary concept and it will remain so until its actualization. African nationalism is its ideological vehicle. The two are, therefore, inseparable. They are instruments for Africa's defense and offence in the theater of ideological war, imperial exploitation and global racism. When one accepts the concept of African unity, one has also accepted a revolutionary course that would not only change the historiography of Africa and Africa's social landscape, but also radically alter the international relationships that Africa currently has within Africa and outside Africa regarding economics, politics, national defense and history. African unity and African Union organized on the principles of African nationalism and personality will alter the global political and power landscape that has been Africa's downfall as well as working against every ounce of African true interest.

The concept of African unity threatens the existing global environment because its ideological foundation conceives of a new world order that is organized around the principle of freedom, justice and fairness under true democracy domestically and internationally. It rejects the permanency of the current African partition as well as the socioeconomic and political relations between Africa and the rest of the existing world order. It conceives of a new socioeconomic construct of the world and a new African world. As a revolution toward Africa's complete emancipation, African unity is a program. Such a program must be designed and organized, its course uncompromisingly charted, and needed actions strategized for the application of mass positive actions toward its realization. It is also the challenge of the survival of the race, the African race. It is because of this revolutionary character that the thought of African unity strikes fear in the hearts of Africa's predators and separatists to evoke dislike and hatred.

The logical process of actualizing the potential inherent in nature and society does not permit one to accept the good and benefits in a potential and at the same time find reasons to justify why that which is good and beneficial must not be created except on the basis of real cost analysis. This is a contradiction in the process of replacement of the old by the new. This contradiction leads to an action impasse of sit and wait, a position of do-nothingness which is a typical characteristic of the African separatist who is always comfortable in explaining his or her inaction or negative action by the principle of impossibility (of African unity realization).

To the African separatist this position of do-nothingness is the minimum effort one. It is the least troublesome because the principle of impossibility always keeps him or her in his or her state of social pre-maturity, intellectual sterility and cognitive stagnation. He or she fails to create the inertia for self-motion and hence will rot in his or her relative state of affairs in perpetuity.

The mental state of do-nothingness seems to be a cognitive bliss point for the African separatists. They, therefore, accept the current African divisions as constituting countries and nations where their sovereignties have been ordained and cemented to be permanent landmarks of Africa by gods of Europe. They dance to these sovereignties and worship the gods of Europe while the African masses live in the most deplorable conditions in this world. They reject the challenges of consciously creating history because their education and personality lead them to believe that Africa has no history to create. The African separatists, therefore, are in perpetual bondage and are at the service of their European exploiters and predators. They are of no use to Africa and her children.

Ironically, the African separatists overlook an important organizational fact that just as the European powers at the Berlin Conference partitioned Africa in accordance with European interest, the European colonial powers could just by strokes of their pens have created African mega-states. France could have consolidated the whole of its different colonies in Africa as one colony composed of Senegal, Togo Land, Dahomey, Morocco, Mali, Ivory Coast, Chad, Guinea, Algeria, Tunisia, Upper Volta, Mauritania, Niger, Cameroon, French Equatorial Africa and others. Similarly, Great Britain could have consolidated her African colonies like Anglo-Egyptian Sudan, Egypt, Kenya, Gold Coast, Nigeria, Tanganyika, Nyasaland, Southern and Northern Rhodesia, Gambia, South Africa and others into one mega-colony. Portugal could have done the same thing by consolidating her occupied African territories into a mega-colony. In all these cases the African separatists would have nothing to say about the consolidations.

The political reality is that each of these territories had a governing colonial entity that was controlled from the center of the government of the imperial country against the will of the colonial subjects. It was an undemocratic setup like that of any other occupied territory. The administrative fact was that these colonies were organized and managed as federal states within the respective empires. What then are the reasons why the decolonized Africa cannot be organized on the principles of unity and administered on the principles of federation? This is a question that must be answered by the African separatists. The essential point that is being magnified here is simple. The African separatists constitute a liability rather than an asset to Africa's progress and sustainable freedom. They have simply become useful idiots for European propaganda. They fail to understand that Africa's emancipation and sustainable development rest on seven basic principles of unity, freedom, justice, peace, creativity, faith and progress; all of them are organized around respect for the individual and the collective as African traditions demand.

4.3 The African Nationalists and Separatists in the Unification Process

This position of the African separatist is one opposing African unity and hence African nationalism. It should therefore be rejected completely by the African nationalist. The African nationalist, like the African separatist, accepts the concept of African unity. Unlike the African separatist, however, the African nationalist accepts all the challenges of actualizing the concept of African unity. His or her immediate task is to become a prime mover of African history and mold it by creating the necessary and sufficient conditions for Africa's self-motion. The African nationalist understands clearly those things that are at stake. The African separatist is a sitting duck who fails to understand the dual character of state-specific nationalism. It must be pointed out that proper understanding of the ideological system of Africa's emancipation as implied in Nkrumaism requires state-specific nationalism and African nationalism to be not only complementary but operationally and conceptually inter-supportive.

The logical system of Nkrumaism and the conceptual and operational position of the African nationalist see the first character of state-specific nationalism as providing an ideological guidance for territorially specific political decolonization because of the nature of the political partitioning of Africa. The second character is then seen as providing the ideological guidance toward African unity and Africa's complete emancipation. The first character of state-specific nationalism is a necessary condition for both African nationalism and African separatism. The second character is the sufficient condition for African nationalism. The first character is a necessary condition for African separatism, and hence the lack of the second character of the state-specific nationalism is sufficient for African separatism.

The lack of the second character puts any state-specific nationalism as an ideological adversary to African nationalism as well as indirect opposition to the charted course of Africa's complete emancipation. Its presence is sufficient for the state-specific nationalism to have an inter-supportive relationship with African nationalism. The most important thing to note here is that state-specific nationalism may have either an adversarial or an inter-supportive relationship, but not both, with African nationalism. While an African separatist can be a state-specific nationalist, he or she cannot claim to be an African nationalist. One cannot be an African nationalist and oppose African unity by thought or action.

It may be added that the practice of the ideology of African separatism creates the necessary conditions for the destruction of state sovereignty as well as jeopardizing the chartered course of Africa's emancipation. In fact, it undermines the political independence of the states and reduces the states to international beggars, making them not only subservient, but complete twenty-first slaves to the same colonialists and imperialists that our forefathers and mothers fought so hard against, leaving their sovereignties in laughable state. There is no glory in trading off nineteenth-twentieth century slavery for twenty-first century servitude, for there is no victory in winning over direct colonialism and being completely conquered by indirect colonialism; and there is no pride in flying flags and being international beggars. This is not only contrary to the African nationalist position but also to that of the Africa masses whose future must be balanced delicately against the forces of international predators and their domestic rent-seeking collaborators. What is this position of the African nationalist?

By African nationalism, we mean something positively uniting and liberating all Africans and their descendants; something revolutionary in thought and in practice. It is a rebellion against the existing African divisions and those that maintain and practice them. It is also a rebellion against African's current global socioeconomic relationships where the Western nations, particularly the neocolonialists, return a small portion of things they steal from Africa back to Africa under the pretext of philanthropy through trivial gifts, aid and loans, poverty reduction, debt relief and deceptive trade preferences while at the same time encouraging the African political and economic elite in collaboration with foreign predators to siphon the African resources and deposit them in the financial capitals of the Western countries. African nationalism is a rebellion against the situation where Peter is robbed not to pay Paul, but to make Peter so poor and helpless that he becomes mentally, emotionally, physically and spiritually dependent on his thief in the name of democracy, good governance, and rules of international order, development, civil society and humanitarian militarism. By African nationalism, we also imply an ideological channel of anti-colonialist and anti-puppet struggle to melt the imperialist ice covering and set free the frozen creative energies of Africa. It is the ideological principle conceived to guide the second phase of the African Liberation Movement (ALM) from decolonization to independence, from independence to unity and from unity to sustainable progress and complete emancipation.

This phase is the unification of Africa on all fronts of human endeavor. It is the most difficult phase of the charted course of Africa's total emancipation. It is the action center of African nationalism. By African nationalism, as an ideological guide, we also mean a logically consistent system of beliefs, thoughts and ideas, to intellectually arm the Africans irrespective of place of birth and residence to fight against the so-called "special warfare" of the Western nations, a concept of General Maxwell Taylor of the United States Armed Forces and a military extension of the creed of John F. Dulles [127b, pp. 364-389]. Let the Vietnamese fight Vietnamese, while the Africans fight the Africans not for any meaningful purpose or principle of African progress that the Africans believe in, but for the joy and interest of neocolonial powers and international predators. It is also an ideological foundation the logical system of reasoning to arm the Africans in oder to place in a proper ideological perspective and global conflicts the strategies of "low-intensity warfare" and humanitarian militarism of the United States of America. These concepts are extensions of the "special warfare" mentioned above, where by the method of divide and rule, United States, supported by other members of NATO creates miniature terrorists of a country's nationals to cause mass terror and destruction, to disrupt the economic and social fabric of that society. The objective is to create socioeconomic conditions that will lead to an overthrow of weak governments in the developing world that would not become puppets of the West. If America or an imperial country does not succeed in overthrowing these governments, the American or imperial government attempts through the CIA operating machine to get rid of the leaders, finds pretext with support of other Western nations, activate and use the NATO war machine to deliver humanitarian bombing and cause mass terror, and collective punishment for the innocent masses (just revisit the historic events in Panama, Granada, Chile and then observe current unfolding events in Iraq).

The cases of Libya, Angola, Congo, Algeria and others such as Iraq must not skip our memories. The unfettered support of the Western nations for the apartheid system in South Africa, Namibia, and Southern Rhodesia should not skip our minds in terms of historic instructions. The history of South and Central America provides classic examples of imperialists and colonialists at work. The history of Haiti is especially instructive to the African nationalist as to the hypocrisy, politico-economic violence, and the mindset of the imperialist predators.

All of these atrocities against humanity are done in the name of deceptive concepts of God, peace, democracy, human rights, freedom, terrorism, development, poverty reduction, law and order, while the Western practices are merely imperial, seeking subservience and full spectrum dominance. Justice and fairness are always left out of the question and social equation. Freedom and justice are always the casualties of imperialist implementations of these deceptive conceptions. It must be noted that special warfare, low-intensity warfare and humanitarian bombing are all state-sponsored terrorism even though they are presented to us as actions of goodwill. They are practiced by the imperial and colonial powers by creating ideological conditions favorable to them. Here true freedom fighters are defined as terrorists while true terrorists are ideologically made to be freedom fighters, all in the name of law and order at the level of decision ignorance of the African separatist. There are always practices for the overthrow of constitutionally democratic governments that are not slaves to the imperial order, assassinate legitimate leaders, and produce suffering to the innocent people who can least help themselves. To stop these practices requires the creation of an opposing system of conditions. On the continent of Africa, these conditions are provided by the Africentric views and beliefs embedded in African nationalism and African unity but not in African separatism.

To the African separatist, we should point out that the ideology of African separatism is an indirect support for Western low-intensity or special warfare or humanitarian bombing against innocent Africans. The reasons for this statement are found in the military and economic vulnerability of the African states in their current territorial forms and the vacuousness of state-specific sovereignty that is based on separatism in Africa. Low-intensity warfare and humanitarian militarism cannot work against India, neither can it work against Russia or China, countries whose governments are considered adversaries to the USA and other Western imperial predators.

To the African nationalist, we should point out that there is a third phase of the process of Africa's complete emancipation. This is the phase of total mobilization of human and non-human resources to create the better life for all Africans irrespective of the place of birth. But we must hurry because time is running out and the clock of African destiny is ticking with an unbelievable regularity. The imperialist and the neocolonial predators with the support of internal parasitic elites are constantly organizing and reorganizing as well as changing terms of the theater of exploitation and the appearance of the predators.

The immediate implementation of the second phase is necessary for the implementation of the third phase without which our people, the African masses, will live in perpetual international servitude and in poverty and shamefulness, racial underdogs and beggars for the world's leftovers and even what Africa has produce or has. The successful implementation of the second phase, African unity, and the third phase, resource mobilization to create better life and happiness requires the complete rejection of the position of African separatists. After which the conceptual position of African nationalism must be accepted unconditionally and the required organization carefully crafted for its implementation and practice. We have more work to do in that the institutional arrangements of political, economic and legal organizations consistent with the creation of African unity must be designed and implemented. In this respect, the African Union must build institutions through which integration policies can be administered. Let us turn our attention to the concept of state-specific nationalism itself and its relationship with ethnicity and tribalism and the positive and negative roles that they can play in the process of

African emancipation and progress under the ideological guidance of African Nationalism and supporting African personality.

5

STATE-SPECIFIC NATIONALISM, ETHNICITY AND TRIBALISM

We have dwelt extensively on African nationalism in its various dimensions and how these dimensions relate to one another and to Africa's complete emancipation. We have also related these dimensions, perhaps not fully, to the opposing positions of African separatism and state-specific nationalism. Now, we turn our attention to certain stubborn realities of contemporary Africa. Stubborn because these realities are misunderstood and minds misguided, leading to mass suffering and exploitation for personal riches and gains by some myopic African rulers whose actions and decisions are supportive of the imperial order that exploits the African masses.

These stubborn realities are the relationships among tribalism, ethnicity and state-specific nationalism and the role they play in African nationalism and the suffering of the African masses. We have to say from the onset that tribalism and ethnicity have incredibly positive elements in speeding up the liberation and decolonization process toward African unity and Africa's complete emancipation. In order to show how, we must isolate those positive elements in tribalism and ethnicity from the negative elements and then specify their theoretical and operational contents to a positively charted course of Africa's complete emancipation in the context of sociology of African Union.

5.1   Language, Ethnicity and Tribe

First, we must state that racially, Africa is more or less a homogeneous society with patches of foreign intrusions such as the Boers in the southern tip, Arabs on the northern strip, and some Indians on the east coast. They were intruders and are still intruders whose current permanence we must consider as an integral part of African experience. There can be no question in the mind of a visitor or any objectively minded researcher that Africa is the land of the phenotypic African (Blacks). The Arabs and Indians are our brothers; at least we should regard them so as one can understand by looking at the population of Southern India and the Arabs in addition to our joint history [10b] [10c] [10d] [14] [36]. The original Jews (Falasha Jews) were Africans by all historic accounts.

Africa is, however, divided into pseudo-linguistic zones and sub-zones. But it stands to reason that Africa is one racial zone by all accounts and by any analysis with cultural unity. It is therefore either intellectual irrationality or cognitive ignorance or ideological deception to speak of Black Africa except in the sense used by Anta Diop [37] [38]. This term which presupposes another Africa is coined by the modern European intellectuals as they witnessed the dismantling of their colonial holdings. It is a term that also reflects the European treachery of divide and rule. Ironically, we must admit that a number of African students and intellectuals, dwarfed and colonized by their perceived superiority of European mind, have bought into this concept without examining the social psychology and historical significance of it. We should state at this point that to the African nationalist there is nothing, and there should be nothing like Black Africa. This term must be rejected vehemently by African nationalists without reservation.

There is one Africa and one Africa only. No amount of either Arabization or Francophonization or Anglophonization can change this factual reality. The sociological term "Africa South of Sahara" is just as silly and stupid as its complementary term "Black Africa". There is no intellectual credibility to these terms; they are simply meant to be another means of propaganda against Africa so as to divide her people as a strategy designed by the predators to deceive and to exploit. The idea of Africa south of Sahara is again a treacherous attempt to divide the north from the south and set us against each other in a special warfare: let the Africans fight the Africans for a power that they individually do not have but can collectively have if they unite and stay in unity. These two terms, "Black Africa" and "Africa south of the Sahara", and the connotations they politically carry are diametrically opposed to the principle of African nationalism and the charted course of Africa's complete emancipation. The concepts of First, Second and Third Worlds may also be looked upon in the same intellectual light.

The acceptance of the term "Black Africa" concedes to the implied acknowledgement that there is either a White Africa or some other Africa which we have no knowledge as yet. Africa is indivisible in race. South Africa, for example, is not White Africa, neither is the coastal strip of Northern Africa. The sooner we Africans abandon this intellectual deceit of the indirect colonialists of the West and the supporting predatory system, the better shall we come to understand the true obstacles that must be overcome in developing relevant concepts and strategies for Africa's complete emancipation for Africa's glorious future.

The treacherous design of European indirect colonialism is to first divide, set brother against brother, sister against sister, and brother against sister, and vice versa by manipulating the factions that they have succeeded in creating out of the whole. The objective is to make the whole impotent so that the parts can be aggressively exploited to the full advantage by African adversaries and the international profiteers. The Westerners are once again on the ideological offensive just as they were during their treacherous campaign to colonize Africa through civilization, Christianity and a false conception of God. They have created ideologically and racially loaded propaganda concepts for a new style of disinformation campaign against the African and Africa. The concepts of democracy, human rights, freedom, liberation, good governance, terrorism and others are ideologically coded with meaning reversals to become instruments of neocolonialism, exploitation and predation at the disposal of the imperial predators.

The process is simply to replace direct racism with indirect racism, just as European indirect colonialism has replaced direct colonialism. The intent is to further distort African history and intensify the confusion of the already confused Africans and divided Africa. They emphasize disunity and separatism in Africa while they promote unity in Europe and the United States of America. They pronounce the perceived differences among various African states as a technique of social destabilization. They emphasize tribalism, ethnicity, language differences and religious differences while they emphasize uniformity in Europe and the members of the Western Alliance given all the intense differences that cumulated into the imperialist wars. They characterize some Africans as rich and some as poor while they overlook Europe's deep-seated differences. They construct social theories around racism. The objective is to divide and control Africa where the Africans spend their energies and resources to fight one another not for any principle of African progress but simply for the support of neocolonialist strategies for predatory activities.

In taking this approach, the Europeans and their descendants have managed to form a solid alliance with the African separatists. They search for the African separatists, identify them, bring them through their mass media into social prominence, elevate them to leadership and turn them into useful ideological tools that are then used against Africa and her children. They have succeeded in arming the African separatists and state-specific nationalists in Africa with intellectual munitions to actively carry on the European propaganda wars and battles against the separatists themselves and other Africans, and in favor of the authenticity of the intellectual rubbish of European race supremacy.

Intellectually colonized by Europe and armed with the logic of the art of European deceptions, dis-information campaign and racially loaded social theories, the African separatists and state-specific nationalists take on the battle helmets and fighting boots of their colonial and neocolonial masters to wage low-intensity warfare and battles against Africa and her people in the theater of struggle for freedom. The African separatists now assume the leadership of this dis-information propaganda campaign against themselves and the people they are supposed to lead out of the tunnel of darkness. They tell the Africans the degree of their worthlessness, how poorly they communicate with one another because they have different languages. They amplify these by insisting on how each tribe wants to dominate the rest. Some of the African separatists even argue for further territorial disintegration into unviable tribal states.

By advocating this position and fighting the war and battles of their colonizers and predators against their own kind -- and ironically themselves -- in the theater of ideological war, and having disgraced themselves at the feet of their European intellectuals, these African separatists hope to earn a place in the history of the Western intellectual kingdom by acceptance to the fact that they also belong to the intellectual traditions of the imperial predators. They, however, end up as laughing stocks of their Western intellectuals. They neither earn a place in the Western intellectual kingdom nor gain respect and acceptance by their own people. These Africans must be viewed as dangerous to Africa. Their treachery must be exposed without mercy and without pardon by the African nationalists through the establishment of institutions of Africentric think tanks and the application of positive action on all fronts against them.

It is a fact that Africa is partitioned by different languages into language groups, but this is of no serious consequence because one may be surprised to find out the degree of commonality among a number of African languages. Europe is partitioned by different languages, so also are Russia and many other countries. Language differences among African people must be viewed as an asset rather than a liability. The African must accept the concept and practice of a natural principle of diversity in unity as central to Africentric cosmology. Nature itself resides on this principle and the beauty and strength of nature are built on this principle where diversity is nature's strength which accords it an ecological and rhythmic balance. Diversity is not nature's weakness. It defines the conditions for nature's organic unity. Unity does not imply homogeneity and logically it cannot. Unity implies differentiation of parts of a whole where such parts are welded together by a set of common objectives or one common purpose or a principle or creed. The human body itself, perhaps, the most perfect machine, is not made up of homogeneous parts. The hand is different from the stomach and yet they manage to work smoothly together for one purpose, the maintenance of life. Nature itself is a unity engulfing diversity where such diversity by certain logical processes defines, asserts and maintains nature's unity and beauty. The concept of unity, then, implies the existence of diversity and potential of harmony, co-ordination and integration (see the discussions in a companion book [43b]).

Someone may be quick to ask whether I am not confusing functional operations with differences in communication. My simple answer is no, for wherever a common purpose is defined, channels of communication can be established. When different parts are in isolation without common purpose they will have different channels of communication and hence different "languages". Linguistic differences do not define or establish differences among people. Goals and objectives do, in the arena of decision and choice. The implied idea in this analysis is an emphasis on organization and channels of information flow that allow diverse units to be glued together as a whole. The Western military alliance, NATO, is established among people with linguistic differences. They are, however, united by one common goal to dominate, oppress, and exploit other human races that are outside the Western Alliance and to kill people if they go astray. It must be added that they all belong to one common race, linguistically divided but united by a common goal and purpose.

Differences in language do not establish differences among people; goals and objectives do. History teaches us that wars are not fought on language differences. Wars are declared and fought on differences in goals, objectives, purposes, interest and convictions through ideology, religious doctrines and fundamentalism of all forms. Conflicts result not from language differences but from perceived differences in creed. Common purpose, goals and objectives define channels of unity and cooperation; common language does not. For example, the United States of America and the United Kingdom are connected by one common language. They were, however, the greatest adversaries in the 19th century and the beginning of the 20th century. Admittedly, language may facilitate initial communication and ease the task of organization. A British and a French person, with different languages and no immediate linguistic channel of communication, faced with a danger of being destroyed by Germans are not driven apart by their language differences but are driven together in unity by a common goal of survival. They unite not on a common language but on a common goal, the goal of destroying their common enemy. They know that if they fail to unite in creating a common front for the protection of them both, neither can be saved.

In the eyes of the Germans, the British and the French are materially indistinguishable. They are objects of their exploitation to the satisfaction of their insatiable hunger of imperial expansion. They represent nothing but opportunities to be exploited by the Germans. This realization propels the British and French, irrespective of their language differences, to join hands in order to create a common front to deter the German or to destroy him so as to dissipate the circumstances of either of them falling as a victim. Similarly, the European Union and the NATO Alliance are formed not on the basis of common language but on the basis of common creed and the ideology of global dominance. Why cannot the Zulu and Yoruba do the same? Why should the Zambians and the Senegalese allow themselves to be separated by language differences? Why should Ghanaians and Zambians or Tanzanians and Egyptians or Mozambicans and Algerians view themselves as separated into opposing groups by language differences? In terms of language Africa is blessed with Arabic, Hausa and Swahili and others that may be given a continental value. The point here is that Africans have so much in common, share a common historic path, common philosophical traditions, common cultural values that overshadow our language differences.

Are you not suffering, exploited and racially discriminated against because you are an African or a descendant thereof? Are you suffering because you speak either Setswana or Swahili or Twi or Hausa or Arabic? If that was the case the Africans that were transported as cargoes to United States of America would have no problem regarding discrimination, racism and oppression. The degrees of common suffering, exploitation, degradation, and abuse of all Africans, irrespective of their places of birth or their places of residence, far outweigh the degree of pain, if any, in communicating with one another in a common language. Just travel to Europe, the Americas, Australia and others and observe for yourself that the common language of Africans and all their descendants, without qualification, is not our common suffering, our common history, and our common destiny but our common racial identity. This common suffering, history and destiny should provide and cement our channels of communication irrespective of the language that we speak. We have dwelt on language and related matters quite at length as if we have abandoned the question of tribalism and ethnicity and how they relate to the struggle of a race to emancipate and uplift itself through self-reliance and internal self-motion as demanded by African philosophical tradition.

What does language have to do with tribalism and ethnicity? The fact is that the acceptable definition of tribe includes a common language that binds a section of the human race together and sets them apart from other members of the human race. Since language performs a function in human endeavors, as a medium of communication and as a carrier of culture, it encompasses a great portion of culture itself. Language as an element in the definition of tribe also applies to defining a nation. There is, however, a difference between them. A tribe is viewed as a small community lacking effective political and military characteristics that are associated with a nation. A tribe also lacks the basic resources for economic viability relative to its population characteristics. The lack of economic viability also deprives a tribal community of the material channels for effective technological, scientific, political and military organization that can ensure the tribe's survivability against even the smallest external aggressor without surrender. A tribe will always be a tribe, an unwilling dependent on the generosity and cruelty of other powerful groups with efficient political and military organization that can effectively enforce the boundaries of their sovereignties and project their economic and military power over other people. When a tribal community reaches this stage of organizational complexity it will no longer be a tribe but a nation.

The existence of a tribal community in isolation from others organized around a concept of a nation is itself an instrument of her own death.

The survival and preservation of a tribal community require the tribal community not to pursue a policy of tribal purity and isolationism but to seek to unite with other tribes with common characteristics and interest irrespective of linguistic differences, where mutual respect can be found. This is particularly an imperative for contemporary Africa which must be reorganized to face global hostilities and racial antagonism. This is particularly important for the success of the African Union. For the unity to be strong and long lasting the tribe must belong to the same racial origin with the basic interest of race preservation as well as its development. The common goal is race preservation particularly in these modern and difficult times where other races such as the Indians of the Americas and Aborigines of Australia have been almost completely exterminated by the European settlers. These are facts and not fictions. Race preservation does not imply racial hostilities toward other races. Race preservation becomes racial hostility and moral evil when it implies the annihilation of other races as occurred in the Americas and Australia at the hands of Europeans. In fact race preservation demands racial harmony that must flow from mutual racial respect and laws of bio-diversity.

The process of ensuring the survivability of the tribal community and the race demands the formation of a community of tribes out of which a nation is born through peaceful arrangement or otherwise. We must emphasize that the driving force for the formation of a community of tribes is tribal self-preservation as well as the preservation of the race. For such a community of tribes to exist it must develop mutual respect for one another on the basis of shared responsibility, freedom and justice irrespective of the level of social development, as well as the creation of a means of communicating with one another on a mass scale. In other words, the development of a language of common understanding for the community of tribes must be created. The argument holds for weak and small nations that individually hold no power but only illusions of it.

5.2 Affinity, Tribal Unit and the Size of the Family of Tribes

One may ask the question as to how large this family of tribes should be. The question alternatively translates to a question of how large a nation should be. This question belongs to the politico-economic theory of the size of nations. There is no logically specific answer to this question. The answer depends on many factors including the population size, its "quality", technological capabilities, multiplicity of natural resources, organizational skills, actual or perceived external threat and the global politico-economic dynamics. While each of these factors is subjectively equally important, the chronology of their developmental importance varies. First and foremost are the people of the land. Next comes the development of the required organizational skills blended equally into the development of technological capabilities that will provide the potential for increasing efficiency in organizing human and non-human resources for the survival of the family of tribes. In this respect the contribution of each tribe must be equally respected, supported, enhanced and shared.

The underlying current for discussion is the survivability of the tribe and the race. Each tribe brings into the family of tribes, a people and a culture, land (except an invading force), a level of aggregate organizational skill, a set of technological capabilities and a means of communication that may be different from other tribes in the family. These different elements of tribal communities must then be integrated and reconstituted to meet the new realities of the family of tribes in terms of the family's internal harmony, the survivability of the individual members, the tribes and the family against internal strife and external adversaries. How large the family must be depends, therefore, on the perceived relative strengths of external adversaries and the general ability to meet the complex material needs of the members of the family and maintain internal stability and harmony on the principle of freedom and justice for all. Certain qualifications would have to be made to the argument if forced territorial occupation and tribal annihilation are contemplated by invaders such as those that occurred in the Americas, Australia and New Zealand.

Each member of a specific tribe has a general affinity toward its tribe before entering the larger community, the family of tribes. This must be the case; otherwise he or she will not be a member of such a tribe for long since loyalty to the tribe to which one claims to belong is an important prerequisite for lasting membership. The ability to speak the tribe's language is secondary even though it might be a first sign of trust. The tendency for one to gravitate toward one's tribe is merely tribal affinity. Tribal affinity is always developed before entering the larger community. Tribal affinity, a sense of loyalty and devotion to one's group of belonging, is that which guarantees the individual tribesperson a sense of security of the tribe. The individual tribesperson has a responsibility to himself or herself as well as to the tribe and its members. Similarly, the tribe has responsibilities to its members at all levels of human activities.

The basic responsibility of an individual member of a tribe to his or her tribe's survival overrides his or her responsibility to himself or herself. He or she must be willing to sacrifice self for the survivability and continuity of the tribe. The collective consciousness of the members of a tribe for defending each other and maintaining the survival of the tribe may be referred to as tribe-specific social consciousness. Tribal collective consciousness is therefore, equivalent to nationalism defined in a sense of strong devotion to what one considers as his or her national origins. Tribal affinity is used here to capture tribal-specific collective consciousness or a sense of devotion to tribal ancestry. Tribal affinity is positive and carries with it a positive action role for the survival of an individual tribe's person as well as his or her tribal community. It carries with it a sense of belonging that provides assurance as well as insurance for the individual and the tribe.

When a tribe joins a family of tribes or it is incorporated into the family by whatever means, the individual members do not abrogate this sense of belonging and loyalty to their respective tribes, so also the tribe as a unity does not abrogate the sense of collective responsibility to its members. In fact, it would be suicidal to do so. Tribal affinity, however, assumes a new and important character in the family of tribes. In order to examine this new and important character, let us scrutinize the conditions that must foster the change in the character of tribal affinity within the family of tribes. Similarly, when a leadership by whatever means brings its tribal members into a family of tribes, it surrenders the tribal autonomy to the reconstituted leadership of the family of tribes. The leadership of the family of tribes is determined by the fundamental rules (that is the "constitution", written or not) of the organization of the family. The members of each tribal unit, therefore, agree to abide by the fundamental rules of organization and the mode of social decisions. They pledge a new and superior allegiance to the family of tribes. Each of the members of different tribal units becomes responsible not only to himself or herself and his or her tribal unit, but also to the family of tribes and all the members that belong to the family. They all pledge directly or indirectly allegiance to one another as well as loyalty to the reconstituted family of tribes. In this process, a dual affinity emerges. These dual elements are affinity to the tribal unit and affinity to the family of tribes.

To the members of each tribe in the family of tribes, the old tribal affinity does not immediately vanish, neither does it diminishes in intensity; it rather assumes a new form. It becomes subordinated to the affinity to the reconstituted community which is the family of tribes. If such a community is to survive against internal strife, tribal animosities and external adversaries, then affinity to the family of tribes must over-shadow the tribe-specific affinity. The old tribal affinity plays a new role as a check and balance on freedom, fairness, equity, and justice in the larger community. The tribal units provide a sense of security and a support mechanism for each unit and its members as well as the family of tribes. There is, therefore, an established hierarchy of support mechanisms and there is a hierarchy of sense of belonging. In such an organizational framework of humans, we speak of tribe-specific affinity and tribal-unit affinity. The tribal-unit affinity is the newly constituted collective consciousness that must guide reason and actions of the members of the family of tribes under the fundamental rules. In the new setting, the tribe-specific affinity plays a new and positive role, and hence possesses a positive character for checks and balances.

In so long as this role of tribe-specific affinity continues in the day-to-day organizational logistics of politics, science, economics, commerce and military defense without having a destabilizing effect on the internal organization of the family of tribes, tribe-specific affinity is unity-supportive. Note that in tribal isolation, we speak of tribal affinity. In a family of tribes, we speak of tribe-specific affinity and tribal-unit affinity. Tribe-specific affinity immediately ceases to play a positive role when it acquires the social character of tribal favoritism and nepotism even in one of the endeavors of the organization of the family of tribes. When this happens, tribe-specific affinity becomes tribalism that operates on the ideology of discrimination and injustice.

When tribe-specific affinity becomes tribalism, it acquires a confrontational property destructive to the collective consciousness of the family of tribes. It thus rallies together forces of destruction and internal strife for the family as well as the tribal unit. It sets in motion elements of self-destruction not only of the family of tribes but also of the particular tribal unit to which the "tribalist" belongs, because the elements of tribe-specific affinity of other members in other tribal units will force them to do likewise in defense of their units and their members. The practice of tribalism tears asunder the center around which all tribe-specific affinities gravitate. The results of tribalism in a family of tribes are conflicts, wars, social unrest and mass suffering.

In respect of the sociological process of nation formation, when a family of tribes has reached the stage where its economic, technological, organizational and military strength allow it to stand on its own and reinforce the boundaries of its sovereignty and territory that it claims, a nation is born. The argument we have advanced so far on the relationship among tribal affinity, tribalism, loyalty and general collective consciousness of the tribal units to the family of tribes also holds when the family of tribes acquires the social character of a nation. Tribalism is only possible in a family of tribes and in a nation that is constituted by a family of tribes. It acquires no logical and analytic meaning in an isolated tribal existence. Just as there cannot be racism in a nation of one race, so also there cannot be tribalism in a community of one tribe. It must be pointed out that the optimal size of a nation depends, among other things, on external threats. This external threat may be enhanced by tribalism.

Tribalism, just as racism, is destructive. In a family of tribes, tribalism does not only inflict physical and emotional pain on those against whom it is practiced, but it warps, perverts and injures the very people who hope to benefit from it and hence practice it. This is equivalent to Nkrumah's view of racialism [102]. The strength of the argument lies in a distinction between the fundamental rules of the organization of the family of tribes on one hand and the decision and choice practices that generate costs and benefits within the boundaries set by the fundamental rules of behavior.

The members of any tribal unit in a nation or a family of tribes will experience no peace as long as they practice tribalism even if they constitute the majority, since peace and harmony have no lasting anchorage in an unjust order. Just as the practice of tribalism tears asunder the center around which all tribe-specific affinities gravitate, so also the practice of injustice destroys peace, freedom and harmony required for internal tranquility and sustainable development of any nation.

The interest and peace of any nation of tribes, therefore, compel every tribal unit, large or small, in that nation to take active steps against tribalism and act in consent to eliminate it from the nation. Tribalism destroys trust and genuine co-operation and steadily builds a wall of intense hate which will, unquestionably, result in the most violent, destructive and regrettable consequences in the future of the nation (such as what happened in Rwanda, Liberia, Sudan and others) unless each tribal unit comes to understand that democracy, peace, freedom and unity are only possible in the absence of tribalism, intolerance and injustice. This is also true of a nation composed of races as observed by Nkrumah. Furthermore, tribalism cannot ensure political and organizational stability and tranquility required to create the material conditions for the maintenance of the nation to pursue liberty, stable democracy, social progress and happiness.

Tribalism in the last analysis, therefore, diverts the resources of the family of tribes away from development, social construction and progressive institution building to the creation of conditions of destruction, suffering and misery. Tribalism is abomination just as the fundamentalist affinity to religious doctrines where there is only right or wrong is a travesty of Divinity. It must, therefore, be understood by all in the tribal units of a nation that whenever there is a slightest possibility of conflict arising out of tribalism and nepotism, the nation's social fabric and unity are threatened. The collective consciousness of our race involves preservation of the race. The task of preservation of the race is not only a moral obligation but a duty required of all Africans. Within the race, there are many tribes whose tribe-specific consciousness must be subordinated to race consciousness and affinity, otherwise to fight against racism as practiced against Africa will be in vain.

In other words, since tribal communities lack the resources to create the conditions of real self-survival on the basis of modern production and lack the strength and capacity to compete for the world's resources, they become unwilling dependents on the material generosity and cruelties of other nations that have the military power, technological complexities and material bases to dictate terms of global competition, survival of the fittest and what nations may or may not fall victim to predation and imperial violence against the citizens of the country. Since tribal communities lack organizational complexities in terms of armed forces, the defense of their population and non-human resources is at the mercy of other nations and hence they become unwilling dependents on other nations including their adversaries for the protection of their population and resources. In fact, the most precious elements of the small resource base they have can be exploited freely without compensation by other nations because the tribal communities lack the desired organization of defense. This should remind us of the aspects of African history of catch-and-sell of African people.

In the modern age, the economic and military viability of tribal units viewed as nations depends heavily on a system of dependency and begging in the sense of submission, if the tribal communities are to survive. The members of each tribal unit are thus reduced to unwilling international beggars where the act of begging is undertaken by their leaders under all kinds of names such as aid, debt forgiveness, technical assistance, cut-throat loans and others. Their leaders beg for goods, for arms, for technology, for miseducation, misinformation, shelter, clothing, and the like, without either knowing or admitting to it. The price to pay is the sacrifice of their self-worth, independence and freedom. It is an illusion to speak of African national sovereignties under these conditions. At this moment, what African states have are sovereignty potentialities that must be actualized through an effective system of organization with a vision of nation building and the objective of Africa's complete emancipation. Anything less than this is unacceptable to the African nationalist.

To sustain this system of begging, the leaders abandon their pride and the pride of their tribal communities and the composing members, accept humiliation, become abjectly submissive or servilely compliant in such a manner that most of the time they become useful idiots and mouthpieces for the promotion of the propaganda of other nations against their own people. They then develop repressive machinery for containing their tribe's people without shame, and in the process, gain nothing of significance for their communities or for themselves. Is it not a shame to Africa to hear the Western press describing the efficiency of torturing machines of some African countries such Egypt? If a family or a nation of tribes is economically, technologically and militarily non-viable, and possesses all or some of the above characteristics, then such a human organization can abstractly be considered as being still in its tribal stage requiring further consolidation and a critical restructuring of its existing institutional configuration and political arrangements. This is the situation in Africa, we believe, unless somebody can convince us to the contrary.

5.3 Redefinitions of the Concepts of Tribe and Nation

The concept of tribal community used here has a specific sociological meaning and general implication for social organizations. It is relative and dynamic. As some nations either modernize their institutional configuration or consolidate themselves by mutural incorporation of other states and tribal communities into larger economic, political and military organizations, other nations degenerate into tribal states. In this respect, all African countries without exception, we think, are in their tribal states, requiring either further consolidation of tribal communities or critical restructuring of the current institutional configuration of economics, politics, law, defense, and territories in the African Union. This is the position that must be held by the African nationalist.

The African Nationalist must accept the position that all the so-called African nations either are in the state of their tribal communities, or are non-viable units of family of tribes belonging to one common race, a race of people whose history is a unified one, whose cultural tapestry is engulfed in unity; and whose struggle is common and linked together by one common destiny in the contemporary world (see also [37]). This destiny is nothing more than to reclaim Africa's place in world history. It is nothing more than the complete emancipation of all Africans irrespective of their place of residence, and the creation of conditions where freedom, justice, peace, and pursuit of happiness flourish for all Africans, wherever they are, and whatever their creed, religion, or tribal affiliation. This destiny is a right and not a privilege for all Africans. However, the current sociopolitical conditions of African countries, being in their tribal stages, prevent any meaningful and effective process from evolving to reclaim Africa and set her children free.

African states in their current territorial forms and boundaries set and established by Europeans according to their imperial interest are operating in a stringent global system of exploitation by mega-groups without the needed instruments of economic and military defense. The people in Europe and in the Americas are working hard and continuously to consolidate themselves into larger groups so as to strengthen their positions in the global system of resource flows and output distribution, while the Africans on the other hand are working intensely not to consolidate but simply to further disintegrate their current nonviable units into super micro-tribes that will further weaken their overall defense and send their citizens into servitude, poverty and hopelessness .

We are sure that some readers may be uneasy with any unconventional and unorthodox usage of the term tribe. This is both anticipated and welcomed. Our usage is adopted intentionally and provocatively. We are using the term in an organizational sense of economics, politics, law, defense and survivability of the community. Here, we see a family, tribe, family of tribes, and nation as an evolutionary process induced by the dialectics of struggle and survival to preserve life against destruction and cruelty that may be brought by either other nations or nature. A state, for that matter, a country, is thus said to be still in its tribal stage if it possesses some or all the characteristics that we have defined and listed above relative to the global system of social formation and power distribution. It is in this context that we have characterized the African states as still in their tribal stages. Important conceptual distinctions are being imposed on the forgoing analysis. State-specific affinity is distinguished from state-specific nationalism; tribal-unit-specific affinity is also distinguished from tribalism within a family of tribes or a nation.

The tribal stage of these so-called African nations implies that the concept and practice of state-specific nationalism is synonymous with the concept and practice of tribalism. The practice of visa requirements from Africans in order to enter other African states in which they are not resident is a practice of tribalism. The failure of the African states and African leaders to put into proper historic context the reestablishment of the motherly affinity and fatherly guidance to those Africans that were forcefully removed and sent without passports and visas into slavery in other parts of the world, where they were condemned to the prison of exploitative hell with hard labor, is a travesty of African ancestral continuity of great social and spiritual significance. No excuses can be made to justify these practices.

Mother Africa will not rest and Africa will have no peace until all her children are reconnected and brought together under the roof of spiritual unity and harmony. It is even a defilement of the sacredness of the African ancestral tree where offshoots are lost and forgotten. All the African countries were practicing tribalism at the Organization of African Unity (OAU) against each other whether they want to admit it or not. I hope this practice will cease at the reconstituted OAU, the African Union (AU). The important point that we want to emphasize is that state-specific affinity is admissible and compatible with the organization of a family of tribes. For example, the concept and practice of African nationalism not only accept the idea that a person from either the state of Nigeria or Egypt or any other African state has affinity to that particular state, but encourage him or her to do so. State-specific affinity and tribal-unit-specific affinity are concepts and practices that are compatible and in harmony with the concepts and practices of African nationalism as viewed from a federated state of Africa. The only requirement is that we practice the good in them and avoid the potential evil that will be exploited by the predators and destroyers of Africa to the detriment of Africa and her children as it happened in Nigeria, the Great Lakes Region and others.

Tribalism and state-specific nationalism are not only practices and concepts incompatible with African nationalism, but they are in direct opposition to it and to Africa's complete emancipation. In so far as state-specific nationalism that brought about decolonization of specific African territories is practiced in the form of tribal-unit-specific affinity, the concept and practice are consistent with those of African nationalism and Africa's complete emancipation. In such a situation, the concept and practice of state-specific nationalism leading to decolonization acquire a new and progressive character and hence, Africa-unity supportive. The state-specific nationalism that was decolonization-oriented and collective consciousness now acquires a new liberating force, the force of collective African consciousness, toward unity and Africa's complete emancipation. Its role now becomes positive, complementary but subservient to African nationalism.

A problem arises, however, when state-specific nationalism, such as Ethiopian or Mauritanian nationalism, acquires the social character of tribalism. In this case of tribal character, state-specific nationalism becomes unprogressive, possessing all the evil elements of tribalism in terms of social and spiritual destruction. As such, it performs the same negative role as tribalism in a family of tribes. It becomes divisive within the charted course of African unity. It rallies together forces of separatism, encourages internal strife, arms adversaries, and contributes to the external forces against Africa and her progress. Show us an African separatist, and we will point you to who the true enemy of Africa is. The historic role and mission of the African separatists are to constain the formation of African unity toward African complete emancipation. By supporting state-specific nationalism, the African separatists support the practice of tribalism, ethnic conflicts and the activities of the imperial predators.

African nationalism does not give credence to tribalism nor does it give recognition to tribally oriented state-specific nationalism. The African nationalist condemns tribally oriented state-specific nationalism. He or she knows that state-specific nationalism with the social character of tribalism is not only destructive and dangerous to the charted course of African unity and complete African emancipation, but it deprives the very people who practice it of their sovereignty and freedom while at the same time reducing their so-called nations into neocolonial states by placing their institutions at the service of new and indirect forms of colonialism, all at the expense of the Africans and Africa's progress.

5.4 The Role of State-specific Nationalism in Decolonization and the Process of African Unity

The point being stressed here is that after state-specific nationalism has led to decolonization of an African territory, positive action of the African nationalists requires a new and complete orientation of African collective consciousness away from sheer political decolonization and pseudo-sovereignties of economically and militarily non-viable states and toward the goal of African unity, as well as laying down useful steps for Africa's socioeconomic reconstruction into a true nationhood with true sovereignty backed by military strength in defense of Africa and her children. We should take the liberty at this point to state that it is a complete mental illusion and self-deception for any African to think that the current African states are independent and sovereign. We cannot stress this point enough for critically cognitive reflection. Until this cognitive delusion is abandoned in favor of true and realistic characterization of Africa's current realities, the African separatists, their supporters and sympathizers will always be encapsulated in a dream state where they will try over and over again to reach for an apparition of national sovereignty, development and freedom.

Did not the United States of America with the collaboration of Great Britain take a unilateral liberty to bomb Libya, kill Africans and terrorize the rest, with the hope of intimidating their leaders and try to assassinate the Libya's head of state in the name of a Western civilized code of conduct in 1986? And did not even Israel, no doubt supported by the United States of America, take the liberty in the same period to bomb Tunisia and terrorize the Africans with the hope to intimidate their leaders in the name of a Western civilized code of a good international conduct? And did not the Europeans occupying South Africa in tacit collaboration with Israel and the United States of America, and supported by Britain and other members of NATO (the North Atlantic Treaty Organization), also take the same liberty to bomb Angola, Mozambique, Zambia, Botswana and others, and terrorize the Africans and intimidated their leaders? And in our current experience, did not United States of America and Great Britain supported by the so-called coalition of the willing, which is basically the coalition of the coerced and the bribed, take liberty against international will to completely bomb and devastate Iraq, one of the greatest civilizations the world has produced, in the name of an amorphously changing fundamentalist position of democracy, weapons of mass destruction and "good against evil", with the result of mass killing of innocent civilians of children, women and geriatric people?

Again, did not the United States of America break all applicable international laws and bomb Sudan in 1998, kill innocent Africans, destroyed the country's pharmaceutical plant, inflict terror on the rest and wrap itself inthe blanket of law and order, prevention of terrorism and stoppage of production of chemical weapons? And in all these cases, did not the so-called "civilized "Western people clap and justify their actions on the basis of civilized codes of international conduct and the rule of law despite the spilling of the African blood and the death of innocent Africans who were characterized as collateral damage, that is, viewed tactically, as objects for destruction and not humans for development? And did not most of the African rulers of the so-called

African "countries" sit in silence for the fear of reprisals of all kinds if they open their chilled lips? What is a nation and what is sovereignty? The leadership of the imperial world has not been civilized enough to be trusted with the lives of Africans. The history of the Western nations is plagued with acts of terror and crimes against humanity. They have never paid for them and continue to constitute the axis of violence and injustice. The reasons are clear. They are nations that can protect their people and project their power through violence, coercion and deception working individually and collectively.

Is sovereignty meaningful when a nation cannot enforce its boundaries as internationally agreed and defend her people? It must be clearly understood that when we think of tribe-specific affinity or state-specific nationalism, we must relate it within the broad context of the African experience and international order. In this connection, it must be pointed out that the dominant ideology of the Western nations is not either democracy, freedom or justice as the rest of the world is made to believe; neither is it ideology of peace and racial co-existence and harmony of the human race. The ideology of the Western nations is simply domination, exploitation, oppression and enforcement of the will of the West, at least that is what modern history reveals.

Great Britain did not build her empire on peaceful negotiations, humanism and democracy. French imperialism did not succeed on elements of peaceful negotiations, democracy and respect for humanity. The Portuguese and Belgian colonies were not acquired on peaceful negotiations with the true citizens of the land. The United States of America has never talked its way into acquiring any land that is non-European. Australia was not taken by the European settlers by any form of peaceful negotiations; nor was the original people of Australia silenced by any form of civilized code of diplomacy and agreed-upon protocols; they were rather massacred mercilessly to extinction. The land occupied by the Europeans in the United States of America was not obtained by peaceful negotiations nor was it bought, neither was it occupied by any decent code of conduct. The American Natives too, just like the Australian Natives, were slaughtered to extinction. In fact both of them were racially cleansed. These are facts. They are neither fiction nor ideological in context. The current structural behavior of the Western nations is such that they hold on to state-specific nationalism and act with the ideology of European and Western nationalism that engulfs some important sense of unity. History reveals that the

Europeans have, in barbarity, shot their way to dominance. The prevailing ideology of the West is, and has always been, full spectrum dominance and control by force on the rest of the world wherever they can. This is particularly so for the small communities like African states and South American countries because the cost in terms of men and resource to attain and maintain success is the least expensive to the Europeans and their descendants. This ideology of dominance translates into internal democracy for the West and Western dictatorship over Africa in particular and the rest of the world wherever possible. The Western ideology which has been refined by United State of America is simply ownership. If ownership fails, control; and if control fails, exploit and if exploitation fails, destroy. History of the Western behavior has shown that the imperial predators are not interested in democracy, human rights, good governance and decent cods of international conduct. They have codified these concepts into a religion in support of their predatory activities in the global resource space. This new religion has come to replace or work alongside the European Christian theology that justifies slavery, just wars and others. These are the four Western principles of international operations and diplomacy. In this theater of global power distribution and resource flows, the West understands one language of communication. This language is unity among the member nations of the West and violence for those countries that put up resistance against predation and anti-democratic practices of the West nations. Unity is advocated and enforced by tacit rules and social sanctions among the members of the Western club. They have leant some important lessons from the stubborn facts of the struggle among the European nations to acquire colonial territories, capture African children and expand the individual empires rather than the European dominance. Violence and pain are inflicted on the nonmembers that struggle to separate from the oppressive sphere of Western influence and domination.

Ironically, an African separatist in either Kenya or Malawi or Sudan (perhaps before 1998), acting on the ideology of state-specific nationalism, may even argue when hearing about the United States' terrorist act against Libya that the USA bombed Libya, but not Africa, so why should he or she worry about it? He or she may even add that Libya invited her own suffering, reflecting the view argued by Europeans. Many Africans do not even think that it could happen to their states. The 1998 events, however, have convinced the Sudanese that their country is not shielded from the Western terror and economic sabotage, something that Cuba knows very well. In just a matter of time, other African states will experience that they are not shielded from this type of state-sponsored terrorism as practiced by the West if these African states try to assert their rights to independence and sovereignty. This position of African separatists is contrary to that of the African nationalist. The nationalist knows that the United States of America dared not, and did not take liberty to bomb Moscow, much as Americans disliked communism. It is less costly for United States and United Kingdom to commit crimes against humanity in Iraq than in China under changing justifications that range from possession of instruments of mass destruction to bringing democracy to the people after they are dead. Democracy and freedom have no meaning to the dead.

What do the African nationalists see when they look critically at vast expanse of Africa's territory and history? Three distinct images are revealed to them. One image reflects contemporary African realities and current conditions of African existence. The other image reflects the true, rich and glorious history of Africa's past, Africa as it was, and Africa as it should be understood. The third image is Africa of tomorrow. The past is then linked to the present and the present is linked to the future and by logical extension the future is linked to the past and vice versa as it is cognitively known in African philosophical traditions. The period of slavery and colonialism may be viewed as serious distractions and interruptions that moved Africa from her normal growth and development path.

The contemporary reality is characterized by Africa divided in soul, wounded in spirit, blinded in vision, destroyed in manhood, demoralized in femininity, stripped of courage, sapped of strength, terrified by fear, intimidated by other's modern achievements, deprived of the history of her past contributions, stripped of her dignity and beauty, made stupid by carrying meaningless names of other nations, scrambling for rubbish from other nations instead of the diamonds and gold of her own, and completely confused in her state of being. This is not the Africa that the African nationalist wants. This is the image of Africa that the African nationalist intends to demolish with creativity in organization and statecraft which are characteristics of Africa's ancient empires. The second image of Africa reflecting a truly rich and glorious history is well known to any enlightened individual. It makes little sense to waste time and effort to try and elaborate here. We would, however, like to reference Cheikh Anta Diop's monumental works for those who are unfamiliar [36-39]. The important works of Ben-Jochannan [13-17a], DuBois [47] Rodney [129d], Van Sertima [143a and b] and Williams [150] are also worth referencing. We would like to affirm to the African nationalist and the separatist alike that all the glory of ancient Egypt, the Upper and Lower Nile civilization with the emergence of other African empires that resulted from demographic evolution of people of Akebulan (now Africa) belongs to Africa and her children, the Akebu people. The mighty monuments of pyramids and mummies are African architectural and scientific structures to which the modern world presents nothing that is comparable in terms of their gigantic proportions, creativity and scientific edifice. They are simply indestructible memorials and testimonies of original African genius, organization, hard work, impressive landmarks and historical gift to the world. No amount of rhetorical claims and appropriations can deprive Africa of these achievements. Other important and equally impressive ruins of African cities, cultural and scientific achievements are yet to be unearthed. Like the process of natural order of emergence of the new and disappearance of the old, empires emerge, mature and disappear and in place thereof new ones spring up with changing social centers that express different social personalities for the continuity of life and of the Divine Master Plan just as what the African conception of creation connotes. In human societies these transformations and the creative process take place through institutions and organization that holds them.

5.5   African Nationalism and Africa's Future

Since our main concern, as African nationalists and unitarists, is forward-looking, we would like to dwell at length on the third image. This third image is seen as a continuation of the second image projected into the modern setting. Here the African nationalist seeks to change the course of the current African history, or at least, reposition Africa on its normal path of history before the beginning of the Western disruption. In other words, to obliterate the first image and replace it with a progressive one that is African-centered. The reconstructed image is one that is not linked with the characteristics of the first but reflects a complete eradication of the deficiencies of Africa's recent past and current history. It is an image that projects the triumph of the Africa's creative spirit, the collapse of forces of foreign domination, oppression and subjugation, as well as the emergence of Africa's true glorious effort, reasserting itself, and finally freeing Africa's children from the senseless exploitations and deceptions of imperialists, neocolonialists and their internal collaborators.

The third image of Africa is an image where Africa is both the fruit-producer and fruit-consumer. In other words, the African labor that transforms nature into articles of use is the same labor that becomes fulfilled as a result of this social transformation in nature and society. It implies a new Africa that is completely opposed to the situation where her children languish in poverty while working as slaves to satisfy the ever increasing appetite of others, particularly the "West" and her predators. It, therefore, implies a new reality where the driving urge to succeed and create the new Africa permeates through every aspect of African life, stemming from the leadership which must critically and uncompromisingly combine a high sense of social responsibility, nation building and African nationalism with a daring state of urgency to lead Africa into her glorious and powerful future, the future where Africa is completely emancipated from the shackles of her colonial past and African children have true opportunities to enjoy peace, true democracy, freedom and justice which have always been the foundation stones of Africa's antiquity and statecraft.

This new image sees no boundaries in the way of movements of African children. Neither does it see limitations on Africa's achievements except those that are imposed by herself. It is an image that reflects efficient communication networks in all fields of human endeavor (sciences, technology, art, craft, etc.) merely to serve the interest of Africa first and foremost before Africa's doors are opened to deal on equal footing with the rest of the world. It also reflects a new African collective consciousness and a new African who is driven by African nationalism to expend tireless energy for the sake not of himself or herself only, but of the new Africa that must be constructed, with one aim, a federated African nation that is a worthy place for all Africans born at home and abroad to live. This is also an Nkrumaist position. This new image, however, must be constructed from Africa's recent history and current experiences with global power distribution. The construction requires an active organization of African's integration through institutional building for unity under the ideological principle of African nationalism. The change of name from Organization of African Unity to African Union is not substantive to the African nationalist operating on the ideological principle of African nationalism. The social character of the African Union must be integration on the basis of African interest and nationalism.

The new image of Africa that we have projected is that which must be embraced by the African nationalist. No compromise can be made on this principle of reclaiming Africa and to re-establish her greatness, dignity and beauty for her children. The accomplishment of this image requires the implementation of the goal of the African nationalist, that is, the complete uncompromising unity of Africa as one federated nation. This is the image of Africa that must form the foundation stone of the cognitive system of the African nationalist. What future image of Africa do the African separatists see? This question is left to be answered by the African separatists and those that oppose African unity as well as holding on to the idea that Africa must remain in and retain the organizational structure left by Africa's predators. At this present time wherever you cast your eyes over Africa, either East, West, South or North there are wars, internal conflicts, suffering and disasters that can be avoided through the reconstitution of the inherited colonial order of institutional arrangement. There are masses that are rising up against domestic political elites whose interests are removed from Africa and aligned with the imperial predators. This is creating internal strives and political instabilities that are met with violence of the state which is controlled by the political elite and supported by the imperial predators for Africa's destruction.

There is no place for tribalism or state-specific nationalism and separatism in the nationalist's thinking system. Our culture is called primitive and uncivilized and our dominant religion is called fundamentalism not because we are Senegalese or Namibians, but because we are Africans. Our music, which has become the nourishing base as well as source for contemporary Western music, is caricatured as satanic and evil, not because we are Sudanese or Angolans, but because we are Africans. Our dance forms which constitute the bedrock of contemporary Western social dance are said to be heathenish and immoral not because we are Batswana or Egyptians, but because we are Africans. Our creations are called primitive art and ridiculed as having no artistic value even though they fill the museums and homes of Western nations not because we are Ethiopians, Moroccans or

Ghanaians, but because we are Africans. We are treated as fools, called racially insulting names, considered to be lower than others, and our children languish in psychological and emotional pain, not because we are from the North or South or East or West of Africa, but because we are from Africa.

Wherever and whenever a distinction is made and some of us are separated out to be better or richer or more cultured than other Africans, we must recognize it as a strategy of divide and rule that is always practiced by the predators by emphasizing the state specific nationalism rather than African nationalism. It must be strongly rejected as rubbish. We must always be aware that we are Africans whose contributions to world civilization have not been credited, and whose claim to freedom and the pursuit of happiness have gone unheeded and will not be heeded except by our efforts; this must be recognized. In the land of devils you cannot survive by the acts of angels. The history of human experience has no example where freedom and justice have been secured without cost, or rights have been given, or slaves freed by the masters, or power transferred peacefully. Let those Africans who have ears not only hear but listen, those who have eyes not only observe but see, those who have noses not only smell but sense and those who have minds not only analyze but move for it is raining but Africans are dying from thirst.

The act of violence, the act of war, the act of armed struggle, and the act of destruction of obstructions to one's freedom are strategies that one must not pledge not to use. It is in this spirit that we used the phrase "to fight one's way" to that which is one's right and freedom. Africa has been occupied. Africa is still an occupied continent. Africa has been robbed of her human and non-human resources and Africa is still being robbed of her resources. Africa and Africans are currently in a hopeless bondage to the Western nations who subjected the Africans to exploitative slavery and colonialism, and diverted Africa from her path of development, growth and social transformation. The period of slavery and colonialism was the period of socioeconomic obstructionism whose benefits to the imperial predators are immense, and whose costs to Africa are incalculable.

To change the course, to reclaim Africa for Africans, to liberate African children from bondage, to redefine a new path of African progress and to reassert the true African personality as it was, and as it must be in the current world politico-economic order, will not come about by a simple negotiation even though this is the preferred technique and humane code of conduct consistent with the principle of humanism as held by our ancestors. It is within this context that flexible response, encompassing all instruments and strategies of emancipation and physical retribution, is conceived and assigned a strategic meaning. Europeans do not pledge not to use force or to abandon the use of arms in favor of peaceful negotiations. Non-violence and peaceful protocols are not known characteristics of Western personality. In fact the history of the Western dominance is colorfully filled with the use of brute force, terror, mass violence, collective punishment and uncontrollable greed that cumulate into the imperialist wars.

It is within this context that we assert the concept and the use of strategy of violence wherever and whenever necessary to obtain and protect that which is rightfully owed. Violence should not be used by any civilized people on others; neither should it be pledged away in this bitter struggle to emancipate Africa. This position and the implications thereof, in the process of complete African emancipation, must permeate the minds and souls of all Africans. As we consider a way out of Africa's current dilemma, Africans must think of reconstructing Africa's glorious past, think of consolidating her position as we design strategies to liberate her children from bondage, and to work toward the establishment of the new African federated state. These call for love of self and unity among all Africans irrespective of their place of birth and position in society. They also call for hard work, perseverance, creative thinking, ideological correctness, institutional recasting, courage, optimism, efficient organization and above all a unified principle of thought and action. There is no room here for the African separatist, neither is there any room for dependency syndrome, do-nothingness and subservience. The stakes are high.

In the new Africa conceived by the African nationalists, the federated African nation with continental dimension, ethnic culture, behavior and artistic displays are not only acceptable, but they are compatible with the concepts of African nationalism and the federated nation. The African nationalist sees a cultural tapestry as the greatest natural gift to Africa, not tribalism and ethnic hostilities, but as a *kente* cloth craftily woven together with the finest of Africa's artistry that must reflect her organizational creativity. This cultural tapestry, reflecting also the polyrhythmicity in thought and behavior, portrays diversity in unity which is Africa's beauty and strength but not weakness. The African nationalist sees ethnic diversity in unity where each diverse part plays a unique, important, and supporting role to create the beauty that is truly African in a unified setting. Thus, ethnicity or ethnic affinity, like either tribe-specific affinity or state-specific affinity, generates a positive force that is uniting in the context of African development, social transformation and human progress.

The potential contradiction and antagonistic tendencies in tribal, ethnic and state differences are resolved in favor of African unity and Africa's complete emancipation. Immediately Africans born at home and abroad come to an immutable realization that Africa is one, and that the fight against racism, neo-colonialism, imperialism, and exploitation of our people all over the world, must be fought and won continentally and globally. In this theater of racial antagonism, there is a positive and critical role to be played by the descendants of Africans who were forcefully and illegally removed and placed into slavery in the Americas. A rough estimate puts the total number of these courageous and strategically resilient Africans to a total of over two hundred and fifty millions with the largest concentration being in Brazil. Our strategy is how to forge from our gruesome history a positive link with the descendents of these courageous Africans. Here the work is twofold. One task is from the side of African continent and the other from the side of the African Diaspora.

Every president of the United States of America is fearful of the possibility of unity between the progressive leadership of African Americans and the progressive leadership on the African continent (see for example the Brzezinski's Presidential Review Memorandum/NSC-46, March 17, 1978 to which we have previously referred. See also [142c] [29b] [29d]). We are convinced that total emancipation of Africa on all fronts (economics, science, technology, and culture) can only be ensured if Africa is united. This is an important foundational idea of African nationalism. The emancipation of Africa is not only in defense of the race, but it is the emancipation of human species from senseless racism and injustices as committed by the imperial predators where only the law of the jungle applies. Freedom, justice and peace lie at the core of African unity. This core recognizes that peace and freedom have no opportunity to thrive in conditions of disunity and injustice.

The African nationalist, irrespective of his or her ethnicity, tribe, state or religion, knows that Africa is extremely fragmented into too many small and economically non-viable states. Some are too weak with no ability to feed their people and thus must seek help at the neocolonialist revolving doors of aid, loans and technical assistance with humiliations. Fragmentation is a complete setback to the charted course of Africa's emancipation and any opportunity to reclaim Africa for Africans. Fragmentation dis-empowers the Africans and fosters racism and racial animosities against Africans. It spells doom, produces servitude, and fosters disaster for Africa and her children. African nationalism, therefore, is an ideological light to look for and pick up the precious pieces in this age of ideological darkness and weld them tightly together with the unity flame so that Africa can be detached from the Super-Power framework of ideological idiosyncrasies and rent-seeking activities of imperialist predators.

To any serious freedom-loving African, the struggle for complete African emancipation within the framework of Nkrumaism and African nationalism must be taken seriously regardless of where one comes from. There is a continent to regain, African dignity to recapture, Africa's children to rescue, an African personality to mold, a hope to be refueled, madness to be cured and the greed of the imperial predators to be stopped. The success of the current African Union depends on building institutions where decisions are made on the ideology of African nationalism and where the states' behavior in the decision-choice space are guided by African nationalism complemented with the positive role of state-specific nationalism

In the game of international political and economic life, Africa is not even a spectator. Africa is simply the instrument of play, as a ball is to a game of soccer. Africa and Africans are kicked around for other peoples' enjoyment, bear the brunt of the pain and extensive damage in the global ideological games and resource exploitation. Africa is neither a participant nor is she a spectator; she is the element for the game. What an awkward position Africans find themselves? The answer is not state-specific nationalism, nor is it ethnicity or tribalism. The answer lies in African unity, African nationalism, African personality and Africentricity that point to a new and powerful way of organizing Africans. The answer does not lie in state-specific nationalism, or ethnicity or tribalism. The leaders of the African states operating on the negative elements of state-specific nationalism work so hard to belong to the predators' world instead of working creatively under the ideological principle of African nationalism to create a Greater Africa that will allow all of us to share and enjoy.

These leaders have not embraced the concepts and the creative forces of African nationalism, African personality and African unity as vehicles to Africa's complete emancipation. These are the elements that affect human cognitive actions in the choice-decision space, the outcomes of which establish the path of national progress and history. We have made a case for the creative power of African nationalism that must guide African unity and integration toward Africa's redemption. This creative force depends on African personality which is in turn affected by ideology of African nationalism. We have also made a case for African unity as a strategy for full spectrum resistance against the full spectrum dominance of the imperial predators. This case for African nationalism and unity will be reinforced in the chapter that follows where we will outline in explicit theoretical details that define the modus operandi of the current imperial predators. The objective of this chapter is to define the global institutional framework and conditions of imperial predation. This will allow a full and complete understanding and appreciation of the Nkrumaist strategy and policy of Africa's emancipation that is discussed in chapter seven. Chapters six and seven will further reinforce the case of African unity and African nationalism.

6

THE THEORY OF CRONY IMPERIALISM: THE *MODUS OPERANDI* OF THE PREDATORS

In the previous chapters we characterized the members of the governing class or the decisive core whose individual and collective personalities are derived from cultures opposed to the African way as askari and zombies. At this point it is useful to offer working definitions for askari and zombie. A political, or intellectual or religious askari of a national leadership or ruling class is one who is stripped off his or her traditional sensibility of awareness as to what he or she is, through training and brainwashing, leading to bizarre behavior that is guided by an acquired personality completely foreign to his or her being, and whose decisions and actions are externally motivated to produce results that are inimical to the survival of the members of his or her society. The state in which such individuals function will be referred to as an askari state. A zombie of a national leadership class, either political, intellectual or religious, is one that has swallowed an intellectual opium pill of mind altering substance leading him or her into a state of senselessness that induces him or her to obey commands of external forces of the members of the imperial club who exercise a plethora of controls over his or her actions to destroy his or her nation. The state (conditions) of operations of a zombie is the zombie state.

These askari and zombies, made up of political, religious and academic elites, accept from the outset Western dominance, Africa's current situation and the conditions that maintain both as permanent and natural and even at time as divine. Their perceptions about African's internal difficulties inherited from colonial order, about global events and Africa's experiences of the forces both external and internal to her, and decisions and actions that are taken as a result, are

111

conditioned by such acceptance. They fail to understand that the only thing that is permanent in life and nature is change and change alone is that which induces social and natural transformations. Different forms of life, social transformations, dissolution of empires and the rise of new empires (that is, the whole process of the disappearance of the old and the emergence of the new) are not possible without change.

The askari and zombies have no vision, neither do they have a mission of building a Great Africa and yet they claim themselves to be the leaders of Africa. Such a claim of leadership is supported, maintained and enforced by the predators of Africa. These askari and zombies are always happy to be called as friends of the West while they fail to understand the simple idea that the West has no friends and had never had any but only interests that help to maintain the West's global dominance. The global system of production, distribution and politics is simply a global process of determining who gets what, how much, when and where regarding the flow of global resources: the what, how much, when and where are questions of global production and distribution. The answers to these questions are determined by the global economic, political, and military forces. The institutional framework through which these forces operate and the manner in which these forces operate to bring about global outcomes constitute the international politico-economic order in which power, security and stability of resource flows are displayed. It is in this framework that the members of the imperialist club constituting the incumbent holders of power exert their dominance and power by designing strategies and tactics for maintaining their dominance [29b][64b] [69d] [150b]. One of the strategic arsenals available to the predators in order to create and maintain their dominance and abstract rent in contemporary global existence is the effective utilization of national political askaris and zombies. In this context international laws when they are selectively applied, just as it is done in the United Nations, become mainly instruments of imperial control, Intimidation and subjugation against the weak nations. The objective has always been the control of the global resources and their trade flows.

6.1 The Basic Essentials of the Global Economic Space: The Resource Conflict Problem

At this juncture, let us take a closer look at the social and natural forces that are inducing the creation and the rise of the askari and zombies. These forces emerge from consumption-production duality. To understand the forces at work we must visit the basic essentials of the global economic space.

6.1.1 The Structure of the Global Economic Space and the Theater of Imperial Predation:

Two evolutionary processes engender the nature of the global economic space and conflict zones of our planet earth.

The two processes are geomorphologic evolution of the earth crust and demographic evolution of the earth's people. These two processes induce a set of dualities over the global space whose organic result is the consumption-production duality that spins the dynamics of resource conflicts, imperialism, war, colonialism, subjugation and globalization in the global socioeconomic space. The result is the creation of axes of injustices and oppression that give rise to resistance against the sources of oppression in whatever form possible depending on the state of social and physical technologies. The axes of injustices and oppression are the epicenters of evil that create cronies of global violence. The essentials of factors that encompass the global economic space are shown in Figure 6.1.

The conditions leading to global resource conflict are seen in terms of two major evolutions. They are geomorphological-climatological evolution and demographic evolution. The geomorphological evolution supported by climatological structure brings about distinct distribution of natural resources such as mineral deposits, structure of vegetation, distribution of arable lands and others. This natural resource distribution gives rise to areas of land that are rich in natural resources whose usefulness are conditioned by human production know-how and general state of technology. Alongside the geomorphological evolution is the demographic evolution of the earth's people.

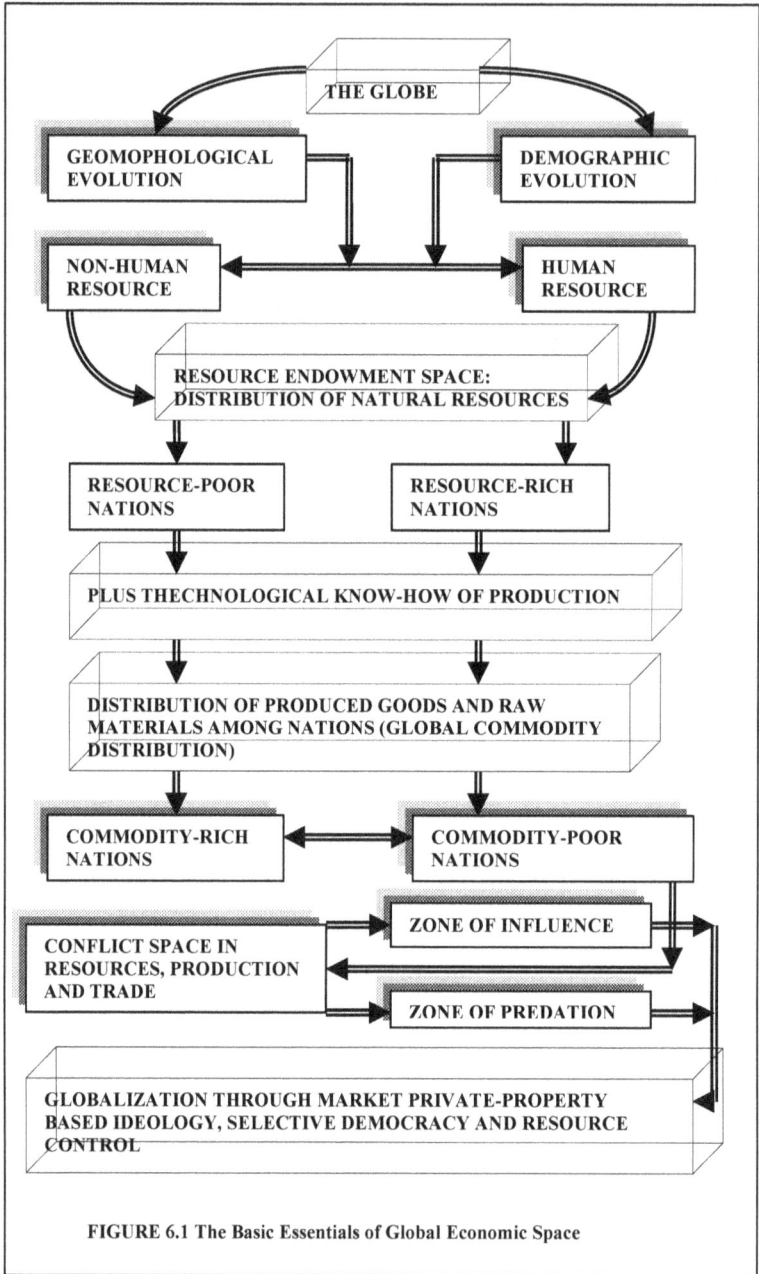

FIGURE 6.1 The Basic Essentials of Global Economic Space

The demographic evolution superimposes on the unique resource distribution a particular type of population distribution over the earth's surface. The two evolutions of nature and human give rise to two distributions of non-human resources and people. The result of the two evolutions and the resulting two distributions is differential distribution of resource endowment where some people have come to inherit differential resource endowment of relatively resource-rich and resource-poor lands.

The global political geography as humanly established has come to define the boundaries of resource distribution and human inheritance as permanent. Given the resource endowment, the use of technology and production know-how, a new distribution of produced goods and raw materials among nations is established. This new distribution gives rise to countries that are rich in commodities (real income) and countries that are relative poor in commodities. In this respect an increasing richness in commodities is constrained by technology and the nature of resource endowment. To maintain the relative richness and its growth of countries rich in commodities, there must be access to resources of global nature given technology and its growth. Global competition for increasing richness gives rise to competition for global resources, creating conflicts in the global resource space. This resource conflict gives rise to the global resource game where the most powerful assert their weight. The result is the creation of a zone of influence and zone of predation that reveal themselves as a predator-prey dynamic game with a process to globalization where more resources are acquired by others at the expense of other countries in competition.

Given the global economic space there arises the conflict-cooperation duality. This duality creates forces of motion that push the global society into constructive-destructive processes toward internal self-destruction or internal self-reconstruction. The constructive-destructive process manifests itself as wars, colonialism, imperialism, territorial occupation and sphere of domination and interest. There are three paths that the global social system can navigate on. One path is that of complete individual national isolationism. The second path is complete global unity, the process of which is a complete globalization. The third is a hybrid of the two in various degrees of closedness-openness duality.

Complete isolation is not meaningful in our contemporary world and hence the path of isolation is out of serious intellectual and policy discussions. We can, however discuss the degrees of isolation or openness. Most nations are traveling on the path of the hybrid with the combination of various degrees of openness and closedness that provide closed-open mix in the policy space. In this framework of openness and closedness there is an optimal mix that is country-specific.

The optimal closed-open mix of one country may, depending on its resource configuration, constrain the optimal mix that other nations seek in other to optimize their internal wealth production as well as their relative power position within the space of international relations to accumulate wealth, global power and control. Relative global power requires wealth. Continual production and accumulation of wealth require access to major resources, broadly defined. Some of the essential and critical resources are not located in the areas of need because of the geomorphological and demographic processes that we have alluded to. Access to the needed resources demands control or international cooperation. The competition to control the channels to these resources creates international conflicts. These conflicts are between nations that own the resources and nations that seek to exploit them to increase their wealth creation for further widening of their relative global power and influence to ensure sustainable control of the access to resources and trade. Here influence and controls, broadly defined, are established through the use of various instruments including diplomacy and non-diplomacy. Instruments of non-diplomacy include force, violence, political and economic destabilization, blackmail and other non-conventional instruments and continual production and wealth accumulation. These non-democratic instruments are available to countries with imperial and colonization tendencies.

6.1.2   Imperial Tendencies, Globalization and the Predatory-Prey Game

The group of nations that seeks to control the channels of resource exploitation and the direction of commodity and resource flows exhibits imperial and colonialist tendencies. There is a tendency for conflicts to arise within this group of nations. The conflict gives rise to forces that bring about cooperation or competition. When competition is engendered among the group of imperialists we have competitive imperialism with competing ideologies in the predatory space. On the other hand when cooperation is fostered among the imperialist predators we have cooperative imperialism with ideological unity in the predatory space.

The previous era, when the European countries were searching for colonies and territories, was marked by competitive imperialism leading to the two imperialist wars toward the completion of territorial acquisitions. This competitive imperialism crystallized itself into competitive superpowers with competing ideologies during the era of decolonization, the rise of national consciousness, wars of freedom, liberation through resistance, independence, claims to sovereignty and self-government. Like any polarity, competition has a seed of cooperation that houses within its confines the seed of competition. Both competition and cooperation house and water within themselves the seeds of their own destruction. Competitive imperialism creates within its path the process of creative destruction that forces the competitors to seek a path of cooperation. The nineteenth and early twentieth century competitive imperialism of Western European nations gave rise to the germination of cooperative imperialism through the process of Europe's self-destruction.

The current trend is leading to an era and a new regime of cooperative imperialism that is fostering the process of globalization. The creation and nurturing of the forces that are shaping the globalization process constitute the objectives and interests of the club of imperialists. The goal is full spectrum dominance. The method of accomplishment of this full spectrum dominance is the waging of total war on the weak and defenseless nations who by geomorphological evolution hold critical and essential resources broadly defined. The strategy of resource control by the established imperialists is to constrain any emerging imperial competitor or neocolonial resistance. The objectives and interests, viewed in an organic sense, are relationally resource control and predation. In a critical material sense we have a predator-prey process. The current process and the objectives are fundamentally no different from those of colonialism. The difference is seen in terms of tactics, strategies and supporting ideological orientation. Instead of colonization we have neo-colonization that is deceptively called globalization. Thus another name for globalization is neocolonialism made palatable. Instead of competitive imperialism we have cooperative imperialism. For the cooperative imperialism to function at optimal level it must have internal and external cronies. The structure of the objectives of the globalization with the predator-prey duality is schematically presented in Figure 6.2 as the predatory-prey game space.

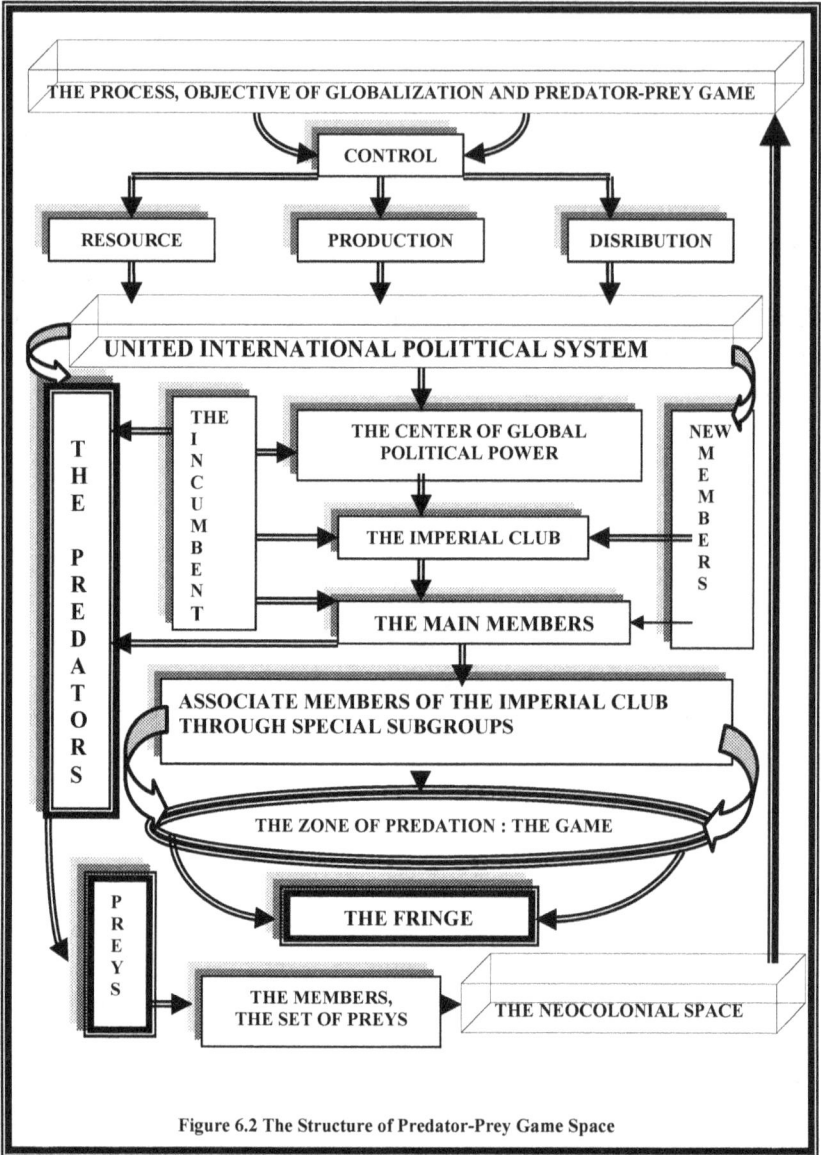

Figure 6.2 The Structure of Predator-Prey Game Space

It is important to note the three groups of stage actors. They are the members of the imperialist club that do the predation, the associate members of the imperialist club that constitute the ideological support and the members in the fringe that form the preys. If you doubt the explanatory process being offered here just ask yourself a simple question as to how one catches a fish with a hook. The process of globalization may be viewed in terms of global resource game that the defines predator-prey space to resolve the conflict of resource supply-demand duality that is generated by geormophological and demographical evolutions relative to national interests and the nature of climatic regime. On the one hand there are distributions of natural resources and population, and on the other hand there are artificially defined distributions of interests of nations whose distributions of resources may not be sufficient to support the defined national interests. A conflict, therefore, arises in the resource space within the dynamics of demand-supply duality that results in a predatory-prey resource game.

The predator-prey space may be viewed as the theater of a pursuit-avoidance dynamic game. Here there are three types of stage actors (players) composed of the incumbent, the cheerleaders for the incumbent, and the fringe whose members are to be prey upon. The reward of the game is the control of the resources and their direction of flows in addition to production and distribution which support life. By controlling the flow of resources, production and distribution the members of the incumbent control who gets what, where and when. The incumbent constitutes the imperialist club with the main members who are supported by the associate members. Allowance must be made in this *modus operandi* of the predators for the rise of new imperial predators as well as some members of the imperialist club losing their imperial status and then becoming members of the fringe. The political process of an effective predator-prey game is the establishment of some form of institutions of a united international political system that are under the control of the members of the imperialist club, which allows them to make the rules, become the referees and control the game. The conceptual space of the game is the zone of predation controlled by the members of the imperialist club and into which the members of the fringe are lured by political, economic and military techniques for predation. The result is to create neocolonial states for continual exploitation until a neocolonial state looses its status of usefulness to the predators.

The process of actualizing globalization is structured around the strategies and tactics of the members of the imperialist club. The degree of extremism of techniques and methods used depends on the free play of the behavioral forces of the associate members and the height of the wall of resistance that may be erected by the individual members and the collectivity of the fringe. The set of strategies and tactics of the members of the imperialist club, the incumbent, operate through configurations of domestic, regional and international institutions that the members of the imperialist club have established. It is worthwhile to note that most of these institutions were established after the Second World War. The basic logical structure of the institutional arrangements is schematically presented in Figure 6.3.

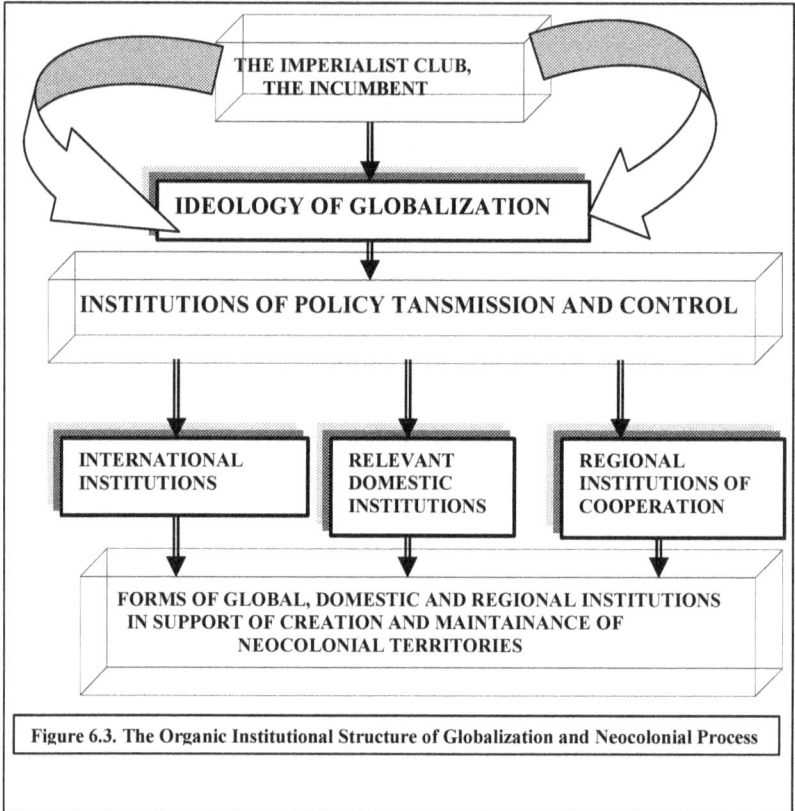

Figure 6.3. The Organic Institutional Structure of Globalization and Neocolonial Process

It shows the macro-space defined in terms of the structure of the current institutional arrangements for globalization, the process of neo-colonization, the management of the theater of predator-prey game in the resource space and the crafting of policy strategies that will support the organic process of the global resource game. Here, given the constitution of the imperialist club we have a supporting ideology of cooperative imperialism and supporting institutions of neocolonial predation where the imperial predators acknowledge only the interests of the members of the imperialist club. The process is such that the interests of the members of the fringe are assumed away or nullified by the incumbent. By assuming away the interests of the members of the fringe, any resistance on the part of the members of the fringe, is viewed in terms of terrorism, anti-democratic or anti-West and such like terms. The supporting institutions of neocolonial predation are vehicles available to the incumbent for control and policy transmission by the imperial predators. The institutions of control are organized carefully by the members of the imperialist club on the basis of internationalism, regionalism and domestic. The specific international institutions are designed in an inter-supportive mode with specific roles and duties assigned to them in the global theater of the predator-prey game in the global resource space. This set of global institutions is powerful in terms of its capacity and ability to support the theater of predatory operations by the members of the imperialist club. Let us keep in mind that the international institutions as we know them now were created by the members of the imperialist club to solve their problems that arose from competitive imperialism. They now control these international institutions for the support of the new regime of cooperative imperialism. There are special characteristics of these global institutions that need to be understood. Each one of these global institutions has the power to convince and entice the members of the set of the preys from the fringe to participate in their own predation.

At this juncture, a note on the organic institutional structure of globalization and the neocolonial process will be useful in further understanding of the role of the international institutions in the dynamics of the predator-prey game in the resource space. The members of the imperial club have developed an ideology of globalization and culture of imperial control to suit the regime of cooperative imperialism. In order to market this ideology institutions of policy transmission and control are required. These institutions are necessary but not sufficient for creating neocolonial states for effective predation. The required set of institutions of imperial cooperation is partitioned into three subsets of a) international institutions, b) regional institution of cooperation and c) relevant domestic institutions in the homelands of the members of imperial predators. The nature of these subsets of the institutions defines the forms of global, domestic and regional institutions in support of imperial creation and maintenance of neocolonial territories. The set of international institutions and the manner of their relational structure are illustrated in Figure 6. 4.

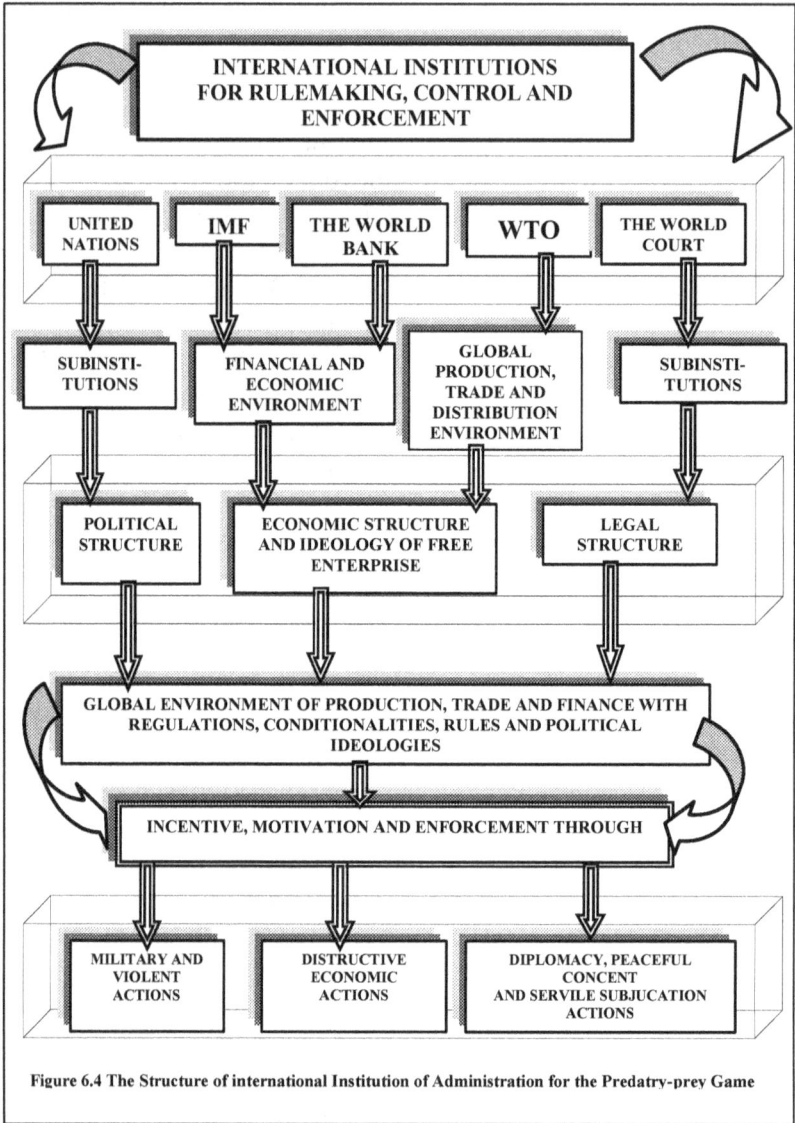

Figure 6.4 The Structure of international Institution of Administration for the Predatry-prey Game

The system of global institutions of control is relationally connected. The actions and behavior of the international institutions define a theater of policy game where the strong and valiant members are the rule makers, the gatekeepers, the police, the witnesses, the prosecutors, the judges and the executioners. The weak and helpless members are rule obeyers, voluntary or involuntary preys and instruments of the imperialist policy game.

The international institutions created by the members of the imperial club are a) the United Nations, b) the International Monetary Fund (IMF), c) the World Bank, d) the World Trade Organization (WTO) and e) the World Court. All these institutions have actual or potential sub-institutions for effective operation and control by the members of the imperial club. The United Nations with its sub-institutions constitutes the international political structure. The International Monetary Fund, the World Bank and the World Trade Organization with their sub-institutions constitute the international economic structure with the ideology of free enterprise and privatization. The World Court with its potential sub-institutions in socio-economic development process constitutes the unfolding international legal structure.

These structures are similar to any national socioeconomic organization of production-distribution dynamics. The international political, economic and legal structures are currently under the control of the imperial club. They define the global environment of resource flows, production, commodity flows, trade, capital flow, finance with regulations, conditionality, rules of behavior, flow of technical know-how in general production and political ideology. The global institutional configuration of resource and commodity environment, controlled by the members of the imperial club, establishes incentives motivation and enforcements through the application of a) military and violent action b) destructive socioeconomic actions and c) diplomacy, peaceful consent and servile subjugation actions.

The strong and valiant members constitute the incumbent as well as the members of the imperialist club under the principles of cooperative imperialism. The weak and helpless members constitute the competitive fringe as well as the preys. The strategies of the international policy game are organized and transmitted through the relevant domestic institutions of the member countries that belong to either the imperialist club or the fringe. Here power asymmetry emerges between the members of the imperial club and the members of the fringe in all levels of domestic organizations of information, technology, finance and economic size. For the conceptual edifice that we are developing, the domestic institutional arrangements of the members of the fringe are too weak to have the capacity on their individual basis to mount out any meaningful and sustainable resistance. In this respect the schematic structure that we are presenting is principally applicable to the members and associate members of the imperialist club.

The configuration of domestic institutions of the individual members of the imperialist club and the associated club bears similarities with that of the international institutions. The institutions are organized in terms of global politics, economics and law with supporting institutions of enforcement consisting of coercion, perks, intervention and others involving terror, bribery and corruption in the international policy space. The objectives of the domestic institutional configuration in the homelands of the members of the imperial club as they relate to the international policy game are organized to maintain the interests of the members of the imperialist club and the survival of the club. In support of this are the ideological machines for dis-information, misinformation, fact distortions, outright lies and cognitive deceptions. The organic structure of the relevant domestic institutions of the members of the imperialist club in the activities of the international resource and commodity policy game is presented in Figure 6. 5.

The structure of the Figure may be explained in relational terms. The governments of the members and associate members of the imperial club work with a common ideology of the imperial-neocolonial order. Besides the international institutional support they have relevant and well-tailored domestic institutions for policy creation that is transmitted through the international institutional organizations that they control. The relevant domestic institutions in support of neocolonial creation and predation are quadruple. They are:

1) Institutions for material and technological production that are relationally connected to international production system and trade. These imperial domestic institutions generate commodities and technology for consumption and imperial control of resource and commodity flows.

2) Institutions for information and intelligence gathering that are used to keep track of behavior of neocolonial or potential neocolonial states connected to the establishment of intelligent bases and operations.

3) Institutions of war, violence and terror which are used in enforcing the will of the members of the imperial club relationally connected in the establishment of military bases in the neocolonial space.

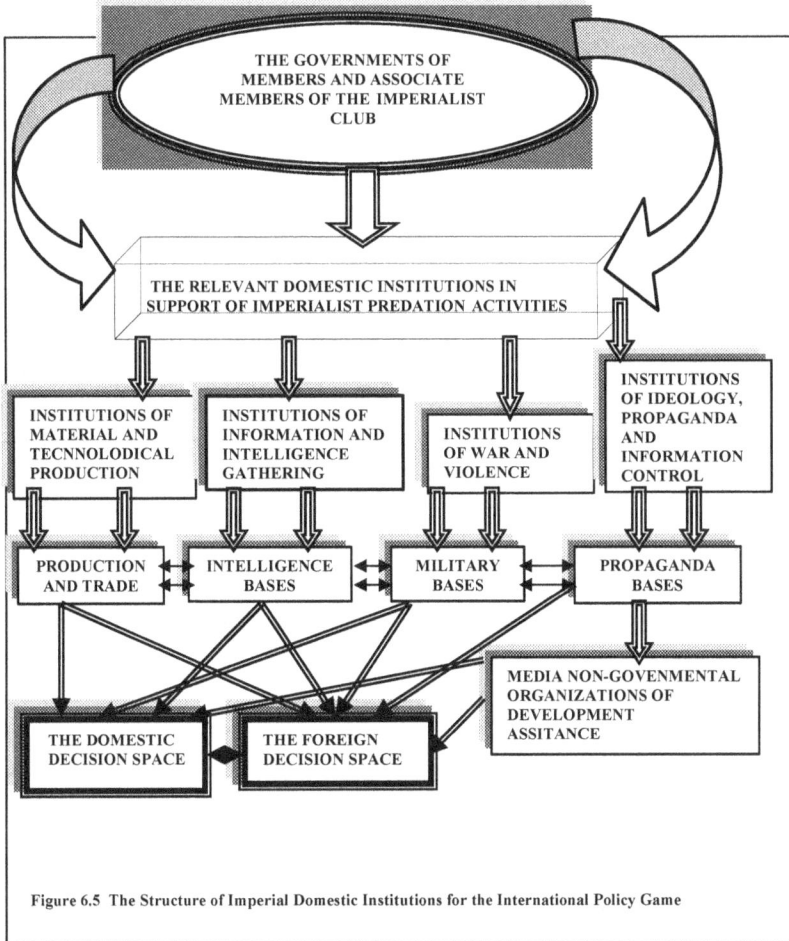

Figure 6.5 The Structure of Imperial Domestic Institutions for the International Policy Game

4) Institutions of ideology, propaganda and information control connected to the establishment of propaganda bases such as radio and television in addition to governmental operations of aid assistance, sabotage through non-governmental organizations and others. These imperial domestic institutions formulate imperial policies through institutions in the domestic and foreign decision space and then transmit them through the set of international institutions that we have discussed under Figure 6.4.

Given the structures of both international and relevant domestic institutional arrangements in the theater of the predator-prey game and international policy space, there is a third group of supporting institutions for the management of the game. This third one is the regional institutions for cooperation that is directly or indirectly set up and controlled by the members and associate members of the imperialist club. These regional institutions are politically manipulated and financially controlled to conform to the interest of the members of the imperialist club. The institutions are organized around finance, the life-blood of obtaining resources that are domestically not available for promoting speedy socioeconomic development. For the reasons of effective control of the behavior of the members of the fringe these regional financial institutions are set up to connect to the financial and socioeconomic control of the financial centers of the members of the imperialist club. The interests of the regional countries are appended to the extent to which they enhance the global interests of the members of the imperialist club. In a sense the members of the fringe are assumed to have no interests. The interests of the members of the imperial club, the incumbent, are the interests which the members of the fringe must work to promote even though such interests are detrimental to the progressive nation-building of the members of the fringe. The interests of the members of the imperialist club are assumed to be good for the international socioeconomic system as a whole and hence good for the fringe in order to do away the true conflicts of national interests. The regional financial institutions are created and supported where the incumbent ideologically preaches the virtues of competition but practically adheres to the fundamental principles of monopoly. The members of the imperialist club like to give socioeconomic aid rather than open up their markets for competition in for example agricultural produce because of food security. Socioeconomic aid is thus seen as cost of establishing influence and dominance. Self-sufficiency by the members of the fringe is not good for the interests of the members of the imperialist club whose goal and objective is full spectrum dominance of the globe. Self-sufficiency takes away an important instrument to create a neocolonial space for resource exploitation. The members of the imperialist club like to discuss terms and conditionality of aid and loans of their control rather than discuss free and fair trade where their markets are opened for the virtues of competition as they preach. All strategies in the creation of regional institutions are designed to castrate the members of the fringe whom the regional set-ups are intended to service. The idea of the imperial strategy is to create dependency and weaken the competitive strength of the fringe. The basic structure of the regional institution of cooperations and control is presented in Figure 6.6.

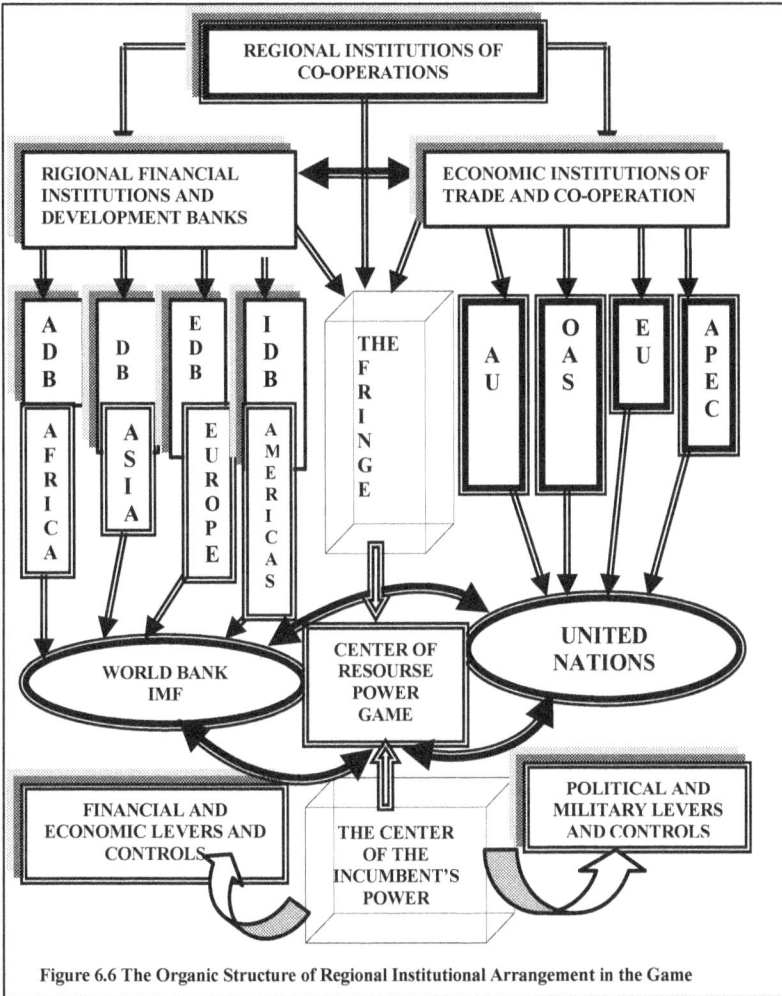

Figure 6.6 The Organic Structure of Regional Institutional Arrangement in the Game

A note of explanation of the content of Figure 6.6 would be useful in the understanding of the role of the regional institutions in support of the imperial creation and predation of the fringe. The regional institutions of cooperation are of two types, composed of financial institutions and development banks on one hand and semi-political institutions that deal with trade, cooperation, conflicts and territorial arrangements. There are four regional financial institutions - the African Development Bank (ADB), the Asian Development Bank (ADB), the European Development Bank (EDB), and the Inter-American Development Bank (IDB). These four regional financial institutions are connected to the financial centers and institutions of the World Bank and International Monetary Fund that are under the effective control of the members of the imperialist club. There are also four semi-political regional institutions which are connected to United Nations. These regional institutions are the African Union, the Organization of American States (OAS), the European Union (EU) and the Asia-Pacific Economic Cooperation (APEC). There may be other sub-organizations but those mentioned here are sufficient to make the relevant points in the argument. We may also keep in mind that new institutions may arise as the global conditions tend to alter.

The interesting thing to note is that the members of the imperialist club control regional institutions of which they are direct members. In addition they seek to control those regional institutions where they are not members. The controls come directly from aid and indirectly form pressures through the leverage that they exercise in the United Nations, the World Bank, the International Monetary Fund and their sub-institutions. These direct and indirect controls are actively supported by the propaganda machines that they have created to spin and promote ideological offensives in the global communication space.

To the members of the imperialist club, the regional financial and economic institutions of co-operation are their assets of strategic manipulation in support of their regional and global interests. The members of the fringe have no interest that must be respected by the incumbent. These regional institutions, particularly those that involve the members of the fringe, become theaters of useless games manipulated and refereed by the members of the imperialist club. In a material sense these regional institutions harbor the seed of the demise of the various members of the fringe. The regional institutions for the members of the fringe become predatory traps where there is a competitive struggle among the powerless for the power that they collectively do not have. Pressure is applied by the incumbent on the members of the fringe within the regional institutions to concentrate on the materially trivial internal game of the powerless to distract them from the basic reality that each one of them is an element of predation at the disposal of the incumbent. It will become clear that the *modus operandi* of the imperial predators are such that the members of the fringe are manipulated to play a sub-game of trivial nature where the members struggle against each other in the regional institutions to become good slaves in exchange for being characterized as a friend to the incumbent, just to postpone their immediate suffering by collaborating with the incumbent for the immediate demise of other members of the fringe.

The structure of the regional institutions, their relationship with the global centers of power and the manner in which they have been infiltrated by the members of the imperialist club render these regional institutions materially useless to the fringe. In their current forms the members of the fringe cannot overcome the monopolistic walls that have been erected by the incumbent or resist its predatory activities by using these regional institutions to assist their development processes or poverty reduction except through a radical restructuring and repositioning. With these conceptual structures of the global institutional arrangements in mind let us examine the *modus operandi* of the predators. It must be kept in mind that these institutional arrangements evolve and change forms as the global conditions alter.

6.2 The *Modus Operandi* of the Imperial Predators

A question naturally arises as to how the internal political askari and zombies are created by the predators, or arrive on the theater of Africa's social life, in order to construct socioeconomic environment of injustice, exploitation and suffering on the African continent. The second question that arises is, what are the basic characteristics of the modern predators and the process of predation? In other words, what is the method of the predators' operations or the conditions of predation? It must be noticed that the predators in our modern times operate through an indirect process where the African governments are constrained by information limitation and held in check by deceptions and lies. Of course these are done not only in Africa but also everywhere the predators go. The areas of predation include Middle East, Asia, Latin America and the Caribbean. This indirect process works through the successful establishment of neocolonial states whose leadership class is transformed into rent seekers. It works well for the predators because unlike direct colonial occupation, it does not directly expose the predator's hypocrisy or their claim to sole custodians of the altar of democracy, decent behavior and good governance (see also the works in [29a])

The theater usually opens with the predators from foreign lands entering Africa with three bags. One bag contains trivial gifts of all kinds including promises of technical assistance, development aid, loans, poverty reduction and many others; the other bag contains nauseous capsules and dangerous tricks (such as conditionalities of various kinds), while the third bag is always empty. All kinds of foreign dignitaries like technical experts, diplomats, and workers of non-governmental organizations, international agencies, and many more carry these bags from the homelands of the predators and into African territories. Sometimes these dignitaries enter with or without the knowledge of the direct or indirect role that they may be playing. With these three bags, the predators operate through their homelands and international institutions that they have established to create an environment for rent-seeking activities. They first corrupt the African leaders and the decision making process with trivial gifts from the first bag or promise of gifts, weaken them and make them impotent as leaders so as to dismantle the effectiveness of established domestic institutions and render ineffectual the decision process that is African centered (a classic example is Mobutu). The process is askarization (many examples may be found on the African continent and other parts of the world). This is necessary, but not sufficient for the predators to succeed in establishing the regime of Africa's destruction.

The predators, therefore, take the most important step of mind control by stripping the leaders of their African personality; giving them the nauseous tricks through disinformation and misinformation from the second bag to break the African spirit, creating a personality vacuum and an anti-African and schizophrenic personality that leads to the creation and maintenance of bizarre behavior. This is the process of zombilization. This technique of control and subjugation has been tried and perfected in United States of America and the United Kingdom on the minority population. In this way, the predators succeed in creating political askari and zombies (Uncle Tom and the political buffoon) who are praised by the predators through international institutions and the mass media that the predators have set up and control. These askarized and zombilized African leaders are then examined for their loyalty to the predators and anti-African thinking. If they pass the test of loyalty, they are then elevated into the status of rulers of Africa who then become or will become good servants to the predators' constructed regime of death and destruction in Africa.

When these askari and zombies are installed as leaders they appear in the African sociopolitical scene with the personality characteristics of rent-seekers but not nation builders. They are then considered by the predators as friends of the West and market-oriented thinkers even if their behavior violates all enlightened rules of democracy and human decency defined in terms of natural and human rights (see a companion volume [43b] for extensive discussions on Africentric philosophical foundations). Mobutu of Zaire, in addition to others that we do not intend to name, is a classic example. The processes of zombilization and askarization are to infect the African leadership with cognitive virus leading to a disease of *negrosis*, the psychological disease of the Negro no matter where he or she is found. This disease is a cognitive one that attacks the thinking faculties and enervates them to create a vacuum of critical deliberation. The disease places the African decision makers in the zone of compromised failure with schizophrenic behavior (see also [43b]).

If this approach of dislodging the African personality and breaking the African spirit of true African leaders fails, the predators revert to an alternative use of the elements from the trick bag. They move the African leaders with strong African personality, for example Kwame Nkrumah, Sekou Toure, Gamal Abdul Nasser, Ahmed Ben Bella, Samora Machel and others onto an artificially created terrain of evil. They demonize them with a pack of ideological lies; call them names such as dictators, killers, terrorists, communists and many more. The objective here is to prepare the grounds to neutralize them, turn the masses against them and reverse the progress of the country (keep in mind the masses operate in the zone of confusion and the rulers operate in the zone of global ignorance and illusions of belonging). With the help of the predators' mass media and propaganda machinery, the predators market these good African leaders as evil and bastards because they do not want to support their intensive and extensive exploitation. The simple goal here is to discredit the African leaders among the African masses just like they did to Kwame Nkrumah, Nasser, Lumumba, Ben Bella, Modibo Keita and may others [31a] [64b]. The general objective in this alternative strategy is to ravage the political structure of the African society, bring about moral discontent among the masses, create from within the African territory a faction of political stooges and puppets who will assume the internal operations of the predators' propaganda machinery to intensely wage an ideological and nerve war unknowingly against themselves and the African personality that the true African leaders possess. For historical examples of corresponding events and data that relate to the theory being constructed here see [29b][29d] [127b] [128b].

Additionally, the predators provide covert resource support to the created political stooges and puppets who act as their internal agents (surrogates) for destabilization and clandestine operations including human disappearances to preempt mass resistance. Simultaneously, the predators undertake low intensity warfare against the African states whose leaders resist conversion of their African personality to that of schizophrenia (example includes Samora Machel's Mozambique and Agostinho Neto's Angola). The intent is to sabotage the political and relevant social institutions that serve the African state and the people. In so doing the predators come to indirectly control the center of the country's power and decision making, and use it to serve the interest of the predators. In other words the decisive core of the nation's leadership is moved to operate in the zombie and askari states.

The predators are vicious, brutal, deadly and inhumane. They have available to them an arsenal of deadly and devastating weapons of mass destruction which are continually being modernized and restructured in response to the changing conditions of global politico-economic complexities and uncertainties. They have established industries geared to the production of instruments of mass destruction, instruments of mass deception and confusion, and killing machines to create fear and contain potential resistance. They do not hesitate to use them particularly on the weak and the defenseless like all the states in Africa and South America. They kill; they exploit; they steal and they have no mercy and no true conception and practice of global democracy except that which supports their interest, politico-economic goals and objectives and the success of ideological war. They market the instruments of death to neocolonial states that are technologically less fortunate, to be used to control the masses and internal descent. The members of the imperialist club establish the rules of who gets what, how and when. In other words they control the distribution of instruments of death in accordance with the structure of their interests. They make rules to restrict competition in the production of instruments of death and mass destruction in other to maintain their privileged position to create and enforce fear in the fringe. The objective is to reduce the members of the fringe to unwilling dependents and passive sufferers of the imperial predation. The potential resistance from the members of the fringe and the production of instruments of defense against the imperialist predation are further curtailed by the imperialist usage of the available international institutions that they effectively control.

This is the morphology of the modern imperial predation. The modern history of Africa, the Middle East, South and Central America with the adjacent islands is full of classic examples of such an imperial predation. This structure of the modern imperial predation, unlike direct colonialism, is a product of European imperial wars against each other in competition to dominate the channels of resource flows. After the two imperial wars there were lessons learnt and to be learnt by the imperial political oligopolies regarding competitive struggle among themselves. They came to see and understand the devastation that they had inflicted on their people, each other's national crafts and Europe itself. From these lessons, the European predators came to an uncompromising understanding of the destructive force of competitive imperialism and the virtues and potential benefits of collaborative imperialism where unity and cooperation flourish among them to reduce cost of European global adventurism.

They have also learnt from the knowledge gains of economic theory about the power of coalition in games to overcome the prisoner's dilemma. On the basis of such lessons and understanding they moved to create a workable unity that constitutes the imperial club which functions through a complex establishments of international institutions (such as the Bretton Woods institutions and supporting financial and development institutions) that are used to strengthen the imperial unity and the control of the fringe. Competition and disunity are encouraged among the members of the fringe that is controlled by monopolistic levers and strategies by the incumbent. Such levers include but are not limited to meaningless economic and technical aid, oppressive loans with development constrained conditionality, corruption of leadership, a program of socioeconomic sabotage and many others.

The imperial predators thus work in collaboration with each other (that is in unity). They bring collective punishment without regard to civilized codes of international conduct either of war or diplomacy. They cut off an important artery of the economy, international credit. They place sanctions on food and medicine that enter the state and torture and kill the innocent. They place embargoes on the freedom to travel in and out of the states and restrict the international flow of commodities into and out of the targeted state. They enforce these actions with military intimidation by mining the ports and harbors of entry and constructing military and intelligent gathering bases in the neighboring states that have succumbed to their will and influence which any of the African states is too weak to contest (many of these bases are littered in Africa, Asia, the Middle East and South and Central America). The members of the imperial club with varying degree of participation are the makers of the rules of the international conduct; they are the judges, the prosecutors, the jury, the witnesses and the executioners.

They do these things with the objective of creating a general economic panic in the targeted state by artificially creating internal conflict, war, hunger, disease and suffering, and then blame them on the true African leaders and their humanistic social policies as irrational, barbaric and stupid. On the basis of this they finally impose international socioeconomic conditionality on the state to further punish the masses, to make sure that the masses know that the incumbent is the custodian and enforcer of international law and order.

These predators are powerful, rich, tactical, strategic and well organized with a plan. They control weapons of mass destruction, weapons of mass suffering and instruments of mass deception which they constantly use against other nations. They do all these things to devastate the economic structure that supports the internal politico-legal arrangements, and to collapse the political order that they consider unfriendly to the West. The process is creating global capitalism where the weak is at the mercy of the villain and strong. The intent is to break the backbone of the African spirit and obliterate the African personality through acts of destabilization of the political structure that holds together the power to make social decisions, provide service to the people and design appropriate development strategies. The predators are successful because of the smallness and weakness of the African countries.

If this third strategy fails, the predators have the final deadly weapon. They turn the political stooges and puppets into proxy armed forces and bring military action through internal coups d'état and execute the members of the leadership class with strong collective African personality (out of over 85 coups d'état, we may mention

Congo, 1960; Togo, 1963; Algeria, 1965; Ghana, 1966 and others). The predators support the proxy armed forces, which may include some factions from the domestic armed forces. They provide them with strategic intelligence, military equipment, and covert advisors on the field. The result of this alternative strategy is for the stooges and puppets to cease power vested in the political structure.

When these stooges seize power to acquire the political kingdom, they become indebted to the imperial predators that quickly turn them into political askari and zombies to either improve or protect the thievery system for exploitation of human and non-human resources of the country, basically for the benefit of the imperial predators with leftover crumbs for the internal askari and zombies. If the internal overthrow of legitimate African leaders is not successful, the predators bring direct military action and justify it with concocted information whose truth is only known by the predators through their documents that they classify as secret. They use weapons of mass destruction, unleash terror on the masses, devastate the territory, bring collective punishment, arrest the leaders with strong African collective personality, and either imprison or execute them (examples include Lumumba of Congo, 1960, Allende in Chile, 1973 [29b] [29d]). A leadership vacuum is artificially created leading to socio-political instabilities (just as one currently taking place in Iraq) and in its place is imposed a proxy puppet government whose leaders have the desired characteristics of the political askari and zombies ready to take and obey orders from the imperial predators and their established international institutions such as the World Bank, the International Monetary Fund and the United Nations. The members of the puppet government are praised as friends of the West and loves of democracy and freedom as long as they go along in protecting the interest of the imperial predators from the West at the expense of the freedom and true democracy of their people.

When these political askari and zombies with puppetry and schizophrenic personality, no matter how they are created, are installed as rulers over an African territory, a neocolonial state is thus born and ready for intensive and extensive exploitation. At this juncture, a regime of death and destruction has been established over the territory and the African masses are on their way to the shores of illiteracy, poverty, famine, sickness and suffering which are then blamed on poor governance, corruption and un-readiness of Africans to govern themselves. The necessary and sufficient condition for the creation and continual maintenance of a neocolonial state by the imperial predators, therefore, is a successful manufacturing and installment to power of political askaris and zombies with puppetry bizarre behavior. The process being described here is also being applied to other countries in South America, Asia and the Caribbean Islands with varying degree of intensity and success. The African case is, however, special due to her rich resources and history.

When the political askari and zombies are created, or installed as puppet rulers over an African state, they become mentally disconnected from the state and Africa itself. They then develop anti-African nationalism, become African separatists, develop illusions of inclusion in the predators' world, and act against African unity. They accept the predators' bankrupt ideology of donor-driven development and neglect the fundamental idea that sustainable motion is internally created and driven. These African rulers travel not on the road of sankofarization (the process of retrieval of Africa's glorious past, understanding of current reality and the actualization of future possibilities) but on the road of further askarization and zombilization. The interests of the installed rulers of African states become bound up with those of the imperial predators. Africa and her children become a terrain for exploitation, and African governments under the control of the askari and zombies become instruments to achieve this exploitation on behalf of the imperial predators and the political askaris and zombies. The existence of the political askari and zombies is the continual maintenance of a neocolonial state, lack of socio-economic development and a socio-cultural regime of Africa's destruction.

The emergence of a set of neoclassical states is a precondition for the establishment of crony imperialism by the predators. Crony imperialism is the last stage of a global capitalism dominated by the imperial predators. The members of the imperialist club constitute a set of cooperative and oppressive international political oligopolies which collectively behave as an incumbent to exploit and limit the growth and development of the members of the fringe and in some cases reverse the development process of a country (for example, Ghana after Nkrumah and Congo after Lumumba). The incumbent acts hostilely against any entry attempt by the fringe (member nations that do not belong to the imperial club) in any important sphere of global production and power distribution. The established power relations between the incumbent and the fringe, channels of resource flows, the right to develop weapon of mass destruction, the right to develop instrument of mass deception, the right to knowledge and the use of knowledge are claimed to be the interest of the incumbent and only a privilege of the fringe with conditionality as established by the incumbent. When a set of neocolonial states is created, each one of them is under a regime of exploitation by the imperial predators that together constitute the imperialist club.

It must be noted that the G-Seven is an imperial club. This is also true of the original OECD countries. The fringe is made up of neocolonial states. The managing of the regime of resource exploitation requires a well crafted calculus of strategies and tactics. The theater of exploitation is a game of resources acquisition where there are moves and counter moves. To ensure the upper hand and dominance by the members of the imperial club, strategies and tactics are created to make it possible to exploit indirectly the neocolonial states as long as it is possible. The space of neocolonial activities by the imperial predators is the neocolonial space which holds all the neocolonial states.

The neocolonial space is partitioned into subsets and ranked according to the decision and operational strategies of the imperial predators. A few of the neocolonial states are strategically elevated to a status of prominence, praised, made into friends and pacified by the offer of feel-good rhetoric, crumbs and token rewards by the members of the imperialist club. The token rewards and crumbs come from the output or the rent from the theater of exploitation and resource game. The token rewards such as aid, grants and access to oppressive international capital markets are simply the cost of international rent-seeking activities that are undertaken by the imperial predators and are paid from the total benefit of predation. These strategically preferred neocolonial states are the cronies and form the set of crony neocolonial states. It is incorrect to think that the crony neocolonial states are less exploited than other states in the neocolonial space. The beneficiaries of the crony neocolonial states are the rulers but not the citizens whose suffering is characterized as collateral damage. In fact they may be exploited more than the members of the non-crony sector of the theater of the game of exploitation and dominance. All the rulers of the neocolonial states are the favorites of the imperial predators because they have access to siphon out the resources of the crony neocolonial states and then return crumbs to the rulers of the neocolonial state for being good slave drivers and putting up no resistance on behalf of their people. Additionally, all the crony neocolonial states are strategic favorites of the members of the imperial club. A crony state is usually offered trivial material compensation such as non-developmental aid, increased military assistance, encroachment of undemocratic practices, disappearances of citizens, and greater kickbacks to the members of the ruling class in other for them to indirectly surrender their sovereignty and collective personality. Examples are Egypt, Morocco, Ivory Coast, Liberia, South Africa and others in Africa, South Korea and others in Asia.

When a crony neocolonial state is born, it becomes a nerve center for the predators' activities against other sovereign states. Some of the members of the imperial club create intelligence posts, military bases and a taskforce for destabilizing other African states whose leaders have not yet become political askari and zombies while at the same time managing the regime of destruction of the nerve center. The imperial predators, having been successful in creating a crony neocolonial state, and using it as a nerve center for their operations, also know that a crony neocolonial state is under a regime of death and destruction where the suffering of the masses may trigger a social revolt against the askari and zombies and render the place chaotic (examples in Africa include Ivory Cost, Egypt, Algeria, Morocco, Guinea; most of the Latin American countries constitute good examples). Its life and usefulness are short. Thus new territories must be brought into the orbit of exploitation and crony imperialism.

Woe beholds the political askari and zombies of a neocolonial state if they either outlive their usefulness as agents and assets of the imperial predators or try to de-askarize and de-zombilize themselves. They obtain harsh treatment from the imperial predators by whom they are quickly moved to the terrain of evil (for example, Mobutu Sese Seko of Zaire, Saddam Hussein of Iraq, Qaddafi of Libya, Noriega of Panama, the Shah of Iran, or Marcos of the Philippines or Pinochet of Chile [153b] and many others that history abundantly provides us) and demonized and called names such as thieves, corrupt leaders, killers, brutal dictators, drug dealers and possessors of weapons of mass destruction and many more names. In this way the imperial predators prepare the disloyal and awakened askari and zombies as sacrificial lambs to be offered at the altar of disgrace and altar of execution to the gods of democracy in order to cover up the predatory evils and rent-seeking activities of the members of the imperialist club. The imperial predators even take higher moral grounds and indict these disgraced rulers for committing crimes against humanity (for example, Pinochet of Chile [29b] [29d]). They put out arrest warrants for them, prices on their heads and make them vagabonds. Their assets in the predators' homelands are frozen and or confiscated. Their children are left in destitution and historical disgrace. The imperial predators are always right and civilized by divine grace and they claim the right to spread this righteousness and the divine grace to the rest of the world population whose nations are militarily weak and defenseless.

The political askari and zombies end up as historical outcasts who are unwanted by the Africans and disgraced by their collaborators, the predators in the imperialist club. As the imperial predators are doing these to the disgraced askari and zombies they are simultaneously cultivating new askaris and zombies as replacements from within the crony neocolonial state. The members of the imperialist club that constitute an incumbent do not like competition inside the club and against their predation in the global system of human organizations, even though they proclaim in their theories of organizations the indestructible value of competition. They have learnt from the common history of mankind that competition has within itself the seeds of Marxian dynamics, the Schumpeterian creative destruction and Nkrumaist transformation dynamics for categorial conversion (see [44]). These seeds are not good for the conditions of dominance of the incumbent. The members of the fringe are viewed as possessing seeds of differential hostility and must be dealt with likewise and contained by whatever means available. One must understand the forces that lead to the formation of the imperialist club whose members were one time or another adversaries and competitors (for example the USA and Great Britain, or France and Great Britain or France and Germany and many others [29b] [29d] [64b] [127b] [128a]).

As a rule, therefore, the imperial predators work not to make friends, and hence have only interests but not friends to defend. These interests are economic while all other perceived interests, whether communicated or not, are nothing but surrogates thereof. The members of the imperialist club are not humanitarians or helpers or philanthropists or donors. They are simply conquerors whose intent is to control the flows of global resources and output to their advantage. To conquer and defend their interest they create zones of influence and control. The members of the imperialist club collaborate with one another by tacitly sharing out spheres of influence and theatrical zones of exploitation. They proceed on two strategic fronts. One front entails the process of keeping the members of the imperialist club together by resolving internal conflict, supporting each other and navigating the path of cooperative conglomerate for full spectrum dominance and exploitation. The other front involves the process of keeping the fringe in disunity by creating internal conflicts, political askari, zombies and neocolonial states for the global control of resource-commodity flows. The political askari and crony neocolonial states are their assets and instruments used by the predators to create and maintain the zones of influence that are needed to protect their predatory activities and interests. These political askari and zombies are defined as friends as long as they are useful as tools and idiots for exploitation, conquering and controlling.

This is the method of operation in the process of creating crony imperialism with concomitant neocolonialism. Crony imperialism is the last stage of global capitalism as designed by the imperial predators and destroyers who collectively act as the incumbent to conquer, control, and exploit the international political market for power and resource. As conquerors, the predators operate on four principles: ownership, exploitation, control, and destruction (OECD). Ownership implies the subjugation of the territory to direct rule, occupation and outright physically taking the territory and converting it into a colony or a settler territory that has an implication of annexation or pseudo-annexation. Exploitation implies intensive and extensive utilization of indigenous institutions and their custodians to siphon out the most precious resources out of the country for the benefit of the imperialist club. Control implies the establishment of some form of sphere of influence that allows the imperial predators to shape and dictate directly or indirectly the terms of the internal and external affairs of a territory. Destruction implies a design of strategies either to collapse the political and economic structure of a country and wipe it out or to completely exterminate the original people that occupy the land, confiscate it and make it ready for resource exploitation for their wealth creation and accumulation. Many historical accounts are available to us in support of the practice of these four principles. We need not go into details of these concepts. One is simply referred to the histories of the creation of United States of America, Canada, Australia, South Africa,

Puerto Rico and the conflict in the Great Lakes Region of Africa, Haiti and other places (see [29b] [29d] [69d] [128a].

The imperial predators' most preferred principle is that of ownership. If the predators cannot establish a regime of ownership they attempt to establish a regime of control. If this attempt fails they resort to different techniques and dubious methods of exploitation. If exploitation is not successful they, by whatever means necessary, establish a regime of destruction. These four principles are interchangeable and are continually being applied by the imperial predators to establish and defend their interests and conditions of dominance. The success of any of these four principles on the African soil depends on the degree of purity of African personality that the African leaders collectively hold and whether they are their own reality or imperialist illusions of belonging.

The African leaders must clearly understand that the destruction of the African personality begins with the imperial predators entering not once and not twice but many times. The predators always carry with them a bag of political and economic tricks that presents deception to their preys. They chameleonize themselves to operate in any social environment. They enter territories in the skins of angels and righteousness. They present development and good life for the future to simply divert attention from their diabolical deeds. They enter the territories in the suites of self-righteousness and present democracy as the panacea of all ills. They also present story lines in a manner that fits the character of a chameleon. The predators working ethics are to confuse, deceive and overcome their preys. They are hunters. They arrest some members of the fringe with their traps, beat, shoot and plant evidence which nobody knows and classify them as secrete for national security. In fact, they act with the same strategies and tactics as the police forces in the cities of United States of America such as New York, Philadelphia, Los Angeles and others where people get arrested, convicted and jailed or punished on the basis of police fabricated and planted evidence for crimes the people did not commit .The current experience with Great Britain and the United States of America regarding accusations and information on Iraq's possession of weapons of mass destruction, leading to the British and American invasion, is a classic strategy of the predators. The imperial predators conceive themselves as the only members of the global system that have interests and that these interests over ride all human rights of the fringe. The role of the United Nations as a supporting institution of neocolonialism and imperial predation is exemplified by its role in the destruction of Iraq's instruments of defense and resistance against USA and Great Britain; supported by a mis-informed coalition, it weakened Iraq's defenses and then watched it being attacked.

For this strategy to work for the imperial predators it has to be backed by divide and conquer, and further divide and rule. The predators' strategies are designed to inhibit coordinated political and economic activities of African leaders, particularly those who are working in the tradition of the African nationalist movement in terms of African unity. They are further designed to distract the African leaders form the cardinal reality that the solutions to Africa's difficulties lie in the Pan-African approach and collective African self-reliance. The solution to Africa's problems does not lie in conditions of dependency on aid, debt slavery, but lies in Africa's self-reliance. The imperial predators know this and hence launch all types of clandestine operations to create distrust among African leaders in order to divide them and set them one against the other. They set fire here and fire there; war here and war there in Africa just to divert African attention away form development, shift resources form fighting against imperial predatory activities and to dealing with internal strives in Africa while the African economic bases are ruined.

These strategies of the imperial predators have worked largely in their favor and against Africa and other places such as South and Central America. The predators' operations of control function through corruption, trivial donations and vain promises where they work on the African leaders by restructuring their minds with sophisticated gimmicks of technical assistance, donations, organizational restrictions, loan conditionality, democracy, individual freedom, good governance, and many more things which they themselves do not practice. They always come to other countries to protect democracy, freedom and justice but not to practice them. They are in other countries to enforce law and order but not freedom and justice. In the process the imperial predators present the fundamental ethical postulate of individual freedom and set it against that of collective freedom in the neocolonial state. The African rulers stripped of their African personality, turned into political askari and zombies and elevated to the status of leaders by external forces are encouraged by the imperial predators to join them and acquire individual wealth at the expense of the African masses, and to store it in the predators' homelands for safekeeping. In other words, they turn the African rulers into imperial cronies and rent-seekers at the expense of nation building.

As political askari, zombies and imperial cronies who are completely devoid of African personality as well as engulfed deeply in illusions of inclusion in the predators' empire of exploitation and axis of injustice and oppression, they become blinded to the way of living for Africa. They acquire the characteristics of the imperial predators as parasites and suckers of the living blood of Africa. They are transformed by the strategies of imperial cronyism into appendages of the imperial predators where their job is not to lead Africa to the glorious future and not to build the African nation but rather to establish a regime of Africa's suffering and extinction. In this way, the rulers of Africa attacked by the negrosis virus are manipulated by the imperial predators to operate in the zone of extreme ignorance. This is not the African tradition; it is not the way to emancipation and a prosperous Africa. It is not the way to create greater Africa. It is simply a way to slavery and Africa's death which is counter to African personality, African nationalism, traditionalism, traditional African greatness and statecraft. The African rulers do not conceptualize the idea that the imperial predators hate competition and building Africa great is to create a competitive empire that would not be easy to exploit by the imperial incumbency.

6.3 The African Intelligentsia, the Clergy, African Personality, Negrosis and Crony Imperialism

We have indicated in the previous sections that the working mechanism of the imperial predators against Africa is to design strategies that bring about confusion and ignorance. Confusion is brought to the masses while ignorance is placed on the rulers and the elite in order to dismantle the true African personality. This does not neutralize all internal opposing forces through cognitive controls. The creation of social confusion and ignorance in African territories operates through the predators' manipulation of information and distortion of knowledge (see [69d] for other techniques of manufacturing consent). After all, the members of the imperialist club control technology and the channels of the flow of information. The imperial predators create conditions where the masses function in the zone of confusion and the rulers operate in the zone of ignorance. The rulers, however, elevated into status of imperial cronies, are rewarded with crumbs and preferential acceptance through the backdoor of the imperial edifice. And just as the askarized and zombilized African rulers are admitted through the back doors into the imperial edifice to be good servants, so also are they thrown out through the same back door to be devoured by the vicious dogs of disgrace and shamefulness that the imperial predators have created.

When an African territory is brought under the predators' confusion-ignorance set-up it is thus temporary swept under the sphere of the neocolonial operations. Ignorance on the part of the political askari and zombies is rewarded with arms and freedom to open bank accounts in the predators' homelands where these accounts are protected against all claims by African masses whose livelihoods are siphoned out. The greater is the degree of ignorance the greater is the size of this reward. The confusion on the part of the populace is rewarded with poverty, degradation, hopelessness, empty rhetorical promises, repression, human and civil rights abuses and mass suffering accompanied by inexplicable mass bizarre behavior against the foundation of their own existence. The masses develop a collective psychology from their confusion and hopelessness that they are experiencing from within their society that the best place to be and live is the predators' homelands. They then spend more precious time not to create wealth in their societies but to find channels of migration into the homelands of the imperial predators. The greater is the degree of the confusion, the greater are the sizes of these rewards. The imperial predators will continually keep such an African territory under their sphere of neocolonial operations and the African rulers as imperial cronies if they succeed in colonizing the collective minds of the intelligentsia and the clergy and turn them into intellectual askari and zombies. We will thus examine how the African intelligentsia and clergy become intellectual askari and zombies, turn into useful instruments for promoting the propaganda and ideological wars against Africa by the predators and destroyers, and thus subvert the true African personality and the African continent itself.

The intelligentsia and the clergy together constitute an important force in the societal dynamics for general social transformation. By their impact on culture and the evolving collective thinking of the people the members of the intelligentsia and clergy play critical roles in defining the direction of social change and the lines of resistance and struggle. The intelligentsia defines the societal thinking system on the basis of which perceptions about social truth and realities are formed by the individual and the collective. The clergy, on the other hand, defines the framework on the basis of which perceptions are formed by the individual and the collective about the spiritual reality of life and the deity systems of the community. The intelligentsia and clergy thus have preponderating effects on the structure on which the national belief system (information and non-information supported) rests. By affecting the national belief systems, the intelligentsia and clergy affect the cultural character and the revolutionary spirit of the nation. In this way, they can play a role either as facilitators or as impediments to the activities of the imperial predators and the forces that can pull into and maintain a country in the orbit of a crony imperial system and state of hopeless dependency.

The important role that the intelligentsia and the clergy play whether in Africa or elsewhere must be seen in terms of the relationship between perception and reality or truth. Perception is a human model of reality or truth. It is defined by human sense formation about events through the cognitive process. Truth and reality are independent of human cognition and will exist whether we know them or not. Truth, therefore, is its own defense while perception has its defense in logic. Thus, perception may or may not be accepted by the individual and or the collective as representing the truth. If the logic is weak, the perception may be revealed to either the individual or the collective or both to diverge from the reality even if it coincides with reality and hence may be rejected as an input into decision making. In the world of human operations, it is the formed perceptions about truth but not the actual truth or reality that motivates and instigates human action. Thus by affecting the perception formation of the individuals and the collective the intelligentsia and the clergy also affect the individual and the collective decisions and actions of the society as well as the nation's destiny and history. This relationship among perception, truth and the activities of the national intelligentsia and clergy must be clearly understood if the evolving social system is to retain its authenticity and rationality.

The imperial predators know the powerful role that the intelligentsia and the clergy can play either against or in favor of their predatory activities. They are also aware that an awakened and uncorrupted intelligentsia and clergy of a subjected or targeted territory can become problematic for their smoothed predatory operations even when they have successfully established a neocolonial state and politically imperial cronies. The smoothed and uninterrupted predatory operations of the imperial destroyers and predators require the support form the intelligentsia and the clergy of the subjected territory. To obtain such a support the predators corrupt the local intelligentsia and the clergy, massage their brains with nauseous conceptions of life, and their pockets with leftovers and meaningless perks. In other words, the predators turn the intelligentsia and clergy into supporting imperial cronies. This is done directly through a system of scholarships and technical assistance or indirectly through the ruling imperial cronies and reinforced through the established system of rules and regulations in addition to latent ones for scholarly publications in the academy. In this way, the predators work to turn the African intelligentsia and clergy into intellectual askaris and zombies whose pre-assigned role is to shape the perceptions of the African masses into accepting illusions, the destructive activities of the imperial predators and false conceptions of the spiritual and material world as the reality and truth that will comfort the masses from their pain and suffering.

6.3.1 The Process of Zombilization and Askarization of the Intelligentsia and Clergy in Africa:

The process to create intellectual askari and zombies is thus similar to that of creating the political askaris and zombies. The imperial predators, by the means of all kinds of deceptive tools, manipulate the intelligentsia and the clergy to operate on the path of askarization and zombilization instead of the path of sankofarization. The process operates by infesting them with the virus of negrosis that is delivered through the established neocolonial institutions of learning and worship. Sankofarization is a process whereby one returns to one's past from the present, to search for the hidden historic treasures, retrieve them, study and learn from them in order to construct the historic monuments of tomorrow from today's experiences. The creative power of sankofarization becomes muted when the intelligentsia and the clergy are under negrosis. They fail to understand certain powerful building blocks of Africa's conceptual system where the concept of sankofarization is the logically indisputable axiom of acknowledgement that the past, present and future are inseparable in continuity of the creative process and in transformations. In other words the seeds of the present reside in the past while the seeds of the future take their roots from the present (foe extensive discussions see [43d].

The objective of the imperial predators' activities in both cases is to control and manipulate the intellectual leadership of the territory that is to be subjected to an imperial predation with a minimum or no resistance from the masses of the subjected territory. In other words the servile consent is manufactured. When the intellectuals and clergy have been successfully askarized and zombilized they become useful instruments freely at the disposal of the predators to carry on their propaganda activities. The members of the intelligentsia and clergy loose the characteristics that make them Africans. They become dismantled from the African personality and take on the destructive characteristics of the imperial predators and justify them in the logic of the predators' thought processes as well as spreading the negrosis virus to the masses.

Having become intellectual askari and zombies and having assumed an anti-African personality, the intelligentsia promotes distorted perceptions of global social currents, history and sociology of life to the masses as to what are the African realities, essential issues and problems of national relevance. They promote the same false conceptions of life as the predators by spreading the disease of negrosis. The masses therefore become duped by the converted African intelligentsia into accepting oppression, exploitation, and debasement as normal part of their life; accepting that their suffering and servitude are necessary conditions for their progress and national development, that without foreign capital, loans, experts, aid, donors help and technological know-how the development of the African states will never occur. They profess the same intellectual foolishness and falsehood as the imperial predators and destroyers before the African masses. Examples of this include the accepted validity of structural adjustment policies, structural adjustment loans, poverty reduction, sustainable debt and many other concepts that have been and are being promoted by the World Bank, the International Monetary Fund and institutions of the members of the imperial predators (for technical discussions on the implied logic of these false claims see [4a] [4b] [44] [107] [128a]). The African political elite, intelligentsia and clergy, unlike the leadership of African traditional societies, fail to educate the

African masses that social progress is a transformation of categories that is made possible through Nkrumaist transformation dialectic where sustainable and continual transformation is engendered by internal forces conditional on the nature of institutional arrangements and efficient organization. In other words they educate the masses to believe in foreign dependency rather than national collective self-reliance, self-determination and self-transformation (see Chapter 4 of [44b]). We now turn our attention to the African clergy and their role in the imperial predation.

6.3.2   The African Clergy and the Spread of Negrosis:

The co-opted clergy, on the other hand, operates to weaken the national soul and devastate the cultural spirit of the nation. The African clergy, priests and pastors preach false conceptions of God, the gospel of the Africa's imperial predators and destroyers, and instruct their followers that the Africans are not God's chosen children but other people and other races are. They present God and good in the images of the predators and ask their congregations to worship directly or indirectly the imperial predators as a symbolic representation of God. They present Satan and evil in dark images of African. All of this is supported from the mythology of the predators' interpretations of the African theological order.   When questions are raised against the manner and content of this kind of teaching, the clergy in cahoots with the imperial predators take refuge in the shelter of righteousness and accuse the critics of the highest crime against God, blasphemy, ungodliness, atheism and sinfulness. Even the most culturally enlightened African theologian in the academy or clergy at the pulpit is guilty of this highest crime against the African mind and traditions.

The members of the African clergy take on the battle boots of the predators and teach the African people about the predators' conception and perception of the Creator and insist to their congregation that the only way to good life and to avoid the rage of God is that of the imperial predators. The imperial predators' way is the truth and nothing but the truth; they say. It is the God's words and nobody must challenge it. They present the heathenish and religious beliefs of the predators as the only accounts of God and God's relationships with His or Her children of which the Africans are excluded. The members of the African clergy stripped of their African essence and doped with negrosis, operate in cahoots with the destroyers, and distort foolishly the African Trinity. Instead of promoting the African icon of the Father, the Mother and the Child, on one hand or the Creative Force, the Spirit Force and the Light Force they promote the false view of the predators where the conceptual Womanhood of nature is completely, conceptually and practically destroyed and in place is erected a heathenish idea of the Holy Ghost simply to distort the conception of the creation by doing away with the importance and the role of the female in the process of creation as conceived in African conceptual system of the spiritual order. Here the Spirit Force is altered in a manner that is logically inconsistent with African philosophical tradition. God is God but not a Ghost. Notice that the Father, Mother and Child represent the totality of mater, spirit and mind. They are also represented by the Creative Force, the Spirit Force and the Light Force in the African conceptual system as we have discussed in the Preface and Prologue in the companion volume entitled *Polyrhythmicity: Foundations of African Philosophy* [43d].

All the African spiritual ways of life from antiquity, the concept of the purity of the pure, the manifestation of the African Trinity where the body, mind and spirit exist in unity, where the Creative Force, the Spirit Force and the Light Force from which Christianity and Islam take their roots and to which they are theologically as well as philosophically indebted, are treated with vain arrogance and contempt by the African clergy who are stupefied by the intoxicants of the religious opium of the imperial predators and destroyers. They see nothing spiritually good about African way of life. The African mode of spiritual communication (libation) to the Creator, the All-encompassing Universal Life Force, handed over to us from Africa's antiquity before Judaism, Christianity, Islam, Buddhism, Hinduism and others, is characterized as paganism and unworthy of practice. The members of the African clergy fail to understand that Christianity as has been handed over to them by the imperial predators is nothing more than a violent appropriation of African spiritual and theological order altered to accommodate the evil and wicked intents of the destroyers. Everything traditional about the rich African culture is projected by the African clergy and intelligentsia in collaboration with the predators as evil and satanic. Even ebony and ivory are restructured and associated with evil and good respectively. At this point, it may be useful to examine how Christianity came to Europe, how the current King James Version of the Holy Bible came into being and what happened to some important spiritual writings that were companions of spiritual documents from which the King James Version of the Holy Bible was translated.

The African practices of reverence to the African Ancestral Tree and Ancestry of which the Creator is the beginning and last in line by the method of reductionism are misunderstood, ridiculed, viewed negatively as ancestral worship and condemned as satanic by the African clergy who, living constantly in the minds of the predators from the imperial club, have become useful intellectual idiots and propagandists in the service of the imperial predators and destroyers of Africa and her people. As religious and intellectual askari and zombies the members of the African clergy fail to point out to their congregations and African masses the similarities between the African practice of reverence to the African ancestors and the imperial predators' ancestral worshiping through heroes, saints, martyrs and many more [34]. Having been co-opted in mind, soul, spirit and pocket by the predators, the African clergy see nothing beyond their social prestige, power and material wealth, and the positive relationship between themselves as imperial cronies and the predators. They have become rent-seekers, exploiters, parasites and free radicals that eat Africa's seeds and Africa's life to extinction.

The members of the African clergy abandon the African masses, the soul and spirit of Africa, the African spiritual traditions, the foundation of Africa's internal strength, and accept the distorted surrogate and secondhand representation of African practices presented by the imperial predators. They become a-historical in their teachings and practices and adopt a violent intellectual attitude toward African ways of life. They fail to point out to the African masses that the greatest calamity in human history (slavery, colonialism and racism[29a] [129d][150b]) as we currently know was committed against Africans and humanity of other races in other parts of the world (for example, the Americas, Caribbean Islands, Australia and others) and by the imperial predators who worshiped and prayed to their representation of God at the top floors of their castles, and raped African women and committed murder against African people at the bottom floors of the same structures (for example in the Cape Coast and Elmina castles [51a] [88] and Goree Island). What a shame!

All the destructive activities of the imperial predators including the most atrocious inhuman acts (slavery, racism, massacre of the

Native Americans and Australians) perhaps far exceeding the greatest imagination of Hitler's work against humanity in Europe are sweet aside by the African clergy and the imperial predators. It is also instructive to recall the continuous lynching of Africans in United States of America after their arrival (see [3b]).

They speak of the evils of Hitler's atrocities and never mention the atrocities of King Leopold of Belgium in the Congo [71a]. The African clergy symbolically project well all the goods, angels, saints and God in the images of the imperial predators and destroyers of Africa. They plant into the minds of African masses conditions of guilt and inferiority complex, thus freezing the creative forces for Africa's transformation. They neglect to instruct the African masses that the imperial predators are the same people that condemned the atrocities of Hitler while they simultaneously condoned and justified on the basis of their religious doctrines the practices of slavery and racism against the African people. Enslaved by the predators' religiosity and infested with the virus of negrosis the members of the African clergy present to their congregations the same religious doctrines that were and are used to justify racism, just wars and servitude of Africans without any reference to the Africa's historic conditions and reality. As a supplementary justification that the Africans are not God's children, but rather part of axis of evil, the members of the African clergy in cahoots with the imperial predators project in their sanctuaries of worship Satan and evil in the images of Africans who are ever ready to commit some crime and devilish acts against God and humanity and hence need punishment, redemption, and perpetual suffering and even annihilation.

The African clergy with their current teachings, instead of teaching liberation theology that will unleash the African creative forces for development and positive transformation, teach the imperial predators' theology for Africa's downfall and death. They, like the imperial predators, even claim that Africa has no history, philosophy and theology. The members of the African clergy are therefore nothing but useful instruments in assisting the imperial predators in the maintenance of neocolonial states and crony imperialism in Africa. Their actions and teachings are inimical to Africa's complete emancipation and progress and hence they constitute an important danger to African's golden future. They fail to understand that emancipation of a people begins first and foremost by freeing the people from the forces that hold them in mental servitude and ignorance but not to reinforce the mental forces that have kept the people in colonial and cognitive darkness while other nations make history on the path of their will. For the purpose of Africa's complete emancipation and her destiny, it is a divine and spiritual duty on the part of the members of the African clergy to conceptualize correctly the interactive relationships between ideas and perception formation by the masses. They must understand that when ideas are advanced and images are presented to the people they become ingrained in the psychic space of the masses. These ideas become part of their belief system and shortcuts on the basis of which decisions and actions are undertaken through life to build a just or unjust society.

Thus by advancing the ideology, doctrine and propaganda of the predators from the imperial club without placing them in the context of Africa's culture, history and progress, the members of the African clergy and intellectuals temporary succeed in numbing the liberating spirit of the African masses against the imperial predators. They forget that in every living thing there is something yearning to be free in other to set in motion the internal forces for creativity and self-change. As long as the predators can continuously create and maintain the political, religious and intellectual askari and keep them as imperial cronies in any African state, the imperial predators will continue to exert neocolonial power and sustain the thievery system that they have established.

By their activities in support of the predators, the members of the African intelligentsia and the clergy have selected to abandon their historic role as leaders of the African masses in Africa's self-transformation. They have also abandoned their role as the intellectual vanguard against the predatory activities of the imperial destroyers. They, sadly as it may be, will thus descend into history's underground and obscurity as worthy of nothing. They will neither be appreciated by the imperial predators because they are mere implements for the predators' craft, nor will they be appreciated by Africa and her children because they have betrayed Africa and assisted the predators to rob Africa off her riches, traditions and beauty. What a shame this is!

This situation of the African intelligentsia and the clergy can be reversed when the members re-Africanize themselves through the process of sankofarization, adopt Africentric intellectual positions, sharpen their African personality. The members of the African intelligentsia and clergy must then dedicate themselves to African emancipation and assume their leadership roles as demanded by history, by creating and advancing paradigms of thinking that elevate the African personality, goodwill, courage, creativity, enterprise and traditions to the forefront of the Africa's struggle to build great nations. Simultaneously, they must subvert the ideological foundations of the imperial predators' mischievous activities for resource exploitation and domination.

In this framework, instead of blurring the collective responsibility to the individual and the society by teaching "each for himself or herself and God for us all," the African intellectuals and the members of the African clergy will place the responsibility squarely on both the individual and the collective by teaching and promoting the age old African principle of each for all and all for each and God as Supreme in judgement, reward and punishment. In this way, the responsibilities of the individual and the collective are placed in an inter-supportive mode in duality which is required by social unity for reestablishing Africa's emancipation, progress and glory. Similarly, the individual-community polarity is emphasized and its relationship to the African conceptual system of never-ending creation is brought to the forefront of social organization.

We have dwelt at length on the negative role that some African rulers, intellectuals and clergy play in setting the tides of history against Africa. The thrust of the criticism is that they have abandoned their leadership role as a liberating force from the colonial vestiges, brutal and merciless exploitation by people from other lands. Instead of becoming the facilitators of Africa's complete emancipation they have selected to become stumbling blocks to Africa's traditions and progress while using the state of mass confusion and suffering to extract rent of the little that the poor have by externally spiritualizing the suffering of the poor. Sustainable development, true and meaningful democracy, and the true freedom cannot occur under this environment.

So far our triumph over the colonial order has failed to achieve the second set of objectives of united Africa, sustainable progress, cultural and economic uplifting of the masses and the true independence that all Africans long for. The poverty of African masses derives its nutrients from cognitive ignorance and spiritual confusion. The most important first steps are to solve the problems of mass ignorance and spiritual confusion. This is our current dilemma where Africa is operating in a terrain of independence and servitude. It is also our challenge and a test of our will and courage to construct Africa's future from our critical understanding of this dilemma. The key to unlock the door of understanding of this Africa's dilemma is effective organization, institutional casting and collaborative effort of all Africans on the basis of Africa's ingenuity, institutions of effective research and problem solving.

Africa's current dilemma and difficulties have been made possible as a result of the colonial overthrow of 1) traditional political systems, 2) selection process of African leaders, 3) moral codes of conduct, 4) traditional collective intelligence, 5) national and ethnic allegiance, 6) cultural traditions 7) social institutions, and 8) technology of wealth creation through which African interests were defined, promoted and advanced not for the individual but for the collective that creates the social defense for individual existence. In the places of these elements we have either superimposed on them, or replaced them with alien political structures, dubious democratic individualism, contradictory moral codes, capitalist greed with no respect and compassion for the collective, thievery systems justified by fundamentalist market ideology and reinforced by theological systems whose operations are contrary to African traditions that project a balance between the relative interests of the individual and the collective with emphasis always placed on the collective. These superimpositions or replacements, even though by themselves they are detriments to Africa and her children, are further reinforced and maintained by the works of political, intellectual and religious askari and zombies of Africa operating from within and in cahoots with the imperial predators and destroyers. The members of the intelligentsia, clergy and political elite have placed Africa on wrong and dangerous pathways to disaster where opportunities for progress as contained in decolonization, independence and acquisition of the political structure are frozen under the activities of the imperial predators and the African collaborators.

The members of the African clergy fail to understand that the religious doctrines and the belief systems that they induce, like philosophy, are not God-given. They arise simply from experiences of human life and social exigencies. They reflect inadequacies of human intellect with respect to ignorance of the working mechanism of forces greater than human control. The religious doctrine and belief system perform two important social roles. First, they allow an explanation of ignorance within the ambit of God and created belief system. Secondary, they become instruments for social control on the psychological basis of divine rage and power to inflict pain or provide reward "hereafter" when an individual or group acts contrary to carefully human-crafted rules that are claimed to be God-given.

Theological explanations of natural and social events that are beyond present human understanding and the religious rules of social control allow the African clergy and the imperial predators to direct the African masses to function in zones of ignorance, fear and confusion in the predators' world. In this way, the members of the clergy, supported by the predators from the imperialist club, can perpetuate their social power as they claim to provide divine mediation between the human and the Divine. The masses are directed away from the fact that religion is simply a product of human experience and hence to be useful its developmental nutrients must be drawn from the cultural confines of the society in which it is to be used. It, therefore, does not make any logical sense to represent God in the images of one's predators. You cannot worship God for your organic freedom and simultaneously fight God as your oppressor. But this is exactly what the African clergy has bestowed on Africa and her children.

To achieve Africa's emancipation and to make socioeconomic progress the African rulers, clergy and intelligentsia must go through a progress of re-conversion from the colonial and neocolonial mind set. They must then go through a process of re-Africanization. In this way, they will come to understand that the fight against injustice, exploitation and racism as practiced by the imperial predators cannot be won by using the same philosophical and conceptual tools that has been fashioned and used by the predators. It requires a well-defined African philosophical position as to the relationship between an African and another African, between one African ethnic group and another, between one Africa and the rest of the world, and between African masses and the governing body. The success of re-Africanization of African rulers as African political leaders, the members of the clergy as African priests and the intellectuals as African thinkers will create forces which will simultaneously bring about united Africa and eradication of poverty as well as the destroying the foundation of the predators' treacherous activities in Africa. The occurrence of this success requires a new thinking system that will allow the African leaders and the masses to see the world through the interest of the African prism. This thinking system is Polyrhythmicity: Foundations of African Philosophy that draws its nutrients from the cultural confines of Africa and to guide African nationalism that is required for practice and progress. The core ideas and concept of Africentricity have been developed in a companion book entitled *Polyrhythmicity* [43b]. Let us turn our attention to discuss a model and African agenda for Africa's complete emancipation.

Finally, we would like to add that the behavior of the incumbent, the imperial club that we described, is guided by an economic logic of self-interest, resource maximization toward the preservation of its global dominance. The economic theory of perfect competition reveals an efficient allocation of resource leading to the greatest overall output under certain restrictive assumptions. However if a monopoly arises within the structure, it could benefit at the expense all other producers by restricting competition through the monopolistic incumbent behavior that will reduce the profitability of all other producers in the industry. At the level of global competition in all levels of human creative endeavor, the emergence of imperial club as politico-economic monopoly in the scene of global competition amasses the greatest benefit of human activities in the global resource, production and consumption space under the ideological conditions of free, fair and competitive trade. The members of the imperial club by continual exercise of their collective and cooperative power in the global space will continually improve their welfare by increasing poverty for all the countries that are in the fringe. The imperial club constitutes an international political monopoly in the global political market on the one hand and international imperial oligopolies playing cooperative game over rent from global predation and as a coalition playing hostile game against the members of the fringe. The ideological principle of the imperial decision is supremacy and full spectrum dominance. This is the *modus operandi* of the predators. The globe is looked upon as a playground where the players are the set of the members of the imperial club on the one hand and the set of the members in the fringe. The game in the playground is a power game. The reward is the control of resource access and the channels of resource flow. The members in the imperial club approach the game in unity on the ideological principle that in unity can we find monopoly strength and power, while the members of the fringe enter the game in disunity on the ideological principle of free and fair competition. The arsenals of the incumbent used in the game to control the outcome are military, economic and technological policies with propaganda through information control and deception. These policies are to force the members of the fringe to adopt suboptimal tactics and strategies at the theater of the game through restraints, constraints and threats.

There are a number of important things going on at the global decision space. Figure 6.4 with the supporting figures presents the three important structure of the global decision space where nations are the actors. We have the political structure, the economic structure and the legal structure. These global decision structures are under the control of the imperial club. In the case of national economies, laws are made to restrict the behavior of monopolies or to break them down into competitive sizes with the view of improving competition and raising the national decision efficiency and welfare. Such corrective measures are not available at the global decision space. Thus there are no checks and balances on the behavior of the imperial club as a global politico-economic monopoly. International laws are useless for the countries in the fringe since these laws are selectively followed by the members of the imperial club to the extent to which these laws support their interest at the expense of the fringe. The members of the fringe acting individually have no recourse except at some level of fringe's unity.

There are important lessons that African countries can and must learn from this process as we have tried to explain. By knowing the *modus operandi* of the predators, Africa can design a proportionate programmed response to defend her interest. The imperial predators work in unity. They have full spectrum dominance over the African countries. Individual African countries are too weak to resist the imperial predation. The imperial predators control international finance, technology, instruments of mass destruction, instruments of mass deception and effective propaganda machinery. The imperial predators have awesome power that can only be resisted by changing the current regime of relationship among the African countries. This regime must be replaced by a regime of unity. Full spectrum dominance requires a full spectrum resistance. This full spectrum resistance demands a committed program of African unity on all fronts of human life if the resistance is to be successful against the full spectrum of imperial predation. The program of resistance must have a *modus operandi* on a different philosophical basis from the philosophical basis of the modus operandi of the imperial predators. Once again a case is made for African unity as conceived by Kwame Nkrumah [105] and Nkrumah's program of positive action that will meet the challenges of the imperial predation. Our task now is to articulate the Nkrumaist model and the implied optimal program of resistance for complete Africa's emancipation with freedom and justice that could support sustainable development for general understanding, criticism and refinement for Africa's future. Let us turn our attention to the Nkrumah's model as an Africa's full spectrum resistance to the full spectrum dominance of the imperial predators.

7

NKRUMAIST MODEL AND AFRICENTRICITY: THE NATIONALIST AGENDA

To present the basic structure of the Nkrumaist model and the African nationalist agenda as full spectrum African resistance to the imperialist full spectrum dominance we would like to point out certain problems of Nkrumah's critics. Much has been written on Nkrumah and Nkrumaist development strategy as applied to Ghana. Most of the literature is criticism of perhaps every facet of Nkrumaism and Nkrumaist development strategy. A number of the criticisms are particularly harsh on Nkrumah's economic development policies. For example, David Guyer states his assessment as:

> On the economic front, there is little doubt that the development strategy of the Nkrumah regime, which emphasized total dependence of foreign capital to industrialize the country, brought almost complete disaster. During this period, Ghana experienced rapid deterioration of its balance of payments position, loss of huge amounts of external reserves and, in the end, the flight of foreign investment. [66, p.81]

Some of the criticisms that seem valid on the surface may be theoretically and empirically questionable. In many instances, not only has the criticism been scientifically lacking, it has been likewise unfair when it is examined against a well structured theory of the development process as well as the empirical reality of Ghana's development experience (see for example Dompere *et al.* [44]). For example, one must answer the question as to what are the appropriate measures of complete disaster, development and social progress. Analytically, it is advisable to distinguish between concepts of economic development and social progress and hence a development of appropriate measures for assessing the successes of policies toward their realization (see Dompere *et al.* [44] for methodological discussions). Failure to do this invariably leads to ideological rather than scientific conclusions, situations that occur often in discussions involving the role, size and relationship between the private and public sectors in national socioeconomic activities without examining the optimal private-public sector mix for nation building.

7.1 Basis of Analysis and Syntesis

In this chapter, we shall present the basic theoretical structure of Nkrumaist decision model for Africa's complete emancipation given the structure of crony imperialism and imperial global aspirations of full spectrum dominance as we have presented in Chapter 6 of this volume. The objective is to provide a theoretical rationale for Nkrumaist development strategies in Ghana. We shall then examine their relevance to contemporary problems of Africa's emancipation, governance, democracy and development. On the domestic front Nkrumah, at least, provided us with a set of measures to judge his performance at home. He states:

> We shall measure our progress by the improvement in the number of children in school, and by the quality of their education; by the availability of water and electricity in our towns and villages, and by the happiness which our people take in being able to manage their own affairs. The welfare of our people is our chief pride, and it is by this that my Government will ask to be judged [110, p. 51].

The discussion in this volume is presented as part of an ongoing examination of Nkrumah's socioeconomic and politico-diplomatic policies. It is also a logical justification of the rights and wrongs of the Nkrumaist development strategy as well as a search of a rational basis for the choice of strategies that would affect Africa's path for good governance, socioeconomic development and emancipation in the reconstitution of the African Union. We shall extend the analysis to the relevance of these strategies to contemporary Africa's global problems and search for unity and unified action to confront the imperialist predation and full spectrum dominance. Thus we would like to do two things: 1) outline a politico-economic theoretical framework of

Nkrumaist development policy; and 2) argue that a) the choice of Nkrumah's development strategy was structurally imposed by the initial conditions of the economy of Ghana and the true independence to be secured; b), the choice was optimal relative to the goals and constraints; and c) all things considered, the Nkrumaist development strategy, when understood in its proper global context, and if properly implemented, is the most viable development strategy for Africa's emancipation on the basis of self-reliance and internal effort. It is the strategy that would offer a path of sustained and integrated economic development that would lead to a sustainable and respectable degree of economic and political independence with a guarantee of degree of national sovereignty of continental Africa.

In developing the theory and practice of nation building we must understand that Nkrumah pursued three different policy tracks. The tracks are: 1) the domestic policy track, 2) the African policy track, and 3) the non-African policy track. Nkrumah's domestic policy cannot and must not be separated from his African policy and his long-run vision of united Africa composed of free and independent states, if one is to truly understand and either criticize or appreciate the nationalist path to Africa's emancipation composed of true sovereignty and socioeconomic development that would create the environment for practicing the core principles of African personality in order to create a just society. The domestic and the African policy tracts must also be related to Nrumah's understanding of neocolonialism, arsenals of predation and the methods of Africa's effective response, whereby he arrived at an analytical conclusion that "the only effective way to challenge this (imperialist) economic empire and recover possession of our heritage, is for us also to act on Pan-African basis, through a Union Government" [114, p. 340]. The critical examination of Nkrumah's vision and theoretical framework for his development policy have become increasingly necessary for understanding the conditions of poverty and wars in contemporary Africa, since the unity of the imperial club is continually being strengthened while the African countries have lost the vision of strength of unity and are fighting to dismantle their nations into tribal states as laughing stock at the joy and benefit of the imperial predators. The organic framework of Africa's emancipation policy may be summarized in a diagrammatic form in Figure 7.1.

In an acknowledgement of the role that initial conditions tend to affect the trajectory of the path of history Nkrumah responds to his critics that: "We reject the carping of those critics who judge us merely by heights which we have achieved and not the depths from which we started" [110, p. 52].

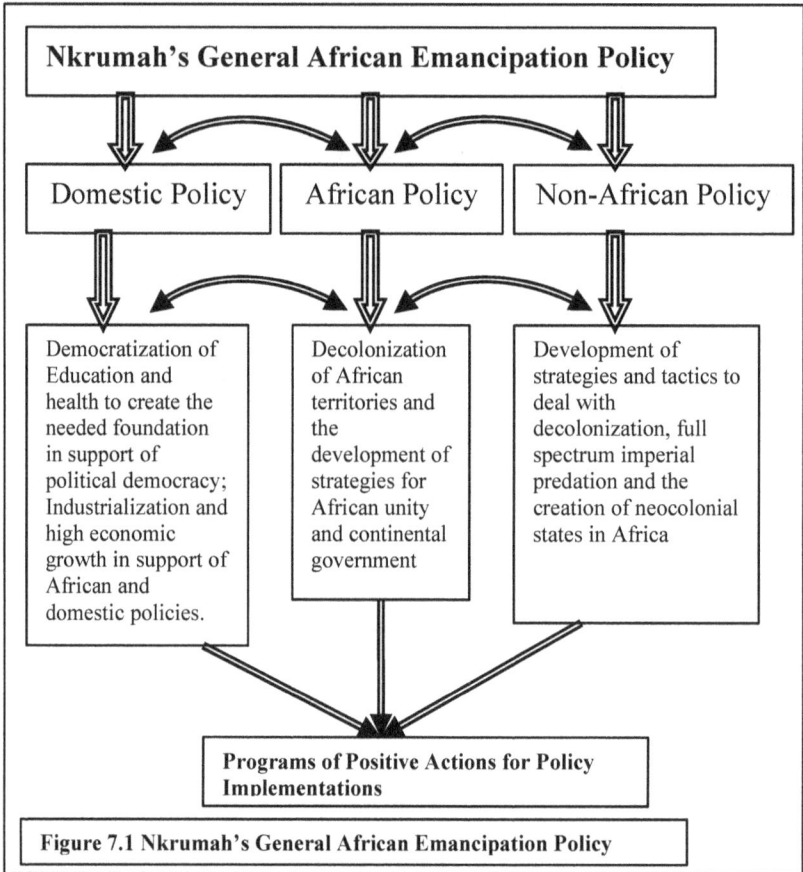

Figure 7.1 Nkrumah's General African Emancipation Policy

The failure of critics of genuine African leaders to understand and link Africa's current conditions to her recent historic path and the *modus operandi* of the imperial predators is a travesty of logical rationality and a ridicule of human spirit to overcome adversities and be free, in particular when these adversities are produced and maintained by global institutions of deception, injustice, axis of violence and production of epicenters of generation of global underdevelopment and poverty.

Considering a number of event periods - a) the period of forced removal of Africans to the Americas (to be enslaved) that led to an incalculable losses of Africa's virile youth who then constituted the energy stream and most important resource of Africa's economic transformation and social progress; b) the periods of wars of resistance against European predatory invaders that siphoned Africa's human and nonhuman resources from Africa's development; c) the period of colonial occupation that destroyed the statecraft of politico-economic management, traditional institutions of governance, democratic decision structure and brought about dictatorship, forced taxation through violent abstraction of unpaid labor, under an orgy of European terror, wars and mass panic; and d) the period of imperialists' violent resource exploitation that increasingly impoverished Africa, not even mentioning the stealing of African treasures to Europe and the Americas - it is even surprising and incredibly resilient with all the imperialist destruction that Africa still have something to show [129d] [150b]. This something to show reflects the age old Latin inscription and saying, *ex Africa semper aliquid novi* (out of Africa comes always something new), that continuously attracts Europeans and others not to leave Africa alone.

In passing, we would like to point out that there is no African that left Africa's shores as a slave to the Americas, at least from the historic account.

Neither can we find a historic account of Africans who left Africa in those days with names like Betsey, Gates, Thomas, Taylor and others. In fact such names present spiritual discontinuity to the Ancestral Tree. The Africans were free people with organizational structures; democracy based on hierarchical system of consensus and statecraft involving systems of governments, production and distribution mechanisms. They left in captivity from the shores of Africa. They then became enslaved where the fruits of their labor were violently appropriated to build and develop other lands. The period of "silent trade" as history reveals did not involve the catching and selling or forcefully subduing people into captivity but rather trading on a fair basis of articles of human production and craft. The conditions and explanation as to what led to the catching and selling of Africans is yet to be brought to light.

The phrases "in its proper context" and "properly implemented" require some notice. The point here is simple. Most of Nkrumah's critics are out of line with Nkrumah and his model of Africa's complete emancipation. They fail to offer indisputable scientific proof of economic disaster of Nkrumah's economic policies and development strategy. The arguments they offer in support of economic failure and disaster are not only logically flawed but at the very best, inconclusive and mostly ideological. The indices for examining the success and failure characteristics of Nkrumah's policies are not explicitly communicated and those that are implied are questionable. In all cases, the critics seem not only to neglect the initial conditions as we have pointed out but also to overlook some important limitations imposed by European imperialism on the choice of strategy. For example, the critics fail to account for the effects of international politico-economic conditions such as the Cold War that are reflected in ever-increasing cost of economic development in the present global environment. In this global environment, political destabilization and economic sabotage operating through an imperialist set-up of international intitutions have become part of the imperialist arsenal of the war of dominance, campaign of terror and brute resource exploitation without regard to human life except those of the imperialist members of axis of terror. All these add to the real cost of nation building (see also [29c] [128a].

The ever-increasing cost of nation building that has become an important binding constraint on the choice of paths of development, true democracy, good governance and economic policy is due to a continual effort on the part of a number of Western economically advanced nations to manufacture political destabilization, economic sabotage, military intimidation, and high intensity warfare against those developing countries that are perceived to stand in the way of the path of global dominance by the members of the imperialist club, as we have explained under the theory of crony imperialism (for example, Cuba, Iraq, Libya, Congo, Angola, North Korea, Haiti, Zimbabwe, Ghana, Algeria, and many others).

It may be pointed out that this trend against the developing countries, particularly small and helpless ones, will continue and become intensified as the ideology of global market capitalism and rent-profit-seeking activities are pushed to the frontier of ultimate success to create global capitalism that is managed by the incumbents of the imperialist club and their cronies to their advantage. In this process of rent-profit-seeking activities through the controls of technology and commodity-resource flows, concepts of democracy, human rights, dictatorship, terrorist nation, weapons of mass destruction, poor governance, failed states and others have become ideological tools used by the members of the imperial club to camouflage their exploitive and unjust actions with the policy of preemption and regime change in the global space. They use these tools to wage psychological war against the weak nations. The space of global injustice, exploitation and dominance is continually evolving and changing its structure and form. This evolving situation was clearly understood by Nkrumah. Nkrumah understood that the wars and battles that have been waged in the second half of the twentieth century in intensity and scope by the United States of America and the imperial members from Europe have primarily been against the less developed and non-European countries. In this respect, he observes that:

> We cannot ignore the fact that the same imperialist forces which exploit and subvert our independent states, and which exploit and oppress our people in the remaining colonial enclaves of Africa, are the very same forces which breed armed conflicts, civil strife and economic impoverishment on other continents. It would be folly for us to dream of Africa as a peaceful and thriving continent in the midst of a world convulsed by armed conflicts, tormented by hunger and disease and continually menaced by imperialist intrigue and aggression [110, p. 73].

Our entry point into the discussion, therefore, is to question certain prevailing conclusions of Nkrumah's critics and push the analysis closer to the frontier of decision rationality rather than ideological appeal. Nkrumah's Ghana was not only historically unique among developing countries but it was surrounded by unusual circumstances in a turbulent world. This, in part, is why Nkrumah stands out as a unique personality in the history of Africa's decolonization process and global system of wars against imperialist oppression, undemocratic practices and activities. And Ghana carries this uniqueness with her. This uniqueness may be seen in terms of how Nkrumah understood the process of Africa's emancipation and the strategies required to effect it. All these were seen in a spectrum of dynamic decision rationality cast in sequential strategies for implementation. The set of these sequential strategies and supporting tactical decisions constitute what is being referred to here as the Nkrumaist model for Africa's complete emancipation. This model also constitutes the nationalist agenda. We must remember as well as understand that the same members of the imperial club who speak violently against human right abuses in other countries are the same people who promote campaigns of violence against the weak in different parts of the world. Similarly, the same members of the imperial club who advocate virtues of democracy are the same people who traverse over continents to support non-democratic governments that are subservient to the members of the imperial club as well as overthrow constitutionally democratic governments that are independent in thinking with program to serve their citizens. The imperial predators strongly dislike human development that is based on collective self-realization and utilization of internal resources that deprive them of control.

From the viewpoint of decision-choice rationality, the success of all strategies should be measured against a set of goals and objectives that is held by the decision agent. While one may disagree with a set of goals and objectives, the fact remains that the modern thinking of decision-information-interactive processes suggests that it is scientifically inadmissible to judge the success of a strategy and choice outcome against the goals and objectives that are not held. Similarly, it is logically unsound to use the disparity between strategic goals and tactical results to assess the success of a choice of strategies intended to realize long-run goals and objectives. It is likewise an intellectual deception to judge anyone on the heights that he or she has reached without accounting for the depths from which he or she has risen and the constraints that he or she has overcome in addition to those that are still binding.

Within the scientific realms of decision-choice rationality, it is incorrect to assess the results of choices of development strategies and tactics of a socioeconomic construction program without critically examining the initial conditions of the program's reference point. The specification of the initial conditions as defining the reference point is consistent with the modern theory of optimal control that allows the abstraction of the optimal trajectory for the control process. Such a reference point is made up of a configuration of factors. Some of these factors include: a) resource availability, composition and physical endowment, b) technical preparedness, c) managerial readiness and the executive capacity, d) the confidence level of the domestic population in assuming initiatives and responsibility in a large scale construction and restructuring program, e) the ideological appropriateness to generate and utilize knowledge and resources to improve one's own welfare, f) availability and suitability of the institutional arrangement for policy transmission, and g) the external constraint that may be placed on the country by the predatory activities of the members of the imperialist club(see Chapter 6 of this book).

In measuring the success and failure of tactical and strategic outcomes resulting from tactical and strategic decisions, we must keep in mind that one of the greatest attributes of a good strategist in decision situations is to know where and when policy switch points occur and to take advantage to alter tactical actions without sacrificing the organic principle. The only thing permanent in life is change, but in social decisions, the change must be purposeful and rational without sacrificing the organic principle. Casual and unscientific writers like Omari [124a] have referred to such decision agents including Nkrumah as opportunist instead of realizing that it takes a good strategist to identify the right environment and appropriate switch points in order to change his or her tactical options.

Given the epistemics of decision-choice rationality [42], any serious assessment of Nkrumah's economic policies and development strategies must a) specify the initial conditions or the initial reference point, b) identify the goals, objectives and effective constraints and c) examine the strategies of Nkrumah. To relate Nkrumah's strategies to the Africentric agenda, the agenda of complete Africa's emancipation, composing of African unity, true sovereignty, self-reliance, and socioeconomic progress from the perspective of the African vision of the world, we will outline Nkrumah's goals, objectives and strategies as may be abstracted from his literally works and speeches. After we have stated and analyzed the goals, objectives, constraints and strategies, we will then suggest a theoretical framework that provides a logical structure for the operation of an Nkrumaist socioeconomic development strategy as seen from the viewpoint of African emancipation process and also as seen by an African nationalist who is confronted with a set of problems of social reconstruction and economic development of post colonial Africa.

This theoretical framework will constitute what we are referring to as the Nkrumah's model of complete African emancipation. It is useful in dealing with the contemporary African pressing difficulties and problems to distinguish between Nkrumah's model and what we have presented as Nkrumaist model for Africa's socioeconomic transformation and complete emancipation. The Nkrumaist model is a refinement and expansion of Nkrumah's basic model to support the African nationalist agenda for Africa's complete emancipation. It is also the Pan-Africanist model.

Generally, therefore, such a theoretical framework must be viewed in the context of Africa's emancipation as well as providing a direction and approach on the basis of which one can examine the empirical realities of Ghana's development experience during Nkrumah's time, as well as the realistic nature of the goals and objectives of Nkrumah, his overall vision of Africa's destiny and suggested strategies to reach them. The theoretical structure of Nkrumah's goals and objectives must establish the basis for assessing his policy success and foundation for epistemic development and practice of Pan-Africanism. It must also provide an example of a model for the African nationalist and a blueprint for the struggle to emancipate Africa through development and democratization on the basis of African traditions. The objective in this analysis is to present a model that is consistent with African nationalism and Africentric thinking. The responses to Nkrumah's critics are just by-products evoked to make explicit the Nkrumaist model of Africa's emancipation. Here a theoretical framework of a sociopolitical decision is presented. We shall begin with Nkrumah's goals and objectives as seen from his writings and actions.

7.2 Nkrumah's Goals and Objectives

Nkrumah's sociopolitical agenda and the required economic support system are extensive, covering the whole of the African Diaspora and the major elements of the accumulated Pan-African agenda. Hence it is not usually easy and straightforward to ascertain his goals and objectives. Many a time writers on Nkrumah, particularly his critics, become confused in the process of ascertaining his goals and objectives and sorting out those that are social and those that are economic. They also fail to correctly ascertain the grand goal. Mentally clouded by this confusion and other ideological preconceptions that they bring, most of these critics, if not all, in the process of assessing the success and failure of Nkrumah's agenda often interchange tactical goals and objectives with strategic goals and objectives. Those who want to critically study Nkrumah and his approach to the African question, the question of complete emancipation, cannot indulge in such analytical carelessness and travesty of reason. It is, therefore, useful to impose from the outset some logical structure of analysis.

Nkrumah's goals and objectives may be classified into political, social and economic dimensions. The economic goals and objectives are viewed as the vehicles through which certain social goals can be attained and maintained. Economics is thus viewed as the material basis of life. As a material basis of life it merely defines future social possibilities and the resources to reach and maintain them. From the material basis arises economic freedom that will support political and social freedom. Economic freedom is thus viewed as a means but not an end. Without economic freedom, sociopolitical freedom is mere emptiness. The grand goal in the new African social order to be established in accord with the Nkrumaist scheme of things is complete freedom for all Africans at home and in the Diaspora. Complete African emancipation has three segments: political, economic and social freedoms. From the position of strategic decision action, these economic, political and social goals and objectives are divided further into strategic and tactical ones. The strategic decision is made up of interconnected consequence of tactical choice actions. To be able to implement actions toward the grand goal, it is necessary that the goal of political freedom must be secured at first. This is the first positive action imperative demanded by collective social action for Africa's emancipation.

The imperative of securing political freedom and the logical grounds of action on which this imperative rests are anchored in the guarantee of decision-making power that the political freedom offers. This imperative acknowledges the idea that he who controls the power to make socioeconomic decisions for a people also defines the content and the path of their history. Here lies the cognitive explanation of the imperial predators to engineer the overthrow of democratically elected governments that oppose to imperial predation on their nations and people. It is this historical materialist imperative that led Nkrumah to assert "seek ye first the political kingdom" [105, p. 50], which became the principal slogan of the Convention People's Party (CPP) that was formed by him. He recognized that "political power is the inescapable prerequisite to economic and social power" [110, p. 78]. In other words, the Africans will not have the power to decide their destiny and the path to it without political freedom. Political freedom will not come without decolonizing the continent. Colonialism is a national slavery that locks all doors to freedom, saps the spirit of democracy, imposes dictatorship, exploits the masses and discourages major national development through national initiative, creativity and courage. Thus decolonization was the first step on strategic path to Africa's complete emancipation.

Nkrumah's emphasis on the political kingdom must be viewed from the understanding that any social system is made up of a) economic structure, b) political structure and c) legal structure. Any other element can be fit into one of the three mentioned. Changes in any of the three structures will affect the state of the social system. Such changes can only be accomplished by those who hold the decision-making power to effect the changes. The decision-making power to make changes in any of the three structures is bestowed on any individual or a group by the political structure. When such a power is bestowed, it can then be used to alter the political structure itself in order to strengthen the power base or weaken it. Therefore, he who holds the key to the political structure also holds the key to mold the economic, legal and political structures in accordance with the goals and objectives as conceived and set. This understanding is fundamental to every revolutionary struggle and is reflected in the historic outcomes of decision-information-interactive processes. He who controls the political structure wills the power to decide on what, how and for whom whether it is resource, justice or works that is being considered.

We must, however, keep in mind that political freedom quickly dissipates into a thin air when it lacks the material basis for its support. Poverty encourages slavery, subservience, emptiness, begging and hopelessness. Given the attainment of the objective of political freedom, therefore, Nkrumah's second objective is economic freedom. He observes that "whenever there is economic dependence there is no freedom" [100, p. 17]. The importance of economic freedom is emphasized by Nkrumah when he says "what meaning can independence have for the people if we throw off political bondage only, and remain in economic and mental subservience" [110, p. 82]. The decision linkages that connect the political and economic structures are made explicit and rightly affirmed when Nkrumah states that "independence must never be considered as an end in itself but a stage (in the decision process toward true and lasting freedom), the very first stage of the people's revolutionary struggle" [112, p. 16]. It is a first stage, a stage that provides the people with the decision-making power to alter their conditions of existence and redefine the path of their national history.

Within the morphology of the problem solving sequence, Nkrumah states the second positive action imperative. The second positive action imperative is the attainment of economic freedom. Together, the two imperatives translate into the statement that the attainment of national political freedom is a prerequisite but not a guarantee for the attainment of economic freedom. The attainment of economic freedom, on the other hand, provides the material basis on which the political and social freedom can be nurtured to maturity thus further strengthening the structure of the decision-making power for shaping the people's destiny; in this case, the African people's destiny.

The attainment of economic independence and the complementary freedom requires developing the domestic material and economic conditions that will support and maintain the national political freedom. This calls for an economic restructuring and construction where tactical goals must be set before strategies are made into actions for economic development and the strengthening of the material basis on which political freedom must be secured and maintained. Political and economic freedoms are not mere articles for display in the global museum of competitiveness. They are the vehicles to improve the social conditions of the people. The people, therefore, have no claim to the political and economic freedoms if such freedoms when attained do not uplift them spiritually and materially. It is by the people's sweat that such freedoms are attained and maintained. It is also by the people's ingenuity, creativity and courage that such political and economic freedoms are translated into social improvements that move the society to higher levels of culture and welfare. The welfare improvement possibilities are mere potentials whose actualization requires the attainment of economic possibilities.

The people have not mastered the power of political and economic freedoms if their attainments fail to yield social improvements for all. Economic growth and material improvements are not for profits that satisfy the pockets of few rent seekers and profiteers but rather for the improvement of the productive base as well as social improvements of the masses of the people whose sweat is the foundation stone of nation building and national greatness. The masses of the people are left in economic servitude and subservience if economic growth fails to translate into mass social development. In fact the existence of rich and dominating class is domestic colonialism. The people are the soldiers at the battlefronts of socioeconomic transformations and nation building on the basis of participatory democracy in all sector of national life. Democracy has no anchorage in poverty, illiteracy and mass ignorance locked in disinformation and information distortions. Both poverty and ignorance just as colonialism and neocolonialism sap the living blood of democracy and consequently render it meaningless and hopeless. Similarly when the lie is lifted to the throne of governance truth becomes the victim of execution and ignorance becomes the operation bases of the masses.

In view of this, the third positive action imperative is social development consisting of welfare and cultural improvements for the African people. The components of welfare and cultural improvements are to be defined and prioritized to establish the kind of vision that the society desires. When the power to make social decisions in all areas of life is organized by the people through the political structure, thus ensuring political freedom, and when the economic basis is strengthened and developed, thus ensuring economic freedom, expanded possibilities are then defined for the general socio-cultural improvements of the masses. These are necessary but not sufficient conditions for complete emancipation. The sufficient conditions must include the will and the collective consciousness of the people in exercising the political and economic freedoms to bring about general social progress. This requires the development of a new and vibrant collective African personality that is creative, self-reliant, self-trusting, self-resilient and self-motivating as well as satisfying the conditions of Nguzo Saba of African-centered behavior (The Seven Principles) that have been discussed in [78] [79a] and given an Africentric philosophical foundation and justification in [43d].

For the attainment of true independence of Africa and the composing states, most of which were under colonial bondage, Nkrumah realized that three positive action economic objectives must be set from the time he assumed various positions in the realms of political power in Ghana from 1948. These positive action objectives relate to the development of the domestic economic basis and the subsequent economic freedom to major strategic goals that will set in motion the road to complete emancipation of the Africans. The economic positive action objectives, as may be abstracted from Nkrumah's decision strategies, may be stated as:

1. The development of an appropriate domestic economic basis in support, maintenance and defense of independence and sovereignty of Ghana within the context of the Pan-African movement and the African unity; and this must apply to all decolonized territories or states in Africa.

2. The development of an appropriate social, ideological and economic basis in Ghana in support of the African liberation movements toward a complete political decolonization of the continent; and

3. The development of an appropriate socioeconomic and ideological basis, in Ghana, to support the African Unity Movement toward a United Government of Africa.

To understand the logical structure and justification of these strategic goals, one simply needs to refer to the Midnight Pronouncement of Independence of Ghana at the Polo Ground, Accra, on March 5-6, 1957 where Nkrumah stated that "the independence of Ghana is meaningless unless it is linked up with the total liberation of the African Continent" [110, p. 77]. The three positive action objectives as have been abstracted from Nkrumah's system of thought are embodied in the Pan-African social thought as well as sequentially integrated toward the realization of the Pan-African imperatives of justice, freedom, and Unity of Africa and African people wherever they are found. Nkrumah's domestic policy is his African policy and his African policy is the domestic policy, in other words the two policies are inseparable. Nkrumah's African policy is structured around the three sub-policies of a) decolonization, b) defense of sovereignties of the decolonized territories, and 3) African unity.

Within the logical structure of Pan-African social thought and the logical system of Nkrumaist decision strategies, each African state when liberated must embrace these three positive action objectives. They, therefore, will contribute their share toward achieving the grand goal of complete African emancipation, sovereignty and freedom with fairness and justice if these three positive action economic objectives are completely embraced as intermediate guiding principles. For the set of positive action economic objectives to have a revolutionary impact and lead to the required sociopolitical transformation of African societies it

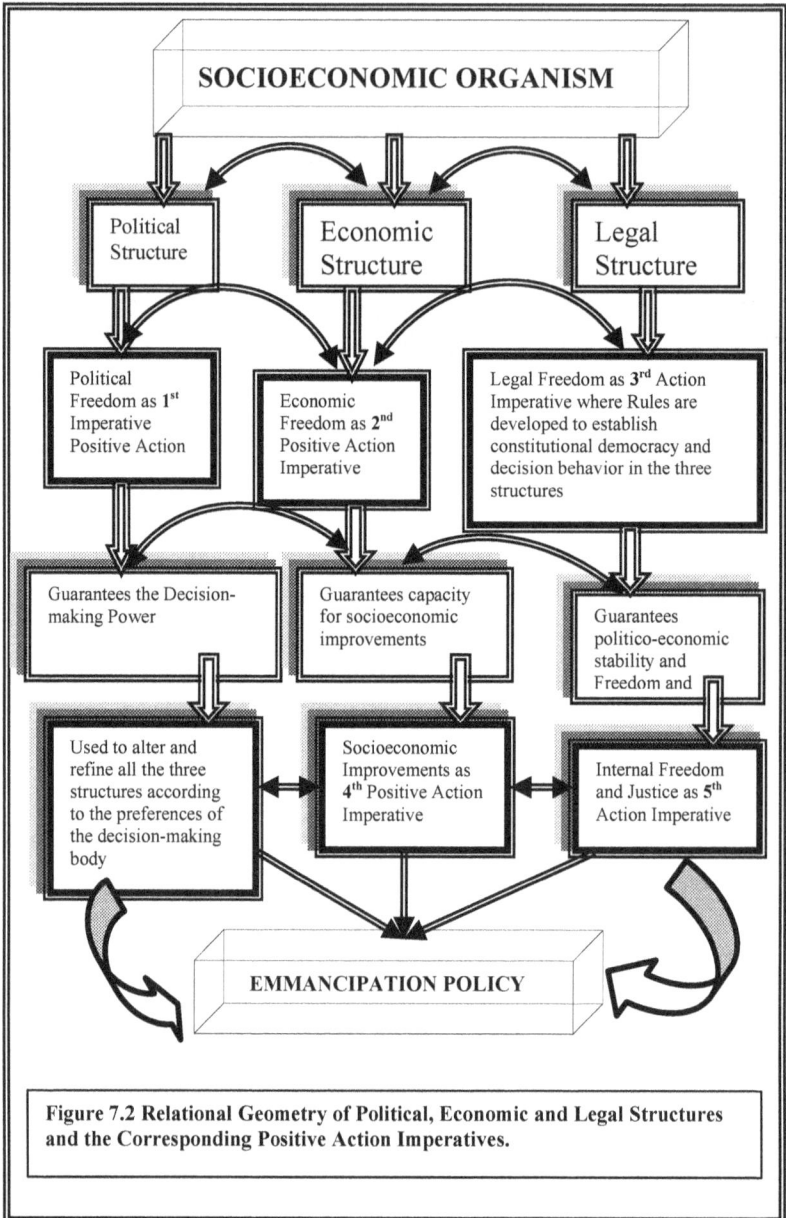

Figure 7.2 Relational Geometry of Political, Economic and Legal Structures and the Corresponding Positive Action Imperatives.

must constitute a program of thought and actions where the decision-information-interactive process is examined with cognitive intensity at all level of African social practice. The social organism may be viewed in terms of its relational building blocks, decision and action imperatives within Nkrumaist conceptual system whose logical geometry is illustrated in Figure 7.2.

7.3 The Goals and Objectives as a program of Thought and Positive Action

How do the abstracted objectives and positive action imperatives constitute a program of thought and a framework of actions? In other words, how do the objectives relate to one another, and how do they contribute to the design of an effective strategy formation toward the grand goal, the complete freedom of Africa and Africans from foreign domination and exploitation? First, the three objectives must be complementary. The required positive actions for the realization of these objectives must be inter-supportive. In a programmatic form, the attainment of the third objective, social improvement, depends on the degree to which the first and second objectives are realized. And obviously, the attainment of the first objective, political freedom, is a necessary requirement for the attainment of the second objective, economic freedom while the attainment of economic freedom is necessary for the maintenance and sustainability of the first and third objectives with the quality of social tolerance.

Here again the African concept of trinity presents itself in unity as a logic of emancipation. To Nkrumah, the creation of a strong economic basis is an instrument for the realization of three major sub-objectives toward an African political kingdom, on the basis of continental unity. These sub-objectives are 1) complete political decolonization of continental Africa, 2) defense of independence and sovereignty of individual African states, and 3) a political union of African independent states after each territory under colonial bondage is decolonized and liberated.

Decolonization of the continent could be done by decolonization of the individual states through the states' own efforts and the relentless support offered by the other decolonized territories. Decolonization does not, however, lead to independence, the political kingdom and protected sovereignty of the individual states. The freedom of the individually decolonized African states is open to danger and destruction that are the results of new strategies crafted by the former imperial countries. The question that arises within Nkrumah's logical

175

frame of Africa's emancipation is how to obtain independence and protected sovereignty and seal them for Africa's liberty and reasonable peace of mind. Studying the history of imperialist predatory activities, it became clear to Nkrumah that there is no security for any African state and no African state can hope to preserve its sovereignty and independence in isolation from other African states. The thought and practice of going it alone by the African states would be suicidal and define a new path of slavery and imperialist predatory activities. The Africa's recent past and current realities have revealed that this is the case. The more the African states have tried to go alone without their sister states, the more imperialist traps they fall into, the more intensively they become exploited, the poorer they become, the more dependent on their oppressors they also become, and the more vicious traps they are forced to face in the future at the global system of imperial predation.

While decolonization can be achieved by individual states of Africa, their independence and sovereignty cannot be protected by the states operating in isolation from one another. The solution, as Nkrumah thought and as is also held firmly by Pan-Africanists, lies in a political union of the African states where the unprotected micro-sovereignties are united into a grand sovereignty for each other's protection and the protection of the grand African freedom. The Africentric philosophical foundation of individual and collective behavior is each for all and all for each. This is the objective on which "Africa Must Unite" acquires its greatest strength and revolutionary character. The work done in this essay provides an analytical foundation and logical basis for Africa Must Unite. It is built on the vision of acquiring the grand political kingdom on the basis on which Africa's emancipation composing of political, economic, technological and cultural independence can be secured. It is a theoretical and practical affirmation of the basic ideas reflected in Marcus Garvey's poem [85, pp. 120-121].

Put in a proper sequence, the objectives reveal the real genius of Nkrumah as a decision strategist par excellence. Once again, we see Nkrumah's emphasis on the drive toward the goal of securing the political kingdom of Africa and hence the political freedom of the continent through an interrelated sequence of positive action objectives. The three objectives, therefore, constitute not only a set of strategies but a program of positive action whose implementation should contribute positively toward the grand goal of Africa's emancipation. The logical system of decision strategies reflects the basic consistency principle in philosophical and political thought of Nkrumah. It also reflects the reasons for Nkrumah's impatience with the pace at which economic development in Ghana was proceeding as well as the speed with which the drive toward African Unity was moving, hence the slogan, Africa Must Unite Now! The cognitive foundation is that without African unity, and collective actions on the basis of a firm collective policy on both external and internal fronts the African micro-states will once again be manipulated by the imperial predators just as they were during the period of catch-and-sell of humans to fight against each other for Africa's destruction so as to move Africa and her children unto a new path of slavery with greater suffering and human degradation. These things are happening right now as the current history is in the making.

As a program of thought, the three objectives form the foundation of African nationalism and the struggle against political, economic and cultural oppression as well as domination by the imperialist predators. From such a thought program, the logical system of Nkrumaist thinking sees African Unity as forming a decision vehicle through which true freedom of African people can be realized. As s decision vehicle, African Unity offers a possibility to shape Africa's own destiny by Africans in accord with their taste and preferences without fear, rather than allowing the imperial predators to pursue the policy of divide, conquer and rule in order to exploit Africa to shape their own destinies. The African unity objective, therefore, is an essential ingredient for the struggle of Africans to be free. It is also an instrument to ensure justice for all ethnic groups and to avoid the possibility of ethnic conflicts and tribalism which usually arise from illusions of power which the Africans collectively and individually do not have at the present time. African unity is a strategy for acquiring needed power to resist the predatory power of the imperialists.

From the modern historic account of brutalities, violence and mass killing committed against Africans by Europeans who claim the divine mission to civilize and christianize Africans, and from the recent history of orgy of violence and mass murder committed by the Europeans against non-Europeans, we must arrive at a conclusion that man in general has not become sufficiently civilized to appreciate the use of diplomacy rather than war for conflict resolution when there is a big gap in the relative global power distribution among countries. The current global direction also points to formations of mega-states, unions and politico-economic co-operations to alter the current global power distribution and the current regime of power application against the weak nations that are endowed with natural resources. These were clear to Nkrumah and to him these trends defined the African challenges for unity, ingenuity and creative organization. It is therefore not surprising that the Nkrumah's leadership seemed to drive a spear through the imperialist predators and their African collaborators.

The drive toward African unity, therefore, is seen within the same program of thought as a necessary positive action toward Africa's redemption. The African unity objective and its redemptive force are viewed as necessary requirements for consolidating and centralizing the decision-making power in order to strengthen the fragile and newly acquired micro decision-making centers of the decolonized African states. The welding together of the politically liberated colonies into one African nation is the African Unity Imperative without which the people in the decolonized territories will trade off direct servitude for indirect servitude, and fight against each other for the benefit of the imperialist predators rather than work with each other for the benefit of Africa's progress and welfare of her children. African unity is an Africentric necessity for Africa's survival and progress for all her children in the Diaspora and Africa itself. It is also necessary to ensure Africa's global interest and effective defense against the predation by people from other lands. African unity alters the existing regime of global power distribution.

Within the program of thought, the decolonization of colonized territories of Africa is the first necessary step toward the ultimate goal of freedom since it allows the political control of the statecraft and the center of decision making. When a colonial territory is liberated, the territory and its people cannot be said to be free. They have merely acquired the instrument of choice-decision possibilities of the paths that can lead to freedom. The newly decolonized territory is immediately under the sphere of influence of the colonial power. Such a sphere of influence involves institutional ties, forced cultural dominance, economic control, mental subservience, and many more including the influence of the selection of people that come to control the state craft and social decision-making processes. The next step toward true freedom for the liberated territory is to break away from this sphere of influence, while at the same time preparing itself against being spun into other spheres of imperialist dominance, control and exploitation. To remain in the sphere of colonial influence is to reinforce the same colonial strangle-hold in an even more effective and destructive manner. To enter into a new sphere of influence of an imperial power will simply be trading off one oppression for another since imperialist influence is indirect colonialism and hence neocolonialism. To stay in the influence of any imperial power is to remain within the tentacles of axis of imperialist oppression, predation and injustice. This was a problem for Nkrumah and it is a current problem for the African nationalists.

All the current African states are under the sphere of influence of imperialist and neocolonial forces at varying degrees whether they accept it as a fact of not. The earlier we accept this cardinal reality and work in unity to break the chains of influence the greater chance do we have in Africa to laid down the concrete and sustainable foundation for Africa's progressive tomorrow. This foundation must involve the development of the three basic building blocks of politics, economics and law. The fact remains that all the international institutions that have been set up by the imperialists, and to which African countries claim proudly to be members of, are effective instruments at the disposal of the imperialists for predatory activities in Africa and other small countries that have resources and no power to defend them. We must observe that critical decisions that affect changes in global socioeconomic, political and military events in our modern times are taken by the members of the imperialist club, such as the G-Seven or the members of the Security Council of the United Nations in an unholy alliance with the World Bank, the International Monetary Fund and the World Trade Organization.

Again within the Nkrumaist program of thought and a framework of action, it is held that the nature of decolonized individual African sates and the corresponding micro-sovereignties is such that the states are economically and politically too weak to generate an effective program of positive actions on their own in order to effect the required break from the axis of injustice. The institutions of the decolonized African states are wretched, their economic foundations backward, their education ravaged by anti-African ideologies and vicious myths, and their technologies too precarious to individually organize resistance against the crafty maneuvers of the former colonizers or against being swamped into another colonial or imperialist sphere of influence for a new kind of exploitation. Problems of continual spins within the spheres of imperialist axis of injustice, evil, predation and exploitation exist after decolonization. The solution that would allow true independence to be secured for each decolonized African territory lies, it is argued and also held in the Nkrumaist logic of Africa's reconstruction, in African Unity; and true freedom and the complete emancipation of Africa and Africans require African unity, and the ideology of African nationalism. Anything short of this will be a betrayal of not only the African masses but also the sacrifice of Africa's golden destiny and the redemption of her traditional greatness.

7.4 The African Unity objective in the Program of the Thought and Framework of Positive Action

Given the generally weak positions that the newly decolonized African territories find themselves and will continue to find themselves in, how can such a break from the imperialist influence be affected? The answer that may be developed to this question by the individual decolonized African states is crucial to the total emancipation of Africa. It is also an important element in the nature of sovereignty that any of the newly decolonized African territories may have. The answer will depend on the nature of how perceptions are formed by the African political leadership about imperialist threats and hostilities as well as on conditions for sustainable socioeconomic development from within. Similarly, if the African leadership is made to believe in the imperialists' propaganda of aid and other things in such a way that the African leaders and political elite come to perceive Africa's socioeconomic development to proceed from without, that is from an external push, then the imperialist propaganda, treachery and traps will be effective in maintaining dependency and the sphere of imperial influence without meaningful sustainable development. The perception formations are themselves under continual ideological manipulation by the imperialists' propaganda machinery that distorts the environment of information input into perception formation and decision making. In this way the African leaders become indoctrinated to a collective mindset to believe less in Africa's internal strength and more in the external dependency that has ruined Africa's socioeconomic development process. We must note that the arsenals of dependency tools and for sociopolitical control include debt traps, meaningless aid, misinformation ideological propaganda and many others(see also 29a] [29c] [128].

Within the logical scheme of the Nkrumaist program of thought and the framework of positive actions the true answer lies in achieving the African unity objective with the final organization of a Continental Union Government of Africa (CUGA) or what Nkrumah calls the United African states (UAS). African unity, therefore, is an imperative for Africa's freedom. And Africa's freedom will survive only on strong internal justice, fairness and democratic principles that reflect African traditions and evolving new society. African unity is an objective around which the African people must be organized. It is also a positive action for the attainment of complete emancipation of the African. It is a vehicle through which we can affirm African traditional greatness and respect for life. It is also an instrument for creating the dialectical moment for speedy transformation of Africa into modernity by Africa's self-reliance and self-motion. This is the nature of Africa unity imperative demanded by Africa's modern realities.

The African unity imperative rests on two logical grounds. The first, demanding the Union Government of Africa, deals with a fear on the part of Nkrumah, who having examined the nature of colonized African states, the history of slavery, the Europeans' insatiable appetite for orgy of violence and the behavior of colonialists and imperialists toward resource acquisition, felt that the true substance of decision-making power when politically acquired by the newly decolonized states would quickly disintegrate and evaporate into a thin air leaving just empty slogans of flag flying, national-anthem singing, national sovereignty and independence as they are observed in the countries of South America. Such disintegration of the decision-making power would be due to a) the regrouping of the imperial and colonial powers with new imperialist strategies and greater cooperation among themselves through the formation of the imperialist club in order to re-enter the newly decolonized territories and control the internal decision-making machine to serve their interest, as may be observed by the activities and behavior of the G-Seven, NATO countries, the World Trade Organization, the International Monetary Fund, the World Bank and many more; and b) the lack of appropriate African institutions that will be used to organize, mobilize and coordinate efforts in the individually decolonized states for resistance against the new imperial agenda which may be presented to the African people as a new world order for their benefit.

In this respect, Africans could be left gullible to delusions of inclusion such as membership in various international organizations that have been strategically erected by the imperial predators to maintain the global exploitative system that they have managed to set up to confuse, with endless debates in which Africa's effort is tapped to make the leadership feel that they are part of global governance. In fact some of their citizens may be appointed to head some of these organizations under imperialists' control. Africans will thus neglect to build inter-state African institutions that will serve as vehicle for their true independence and socioeconomic transformation. Furthermore, the leaders of the decolonized small states could either be co-opted or enticed to develop a donor-dependency syndrome that will blind them into leading the African people into a new kind of slavery without the immediate awareness of the masses (for example the acquisition of useless and unproductive loans). All these are now happening to the African states without exception whether we would like to admit it or not.

Nkrumah's fear translates into his position that "if we [the leaders of the decolonized African states] do not formulate plans for African unity and take active steps to form political union, we will soon be fighting and warring among ourselves with imperialists and colonialists standing behind the screen and pulling vicious wires to make us cut each other's throats for the sake of their diabolical purposes in Africa" [110, p. 9]. The wars and political instabilities in post-colonial Africa such as Angola, Liberia, Congo, Ethiopia, Eritrea, Algeria, Rwanda, Somalia, Sudan, Mozambique, Sierra Leone and others, in addition to countless coups d'état, are important testimonies of Nkrumah's penetrating insight into the working mechanism of the imperialists and their wickedness that we have pointed out in Chapter 6 of this volume. It must be pointed out that when one speaks of an axis of evil, one must speak of the relationship that it has with axis of injustices, and then raise a question as to whether any lasting peace can be established in an environment infested with injustice, exploitation, dishonesty and lies and in a period where true freedom fighters are classified as terrorists and true terrorists are classified as freedom fighter by ideological propaganda in support of dangerous state policy of preemption(see also [29b] [29c] [69d].

The intellectual strength of this Nkrumah statement also lies in the recognition of the relationships among the political kingdom, social decision-making power and how the path of the history of a people is shaped. The ultimate control of the political kingdom, in this case the Union Government of Africa, provides a direct access to the decision-making power. The decision-making power can then be used to alter the history of the people in accordance with their will, for "only a united Africa can redeem its past glory and renew and reinforce its strength for the realization of its destiny" [110, p. 17]. We are yet to find an alternative strategy to that of African unity as a vehicle for Africa's redemption without the wholesale loss of Africa's dignity and soul or without dragging the African masses into a new kind of servitude and subservience. This new kind of servitude and subservience of the African masses is occurring with their politicians and rulers happily cheer-leading the social road to the kingdom of servitude rather than fighting to take the African people to the kingdom of freedom, justice and fairness.

The second logical ground of the African unity objective is that the newly constituted Union Government of Africa would assist in coordinating the activities of micro-decision-making centers for the decolonization movement while preparing the way and strategies for Africa's transformation and complete emancipation on the basis of Africa's collectivity and creativity. By such federated coordination of the socio-political decision-making activities, the Union Government of Africa will be used to strengthen individual state's institutions, assist in the creation of new ones as well as prepare the continent against the re-entry of the colonial powers, in one form or another, and for collective socioeconomic development that is internally driven but not externally dependent. These imperial activities are external to Africa and thus define external conditions for change. They cannot be the basis for Africa's internal change and creative evolution. The actual sustainable change can only come from within Africa on the basis of Africa's self-motion and self-reliance in unity (see [42] [43d] [44] [106] for analytical discussions). Without socioeconomic development, and critical social transformation involving the collective effort of the states with efficient interstate support systems to improve the welfare of the Africans, the African citizens and individual African states will fall victim to the diabolical tricks of the imperial nations of the West and other imperial powers that may arise. Political, intellectual and religious askari and zombies will arise among us as con-artists who will quickly degenerate into useful idiots as instruments for the predators' diabolical tricks.

The diabolical tricks of the imperial nations will now take the form of substituting, in place of missionaries of Christianity and civilization, the missionaries of development, democracy, technical assistance, good governance and non-governmental organizations (NGOS) who appear as human right monitors, field workers, disease controllers and others. These new missionaries will work to destabilize the continent of Africa through misinformation, dis-information and anti-African ideology loaded with new slogans of democracy, human rights, individual freedom, poverty alleviation, debt relief, good governance and many other empty, useless and deceptive concepts that have no relevance to Africa's struggle for self-transformation that will lead to true independence in a manner that would allow Africa to exercise her creative forces to shape her destiny and history. Africans should not forget that the same strategy was used by the imperialist predators in the latter part of the second millennium according to the European dating system. They misinformed the world of Africa's achievement and history by calling it the Dark Continent, forgetting the Latin phrase *ex Africa simper aliguid novi*. The same propaganda machine controlled by the ugly hand of Great Britain is at work. It appears in different clothing by showing the images of starving children and human desperation in Africa just to make a settled racial case. We stand to sell Africa and her children into a new type of imperial slavery without African unity since it is easy for the African political rulers to auction off parts or all of the territories they control through the international thievery system that the imperialists have set up under the disguise of democracy, development, good governance and many diabolical slogans.

The stakes here are the political, cultural and economic freedoms of the African people to control and engineer their own destiny. The objective of independence of African states, the activities of liberation movements, the objective of African Unity and the positive action program for the African unification are strategies conceived within the Nkrumaist logic for the attainment of the grand goal of complete freedom for all African people irrespective of the place of birth and residence. The theoretical and operational problem that Nkrumah faced was how to put together a set of objectives with a rank order so as to organize the African people and resources to attain the grand goal of complete freedom for all African people. The slogan, "Organize! Organize! Organize!" has always been central to Nkrumaist strategy to decolonize and emancipate [114, p. 771]. To the Nkrumaist and African nationalist, therefore, it must be affirmed that good organization is the master of creation and practice of ideas, the practice of organized ideas is the foundation of successful implementations of decisions, and successful implementations of decisions are weapons for social transformation, all of which are reflections of the dominant ideology and collective personality that together have taken hold on the society.

A good organization is judged by the unity of purpose, the harmony in the different parts that constitute the organization, the coordination of activities among different elements, the speed with which tactical actions are executed, the discipline to which the members subject themselves, the collective will and endurance of the leadership, the unfading support of all the members and the ability to mobilize and reach the spirit of the masses. The principle of complete emancipation of Africa should not and must not be sacrificed by any African leader. The success of African leaders must be judged by the road that they establish to communicate this principle. And the violation of this basic principle is a crime against Africans and a betrayal of fundamental principles of African traditions of statecraft. This is the conditions that must be used to judge African political leaders like Nkrumah, Nasser, Nyerere, Modibo Keita, Sekou Toure, Ben Bella, Azikiwe, Haile Selassie I, others and current and future ones.

In accordance with the Nkrumaist logic for complete Africa's complete emancipation, therefore, African Unity is the ultimate vehicle through which the political and economic freedom of individual decolonized African states and the citizens of Africa can be guaranteed. It is thus held within the same logic of positive actions that if economic and social developments are to rest with the African people, they must be anchored in the political kingdom where the Africans exercise complete control. Such a political kingdom must first be sought, thus the Nkrumaist slogan "seek ye first the political kingdom". This is the logically driving force behind Nkrumaist social practice and this must be the basis of strategy formation and the practice of tactical action for the African nationalist.

The necessary condition for the attainment of the unity objective is that all occupied African territories must be decolonized. Thus the liberation of colonies from the imperialist controls in Africa is seen as a

Pan-African imperative. When a colonial territory is decolonized, it acquires a decision-making power and hence a localized decision-making center referred to as micro-decision-making center as we have previously explained. The process of achieving a complete emancipation of Africa through an effective socioeconomic transformation requires that when a territory is decolonized it must make creative plans to unite with other decolonized territories on the principles of Africa's self-determination, collective work and cooperative economics directed to achieve complete Africa's emancipation. It must, therefore, constitutionally plan to surrender part of her decision-making power regarding other matters to the new supra-organization to be crafted through the creation of appropriate domestic and Pan-African institutions. It must also participate fully in the framework of positive-action drive to decolonize other parts of the continent under colonial bondage.

The positive action to surrender certain aspects of decision-making in terms of micro-sovereignty that will affect Africa's overall destiny requires faith, hope, social optimism, political will and collective courage and guided wisdom. The collective faith, hope, optimism, will, courage and wisdom depend upon a number of critically internal factors as seen within the Nkrumaist program of thought and the Africentric framework of positive actions. They also depend essentially on the quality of leadership and its ideological alertness regarding Africa in the past, present and future world history, her antiquity and traditional greatness as well as Africa's true destiny in the world history to come. Such an ideological alertness will reflect the awareness of the leadership of the newly decolonized African territories regarding the relationship among the security, sovereignty and true freedom of individual states and those of the African continent as a whole.

Within the program of thought and the framework of positive actions the leadership of a newly decolonized territory must see its sovereignty, security, freedom and development of the decolonized state as fully connected to those of other decolonized African states as well as the continent as a whole but not connected to her colonizer and imperial predators. As such, an important guiding principle for the formulation of the constitution of the newly reconstituted state is African Nationalism and African Unity. Plans, therefore, must be made within the constitution of a newly decolonized state to surrender individual sovereignty to the sovereignty of the federated state to be formed; this must be clearly understood by all African Liberation Organizations. The shared responsibility, sovereignty and authority between the individual states on one hand and the federated state on the other will be negotiated and worked out in a grand constitution and supporting system of rules, regulations and laws. This principle of African nationalism and a call to unity cannot be partly followed within the Nkrumaist program of thought and the framework of positive actions; it must be followed in full.

It was precisely on the basis of the principle of African nationalism and African unity that the first constitution of Ghana made allowances to surrender the sovereignty of Ghana to the federated state to be formed. Current events and the post-independence history of Africa reveal that the complete logical program for the total emancipation of Africa was not understood, and is yet to be understood by the current African leaders. If it was understood and if it is understood now then the African leaders have lost the African essence and have allowed themselves to be manipulated by the imperialist predators into confusion and disaster in the process of operating in the decision space.

In order for the logic, set of ideas and the framework of positive actions to be understood and translated into applications and practice, the Africans must develop a personality with special characteristics. Such a personality depends especially on the strength of the African cultural institutions upon the basis of which an acceptable ideology and collective consciousness can be formed [1] [5b] [41b] [42] [63] [106]. Hence, another important element within the Nkrumaist scheme is the *African cultural imperative*. Let us turn our attention to the cultural imperative and see how it relates to the whole question of Africa's complete emancipation. Special attention is accorded by Nkrumah on this idea of the cultural imperative [106]. Similarly, the role of culture in the national liberation struggle is discussed in impressive details by Cabral [27], Abraham [1], Nsanze [117], Shorter [131b], and Dompere [42] [43d].

7.5 The Role of Culture in the Nkrumaist Model of African Emancipation

In addition to those Pan-African imperatives already mentioned, there is the cultural imperative on the basis of which the African personality and its development must rest. The importance of the cultural imperative may be seen in its relationships to forces that are hostile to the survival of an African Social System. Such hostile forces as seen within the Nkrumiaist program may be either external or internal. The nature and the character of external and internal hostile forces will be different at each historic point in time. These forces will be defined by the structure and form of the internal social arrangements of institutions and their relationships to all forces internal and external to them. An example of an internal hostile force would be those Africans like the askari and zombies who come to form the imperialist cronies, who place personal interests above those of Africa and Africans and where such interests may be connected to the world imperialist system.

On the external front, there is a powerful relationship between the people's culture and hostile external forces such as imperialists and neocolonialists with supporting international institutions that they have established to maintain their predatory activities as well as global politico-economic dominance that tends to restrict the freedom of other countries to organize their societies in a manner that fits their conception of the future. Anybody that comes to accept the idea that there is only one way to efficiently organize societies to create wealth and happiness is an intellectual fool who has become a slave to an ideology rather than the use of cognitive process. The position is a belief that is maintained by political fundamentalism and social extremism. It is not different from the position of religious fundamentalists who believe that there is only one road to go to the Kingdom of God. Political fundamentalism is like religious fundamentalism. Both of them restrict human freedom, democracy and creativity and thus promote axis of oppression, injustice and travesty of human logical rationality.

Freedom, once won, can be destroyed by external aggressors before it is secured. It can also be destroyed by internal forces that are hostile to justice and collective progress. The rate at which such destruction can occur, and the degree of success of destruction by the external aggressors and internal hostile forces, would depend on the people's culture, the institutions that encapsulate it and the degree of collaborative efforts that the external and internal forces can marshal. Culture, within the Nkrumaist program of thought and the nationalist framework of positive actions, must therefore be viewed as an important and uncompromising element of resistance against external aggressors and internal betrayers. Such resistance operates not through the cultural values themselves but through the institutions that are used to organize the values and the people who hold the values. Investment in cultural institutions is also an investment in defense of national freedom and social development.

Well knitted cultural values and efficient institutions that hold them are preconditions for securing the newly acquired decision-making centers and defending them against hostile external and internal forces. These institutions in the individual African states that have been decolonized, and relative to the magnitude of the African struggle to emancipation, are evaluated within the Nkrumaist program of thought and framework of positive action to be too weak and extremely fragile to withstand the new forces that the imperialists and their internal cronies will bring to bear on their lost colonies in other to render the practice of independence and sovereignty operationally meaningless. The current African experiences are classic testimonies to this Nkrumaist position.

The cultural values of the elite of African states and the institutions that transmit them lack a domestic backbone since most of these institutions were designed to serve the colonial interest and the predators' program of resource exploitation while most of the traditional institutions were destroyed and those that remain are infested with the virus of anti-African ideology. The end result of the process of anti-African ideology is that the institutional configuration left by the imperial predators is schizophrenic in transmitting effective domestic policy that could present formidable opposition to the imperialist propaganda machine and deliberate policy deceptions at international stage where commodity-resource flows become the foundation of progress in the theater of development and nation building.

The institutional configuration left by the imperial predators cannot, therefore, be effectively used to organize the forces of cultural resistance needed in individual nations to defend individual sovereignties and decision centers of the decolonized states. The decolonized African states, acting individually, will quickly crumble under the yoke of the struggle for economic freedom and from the slightest onslaught of hostile forces either external, internal or both. The scale and outcome of resistance against imperialist and neocolonial forces will be different when the decolonized states are united under the ideology of African nationalism to organize this resistance. Current African history is a living memory of this unfolding history while the African states operating as individual countries and in isolation from each other are being devoured one after another by imperial predators that are now constituting the members of the imperialist club and with the support of the domestically internal cronies. In fact much of the current African strife and socioeconomic difficulties are due in part to imperialist maneuvers and lack of unity and effective cooperation to contain the imperialists' predatory activities.

It is, again, in this aspect that the African unity objective and the Continental Union Government of Africa (CUGA) assert their necessity and uncompromising importance in a program to emancipate Africa and her children from senseless sufferings at the levels of matter, mind and spirit. The Continental Union Government of Africa, acting as a supra-decision center, will then become the federated arm that will create the required glue for knitting together not only small differences within traditional Africa, Islamic Africa and Christian Africa, but also to glue together the three different value segments composed of traditional, Islamic and Western elements of the African society owing to the Africa's recent experiences with colonialism and colonial occupation. It will then synthesize and harmonize them into producing an organic culture of unity. This cultural unity welcomes our diversity that will completely support the development of the required African personality and a new African who would become culturally liberated and whose guiding principle to action would be African nationalism and African unity (for extensive discussion on African personality see [43d] and on the role of culture see [1] [27] [106] [126] [142a].

Culture and its relationship to social revolution is important to the understanding of Nkrumah's program as well as Nkrumaist strategies for Africa's emancipation through internal organic transformation on the basis of Africa's internal strength and creativity. First there are living and future categories and secondly there exist processes for categorial convertibility. Thirdly categorial convertibility within and between categories requires appropriate transformational moment to ensure conversion. The appropriate tranformational moment is generated at the social level by the collective consciousness of the society. The collective consciousness in turn is a product of the cultural values and the institutions that hold them. Thus the establishment of cultural harmony in African social existence is held to be an imperative within the Nkrumaist program of positive action where African cultural unity as argued by Diop [37] and extended by Ben-Jochannan [13] is accepted to be true for a continual refinement without question. Africa is considered to be one and nothing else. In fact, it is only through this cultural harmony and the unity that it connotes that the African unity objective, when it is attained, can be nourished and molded in support of the African personality that will define the African nationalism and African social transformation. Thus the African personality is the product and soul of African cultural nationalism. Such a cultural nationalism must find expressions in all sectors of African social experiences and life. It must be the lifeblood of Africa's way of life. It must acquire a true African content attained through the vehicle of the Continental Union Government of Africa; hence the Nkrumaist imperative, "Africa Must Unite!", [105] which is also supported by Diop [40].

Within the Nkrumaist program of thought and the framework of positive action for restructuring Africa politically and economically, culture is viewed as the totality of African history. The material basis on which such culture must rest is the African productive forces, the mode of production and, of course, the people's collective effort. The decision to develop the material basis on which the culture rests is, in the last analysis, governed by the structure and form of the culture through the collective consciousness that it engenders.

The development of the right economic conditions to defend freedom, improve livelihood and maintain the sovereignty of any nation within secured limits rests on the shoulders of the peoples' culture and the institutions that transmit, develop and harbor it. It must be pointed out that the position being presented here is not cultural determinism. It is a position that reflects the idea that social changes and conversion of social categories come as a result of the people's awareness of the environment around them, perceptions they form about current events, understanding of linkage between the past and present, present and future, and their will and courage to change course in accordance with their vision of tomorrow. The people's awareness and will are produced by the interaction of the cultural and natural environments. Thus given the natural environment, the culture finally assets itself as necessary since it affects social perceptions, interpretation of facts and decisions. In such an interaction in the African social context, a question may be raised, what role does the collective intellect play? This question will be examined in terms of the role that must be played by African institutions of higher learning to see how such a role must be related to the culture of the people. Part of the role of the African intelligentsia in the African social and philosophical thought has been discussed in [43d]. We shall now add to it by examining the cultural perspective within the logical framework of the drive to attain complete emancipation of Africa.

7.6 The African Intelligentsia, Culture and the African Unity Objective

It has been suggested earlier that the African unity demands the harmonization and effective integration of different segments of African culture, life and experience by taking cognizance of the cultural unity and differential experiences. For such a newly integrated, harmonized and constituted African culture to be used as an effective force of resistance against external and internal aggression, and at same time defend the sovereignty of the fatherland, it must be anchored in the intellectual life of the people. In fact, culture is the vehicle through which the intellectual output of the African people must be shaped and the coordination of efforts of emancipation explained and organized. In this respect, the African unity objective, the African personality and African nationalism must be completely encapsulated by all dimensions of the African culture while at the same time the culture shapes the African nationalism, molds the African personality and its behavior in the choice decision space and strengthens the African unity objective. African nationalism and African unity are inseparable in concepts and practices within the logical framework of Nkrumaist strategy for securing liberty for the African people and preparing them to defend that liberty and Mother Africa whose history forms the cradle of human civilization [8b] [10b] [10c] [10d] [13] [14] [36] [39] 93a] [93b] [93d]. The character of both African nationalism and African unity is a reflection of African personality which is a product of evolving African culture.

Within the same framework, therefore, the institutions of learning and research in continental Africa, without exception, must be seen not only as an important part but as a moving part of an integrated whole of the institutional configuration that must house, refine, develop and transmit the African culture. The institutions of higher learning and research, particularly the universities, occupy an important and enviable position within the struggle to rid Africa and her people of external domination and technological ignorance. They occupy an important role in constructing alternative domestic socioeconomic arrangements and a sustainable development path for Africa's progress. In this effort, we cannot allow external forces to dictate terms of African cognitive behavior. The African universities must be viewed as the intellectual leadership institutions for the task at hand. This task is simply freedom and development of Africa. The African universities must be reorganized, reconstituted and culturally integrated into the values of African society in order to create a leadership that has Africa's interest at heart, completely devoted to its socioeconomic development and devoiced from colonial mindset and imperial intellectual distortions.

The growth and development of the universities, therefore, must be based on African nationalism, African personality and African unity. All knowledge creation composed of research and teaching must be directed toward Africa's socioeconomic transformation and management. The principles of African nationalism and African unity should be the guiding light leading the African people out of the tunnel of darkness into the world of liberty and general enlightenment. Such general enlightenment must be based on African traditions that are refined to modernity in order to deal with the rapidly changing global competition. Research activities must abstract their workload from Africa's social and natural environment. Education policy must be crafted within the cultural confines to rid Africa of the unfavorable situation that "African education is intimately linked with the international aid and education industry, and that the donor client dependency relationship has inhibited the development of African institutions and the capacity of Africans to develop educational policies which are socially relevant and financially feasible for the last quarter of this century" (twentieth century) as described by Carl K. Eicher [155, p. 27]. In this respect, it must also be reaffirmed, as we have argued in Chapter 6 regarding the *modus operandi* of the imperialist predators, that a similar difficulty engulfs Africa's socioeconomic development and creation of relevant institutions of democracy. The African development and institutions of social transformations are similarly linked with imperialist revolving door of aid, loans, grants, technical assistance and the system of predation to create a donor-client dependency structure that is inimical to sustainable socioeconomic transformation. The donor-client dependency structure has come to constrain the development of relevant institutions of socioeconomic transformation and taken African socioeconomic development as an irrelevant appendage to global development. Worst of all, the donor-client dependency structure has come to inhibit the African capacity and creativity to create internal self-development policies which are appropriate to Africa's needs, culture and resources. The result is the complete and effective arrest of self-reliance and internal self-motion that is consistent with African philosophical tradition. In passing we must note that the main reason for imperialist aid is to create conditions of donor-client dependency structure that allows the existence of sphere of imperialist influence. Socioeconomic aid is sedation of development creativity (for extensive discussions on theories of development see [44] for logical reasoning in transformations see [43d] and for epistemics of decision-choice rationality see [42]).

The intellectual backing of African nationalism and unity must be Africentrically constructed. Here there are two different paths that the members of African intelligentsia may follow. They may choose to follow the destructive path by supporting the ideological and psychological war of the predators, imperialists and neo-colonialists to hasten the destruction of Africa and re-enslavement of her children through cultural genocide. Alternatively, they may choose to wage a counter-war against the African adversaries and help to establish a strong African personality and intellectual traditions true of Africa's creativity and antiquity and thus affirm their leadership in the process of Africa's drive to emancipate herself. We hope they will select the latter path and battle with the odds for the sake of Africa and the masses who are resting their trust on the institutions of higher learning and the intelligentsia that controls them.

The institutions of higher learning on the continent of Africa are thus seen within the program as having a moral duty as well as an historic mission to promote the ideology of African nationalism and African unity that will lead to African social transformation and establishment of new social configuration. The promotion must take the form of content development, refinement and dissemination to the masses. In this respect, even the so-called ideology-free subjects of study, such as the natural, mathematical and mechanical sciences, acquire an African content. The character of the African institutions, and in particular those of higher learning, must be acquired out of the tension of the African emancipation struggle and the conflicts that are generated by creative destruction of the disappearance of the old and the emergence of the new. This character must be self-propelling, liberating and creative as well as educating. The institutions of higher learning have the task of restructuring the true intellectual personality of the African and mold the African into a form that is required to alter the path and direction of Africa's modern history in accordance with the demands of the very nature of transformations and conversions of categories. Anything short of this is Africentrically unacceptable and dialectically vacuous.

This new African must have qualities that fit into the general program of liberation of Africa and its people all over the world from conditions of oppression, enslavement and subordination that have become inveterate characteristics of the African way of life in the current world. The new African must be "a dedicated, modest, honest informed man [or woman]. A man [or woman] who submerges self in service to the nation [the United Africa] and mankind. A man [or woman] who abhors greed and detests vanity. A new type of man [or woman] whose humility is his [her] strength and whose integrity is his [her] greatness" [105, p. 130] (words in brackets are inserted).

The new African must be fully cultured in the Pan-African way of life and traditions, educated to understand his or her environment and corresponding problems and must be trained to find solutions relevant to the problems of his or her environment through the institutions of learning that have been established. The success of his or her struggle to be free from external dominance and material poverty depends to some measurable degree on the institutions of learning and research. As such, if these institutions of higher learning separate themselves from the African culture of which they are part, they set themselves up to propagate ideologies and principles, that are not only counter to the basic ideology and principle of African emancipation, but are inimical to the very survival of the African personality, life and culture. They, therefore, become useless and hope-draining institutions within the African cultural set-up and environment that must nourish them. In this respect, the African institutions of higher learning and research loose their revolutionary relevance and no longer occupy the important and enviable position of intellectual leadership required of them, because they have become alienated from the culture that they must help to develop, and from the people that they must serve.

The cultural alienation leads the institutions of higher learning to train and educate a class of intelligentsia with an alien personality. The interest and culture of this class become completely foreign to the cultural environment that it is to serve by social mandate and contract, to the masses that it must lead to freedom and to the economic basis that provides its livelihood. In this respect the members of the intelligentsia become mis-educated in the sense described by Carter G. Woodson [152], fail to create a thinking society in the sense projected by Attoh Ahuma [2] and plunge into intellectual crises in the sense characterized by Cruse [32]. The management and organizers of these African institutions, therefore, fail to understand a cardinal fact that "the history of human achievement illustrates that when an awakened intelligentsia emerges from a subject people it becomes the vanguard of the struggle against alien rule" [105, p. 43]. And not only that, it becomes the true light that will lead the subject people from the tunnel of darkness and servitude into the land of total emancipation on the basis of freedom and justice but not law and order as taught by African democratic ideals and humanism.

The African intelligentsia and the institutions of learning and research that such intelligentsia controls must enter into the heart of Africa, research on what Africa has done and evolved, study their elements, synthesize the common elements, reconcile the differences and harmonize them into a system of thinking that is unifying of the African people from antiquity to the present while at the same time taking into account the common intellectual heritage of humanity and its African-rooted foundation and contributions [8b] [88] [10e] [93b] [93c].

As far as the recent history of Africa is concerned, the African institutions of higher learning have failed hopelessly to meet the demands that are placed on them by the task of total emancipation of Africa and the Africans. They have also failed to assume the leadership and equip the African people with the requisite intellectual munitions to fight against the mental slavery, physical subjugation and psychological disorientation that have brought intellectual and physical poverty to the African people. Thus there exists an unfortunate gap between the African institutions of learning and the culture from which these institutions draw their existence and livelihood. The members of the learned class have become captives of their colonial training and faked alien personality. They have developed within themselves alien mentality, false identity and beggar's syndrome. As such, they have failed to evolve educational Africentricity, an education that projects Africa and its people as the focus of analysis and Africa as the center of history but not an appendage to other peoples' history, culture and adventurism. The developed alien mentality, false identity, illusion of belonging to a foreign intellectual class and alienation from the African culture lead the members of this class to questions of intellectual research and teaching of social theories that are irrelevant to Africa and her people. They are remotely controlled to accept and teach the history, sociology and cultural values of foreign lands as the only account of man and to completely neglect human experiences in Africa where their livelihood is provided. If this is not an intellectual crime against Africa then we do not know what an intellectual crime connotes.

There are many reasons for this situation. Kwame Nkrumah recognized this cultural alienation of the African institutions of higher learning and also of the dominant intelligentsia that controls them. He also saw the dilemma that these institutions found themselves in. He anticipated the pending intellectual bankruptcy, mis-education and the creation of unthinking society involving the African mind and the corresponding vacuum that would be created by the cultural alienation, the intellectual bankruptcy in the general and specific processes of Africa's total emancipation in post-colonial Africa. To fill such a strategic vacuum in the positive action program toward the objective of reaching the land of freedom and the complete emancipation of Africa, the Kwame Nkrumah Ideological Institute (originally Kwame Nkrumah Institute of Economics and Political Science) was borne as we have previously explained. The mission was to study, abstract by analysis and synthesis toward the understanding of African cultural unity and to develop a Pan-African culture and ideology that could support the creation of a new African and a new Africa. "Pan-Africa and not Eurofrica should be our watchword and the guide to our policies" [105, p. 18].

In other words our policies must reflect Africa's interest and needs but not praises from alien lands, imperialist predators and international institutions that are part of the set-up of neocolonial machine of exploitation, subjugation and dominance. The *modus operandi* of the imperialist predators is about waging a total war on all fronts of human life as Nkrumah understood [107] (see also [4a] [4b]). The set of tools includes tactical and strategic weapons of military, economic disruption, ideological deception through information control and media propaganda, cultural and political hegemony, and education as perpetual mind control. The objective of the total war by the imperialists is to accomplish the principle of full spectrum dominance for effective predation by rearranging the world in their image that bears the colors of their interest. This *modus operandi* of the predators requires a total resistance on all fronts if Africa's complete emancipation is to be achieved.

The logical imperatives of Nkrumaist strategies toward African emancipation demand that if African institutions of higher learning and the intelligentsia that controls them are to play critical, positive and transforming roles within the Pan-African cultural set-up and excavation of the road to Africa's freedom then they must be coordinated to execute complementarily and cooperatively their moral duty and historic mission. This coordination requires the active arm of a federated decision center (the Continental Union Government of Africa) which is only possible when African unity is realized. The active arm of the Federated State will assist in facilitating and creating new relevant institutions as well as the appropriate social environment that would allow the African institutions of learning to develop the right character with the required African content for all Africans.

Within the context of African nationalism and African unity, the historic mission of African institutions of higher learning translates into uplifting the spiritual life of the Africans as well as improving their minds toward rebuilding Africa for Africans. The African mind must be nurtured to think African, to cultivate African identity and to develop an African personality. This requires the development of a suitable ideological and technological guidance that must reflect the activities of all institutions of learning and research. Knowledge without a proper ideological and social consciousness is intellectual bankruptcy; ideology without knowledge is social blindness. In the context of this program of thought and the framework of positive actions, the African people are the backbone of social change, the foundation of their history, and this backbone finds dynamic expression in their collective intellect. The collective intellect reflects the path of social decision-information-interactive processes and economic transformations that knowledge and consciousness impose on us.

It is by the effort of African people that oppression, degradation, suffering and poverty are rooted. It is by the sweat of the African people's brow that African emancipation and unity can be achieved. It is by the will and toil of African people that Africa can be built, and it is by their collective consciousness, courage, creativity, vision and intellectual alertness that Africa's future will be shaped, in that "The people are the reality of national greatness" [106, p. 103]. The vision of the people is their history yet unfolded. It is a potential to be actualized. This vision is anchored in the intellectual life and collective mind of the people. It is simply encapsulated in the culture that defines the boundaries of achievement. The vision is seen as the development of a united Africa through the effort of the African people. The guiding principle is African collective consciousness, where African unity and African nationalism must be the ideological support while Africentricity with its philosophical foundations of polyrhythmicity must be its intellectual support.

African unity, supported by the principle of African nationalism within the Nkrumaist logical framework, is a vision. This vision is conceived as the foundation that will bring about total emancipation, defense of freedom and sovereignty of united Africa, as well as the defense of freedom and sovereignties of individual African states and ethnic units within the general context of the Continental Union Government of Africa or, simply put, the African Union. The objective is to bring about a democratically federated decision center that holds power where an all African Parliament is set up to coordinate continental affairs with some constitutional autonomy to individual states in a manner that does not undermine the power and unity of the Union. The federated decision center is to be used for logistic mobilization of human, mental and spiritual development of Africans within the context of African social experiences. In this way, famine, wars, conflicts and adversities of nature in one part of Africa can be handled collectively, minimizing the possibility of interference by external predators who are always seeking weak moments to deepen their predatory activities. Collective response from our unity will minimize the impact that the adversities may have on Africa's collective life and individual search for freedom and justice.

The same federated decision center will then be used to create the conditions for accelerated technological development of which the institutions of higher learning and research will be the driving force and without which the full effort of resource mobilization cannot be felt. It will also be used to create the military defense system in support and maintenance of independence and sovereignty of a United Africa as well as independence and sovereignty of the individual states and the freedom of African people within the logical confines of African unity. It is only in this context that the principle of non-interference in the internal affairs of states that appeared in the Charter of the Organization of African unity acquires proper meaning. The role of African institutions of higher learning and the intelligentsia is to develop the intellectual guidance for the program of thought and positive action. This requires developing and adopting a philosophy of education that is African centered in the sense of being culturally grounded. Such intellectual guidance should lead to principles of African Unity, Africentriciy and Nationalism, and should oppose vehemently anything else. Keep in mind that the control of educational institutions and the content of education is part of the arsenal of the imperial predators to wage total war against Africa. Through Africa's educational institutions we can maximize Africans' full spectrum resistance against the imperialist wars for full spectrum dominance. Our culture is externally controlled when our institutions of learning are similarly controlled from without, and not only that, our effective resistance to imperial predation is then completely nullified.

7.7 Some Basic Reasons for the African Unity Objective

The African unity objective with the subsequent formation of a Continental Union Government of Africa is a vision. The basis on which it is grounded is derived from ten basic interrelated practical realities of freedom, defense and economic development of Africa as seen within the Nkrumaist program of thought and the framework for positive actions. They may be stated in Nkrumah's own words where the strategic emphasis for operation is placed on Africa's self-reliance and self-transformation on the basis of categorial conversion:

1. Today we are one. If in the past the Sahara divided us, now it unites us and an injury to one is an injury to all [102].

2a. In a world divided into hostile camps and warring factions, Africa cannot stand divided without going to the wall [105, p. 147].

2b. No [African] nation can afford to live in isolation [from other African states] and hope to preserve its sovereignty and independence in the present circumstances of the world. [110, p. 11].

3a. Our freedom stands open to danger just as long as the independent states of Africa remain apart. [105, p. 147].

3b. If Africa was united, no major power bloc would attempt to subdue it by limited war because, from the very nature of limited war, what can be achieved by it is itself limited. It is only where small states exist that it is possible, by landing a few thousand marines or by financing a mercenary force, to secure a decisive result [107, p. xi].

4. If we are to remain free, if we are to enjoy the full benefits of Africa's rich resources, we must unite to plan for our total defense and the full exploitation of our material and human means, in the full interest of all our people. "To go it alone" will limit our horizons, curtail our expectations and threaten our liberty [105, p. xvii].

5. If we do not formulate plans for unity and take active steps to form political union, we will soon be fighting and warring among ourselves with imperialists and colonialists standing behind the screen and pulling vicious wires, to make us cut each other's throats for the sake of their diabolical purposes in Africa [104] (see also [110, p. 9]).

6. Only a united Africa can redeem its past glory and renew and reinforce its strength for the realization of its destiny. We are today the richest and yet the poorest of continents, but in unity our continent could smile in a new era of prosperity and power [110, p. 17].

7a. Unity is the first requisite for destroying neocolonialism. Primary and basic is the need for a Union Government on the much divided continent of Africa [107, p. 253].

7b. There are likely to be more coups and rebellions in Africa as long as imperialists and neocolonialists are able to exploit our weaknesses. Unless we unite and deal with neocolonialism on a Pan-African basis, they will continue to try to undermine our independence, and draw us again into spheres of influence comparable to the original carve up of Africa arranged at the Berlin Conference of 1884 [109, p. x].

8a. Economic unity to be effective must be accompanied by political unity. The two are inseparable, each necessary for the future greatness of our continent, and the full development of our resources [107, p. 30].

8b. The lack of political unity places inter-African economic institutions at the mercy of powerful, foreign commercial interests, and sooner or later these will use such institutions as funnels through which to pour money for the continued exploitation of Africa [112, p.40].

9. I do not believe that the economic development of Africa can reach an effective stage until Africa's human and material resources have been mobilized under a Continental United Government of Africa. But I do believe (and nothing that has happened or can happen will swerve me from my belief) that the emergence of a Continental Government of Africa will immediately make the independent states of Africa a mighty world influence. We shall then be in a far better position to liberate our brothers in colonial bondage and rule, to drive out imperialism and neocolonialism from our continent, to make us a powerful ally of the Asian people in their own struggles against imperialism, and to make us an effective force for world peace [108] (see also [110, p. 18]).

10. The concept of African unity embraces the fundamental needs and characteristics of African civilization and ideology, and at the same time satisfies all the conditions necessary for an accelerated economic and technological advance. Such maximum development would ensure a rational utilization of the material resources and human potentials of our continent along the lines of an integrated economy, and within complementary sectors of production, eliminating all unnecessary forms of competition, economic alienation and duplication [112, p. 26].

Given this vision of African Unity, Nkrumah outlined within the framework of Pan-African sociopolitical thinking that:

a) The case-for African unity is very strong and the instinct of the mass of the people right [107, p. 24].

b)   Africa must unite. We have before us not only an opportunity but a historic duty. It is in our hands to join our strength, taking sustenance from our diversity, honoring our rich and varied traditions and culture but acting together for the protection and benefit of us all [110, p. l7].

It must also be clearly understood within the same framework that African Unity and African nationalism are ideologically and conceptually inseparable in their implementation on the basis of African personality and self-reliance. One cannot be an African nationalist and be opposed to African Unity. An African unitarist, in the true sense, is an African nationalist; an African nationalist, in the true sense, is an African unitarist. Both African unitarist and nationalist are engrained with African personality on the basis of Africentricity whose philosophical foundation is polyrhythmicity and whose logic of reasoning is polyrhythmics. Within the Nkrumaist program of thought and a call to positive action there is no room to compromise on this cardinal principle of African reality. In this respect, not only Africa must unite but Africa must seek and establish a new regime of international relationships.

The establishment of a new regime for Africa's international relationships will require a critical examination, analysis and synthesis of the current regimes of relationships among African states themselves at the levels of both co-operations and conflicts to assess individually how these inter-African state relationships promote or retard Africa's complete emancipation, unity and socioeconomic progress. Similarly, it will require a reassessment of Africa's current regimes of external relationships with Europe, the Americas and Euro-Asia and non-African Arabs to see how they retard or facilitate Africa's vision and interest. In some cases, we may have to downgrade our relationships with our colonial predators, seek new friends and establish the organic Africa's dynamic permanent interest that evolves with the changing global power and economic relations. Our choice of friends and our characterization of our adversaries must be based on this enveloping permanent interest, the interest of Africa's complete emancipation on all fronts of culture, technology, production, politics and law from the conditions of our unity, diversity, strengths, weakness and ancient state craft. The general objective is the development of complete resistance against total warfare of the imperial predators and their supporting institutions in the process of creating full spectrum dominance and control that will bring about an environment for their effective predation and resource exploitation. Here we may suggest that every African state must establish an embassy in Brazil and Cuba with connections to Colombia.

7.8 Choice-Decision Rationality and Intelligence of Nkrumaist Policies

We conclude the analysis with some remarks on decision-choice rationality, the Nkrumaist model and the nationalist agenda. Decision-choice rationality in nation building and administrative management of national affairs is made up of political, economic and legal rationalities. These three rationalities correspond to political, economic and legal decision structures that constitute the decision foundation of the society. The political rationality involves the intelligence of choice and decisions in the political structure of the society in which social decision making power is vested in terms of organizational rules, modes of governance and codes of individual and collective power participation. The economic rationality involves the intelligence of decisions and choices in the economic structure that constitutes the foundation of life in terms rules and institutions of resource allocation and use. The legal rationality, on the other hand, involves intelligence of decision and choices in the legal structure that constitutes the foundation of control and harmonization of the society in terms of appropriate rules of the national organizational system of its governance of the legal, political and economic structures. The type and the character of any of the three rationalities associated with a national leader and the leadership of governance depends on the ideological orientation that affects the conceived vision of nation building, the path of national history and the collective personality of the citizens.

7.8.1 Political Rationality and Nkrumah's Policies

At the level of political rationality and in accordance with Nkrumaist goals and objectives, Nkrumah's decision intelligence reveals that without political control national interest and aspirations cannot be defined and sustainable nation building by internal forces in accord with Africa's vision is impossible. These are also true when the political structure with the decision making power is externally controlled after decolonization. This type of political rationality points to the direction to dismantle colonialism, imperialism and neocolonialism, and the system of internal collaborators and installing democracy by creating favorable internal conditions. It also points to the direction where true sovereignty in Africa can only be enhanced and secured with African unity under some form of continental government. It further points to the direction where true political democracy can only be attained after decolonization by democratizing education, information and health, the landmarks of the governance of Nkrumah's domestic policy in Ghana where education was made free from primary school to the institutions of higher learning and where the national health service was made free and available to all residents. Here we find a different look of the concept of democracy where democracy is not synonymous with voting but many essential elements of life must be democratized in accordance with natural democracy regarding the four elements of air, water, fire and land that form foundation of African philosophy [43d].

The Nkrumaist intelligence embodied in political rationality is that Africa must be decolonized, united and democratized. This intelligence embodied in political rationality is captured in Nkrumah's famous political slogan "Seek ye first the political kingdom" [105, p. 50]. The power of this slogan and its revolutionary relevance toward emancipation and freedom are not clearly understood by either Nkrumah's critics or his admirers. We simply want to point out that the power to shape national history through decision-information processes is vested in the political structure of the society but not in either economic or legal structures. Without the internal control of the political structure the nation is at the mercy of external forces and the interest of the nation is appended to the interests of those external forces that control directly or indirectly the political structure and the corresponding decision making power of the state. In this way the freedom to internally shape national history and the peoples' destiny and to develop the economic forces to serve the people's interest according to their legal structure is externally arrested and taken away from them. The right of people to collectively decide their own destiny, to create freedom and justice and to develop their productive forces according to their needs and to distribute them under conditions of fairness is guaranteed only though their control of the political structure. Thus the political rationality for emancipation at both the individual states and the union of Africa is "Seek ye first the political kingdom".

The basis of the problem of human poverty, hopelessness and external dependency of a nation is economic. The basis of solution to this problem is political. It thus logically follows that the control of the political structure is unquestionably the first and indispensable step toward Africa's emancipation and redemption. This internal political control is a necessary but not sufficient condition to bring the solution into being. The sufficient condition is found in the collective ideology and personality of the society on the basis of which perceptions are formed, information is processed and decisions are made to alter the unwanted situations. The nature and form of the political organization dictate the ideological regime while the ideological conditions shape the morphology of the sociopolitical organization that may take hold of the society as well as defining the power distribution in the social decision space and political rationality that are defined in the political structure.

7.8.2 Legal Rationality and Nkrumah's Policies

At the level of legal rationality, Nkrumah's decision intelligence reveals that legal precepts and emerging rules of individual and collective behavior in the three structures of politics, law and economics must have their roots in the culture of the people. The legal rules must also be related to the national interest and aspirations where freedom and justice operate, without which the concept and practice of democracy is empty. Without legal rules that are culturally based harmony and unity of the society cannot be created and maintained. The implied Nkrumaist decision intelligence in the legal rationality points to the direction of each for all and all for each where the community is the primary element of legal rationality and the individual as a derived category is guaranteed freedom, justice and fairness in the collective and the social organism. It also points to the road of democratization of responsibility, freedom and justice in accordance with the collective interest of the society.

The individual interest rests on the community interest. Here individual freedom, while forming the legal foundation of individual action, does not determine collective freedom in the legal space in accordance with the African traditions. This is one of the puzzles in the foundations of African philosophy regarding social formation (see [43d]). It is on the basis of this type of legal rationality that the coat of arms of Ghana is inscribed with the motto "Freedom and Justice". The implied legal rationality points to African unity in the sense that the only way to bring about unity of the family of tribes and maintain the unity is through freedom and justice with fairness that are enshrined in judicial democracy. The content of first constitution of Ghana is a testimony of this legal rationality where constitutional allowance was made to surrender Ghana's sovereignty to the sovereignty that may emerge from the African Union. Justice without freedom is an elusion, freedom without law is disorder and order without justice is slavery.

7.8.3 Economic Rationality and Nkrumah's Policies

At the level of economic rationality, Nkrumah's decision intelligence is structured in three mega-dimensions. The first dimension is the rational recognition that the people are the backbone of the national creative process at all levels of human endeavor. The people are the actual and potential wealth of a nation. And the youth are the national asset for the defense of today and the construction and actualization of tomorrow's potentials. The second dimension involves the rational recognition that the people's creative force involves mental and physical qualities given their quantity. The mental quality is seen in Nkrumah's decision intelligence as mental labor whose improvement can come about by education and training. The physical labor is seen as raw labor whose improvement can be brought into been by good health services. The third dimension is the rational organization and utilization of mental and physical labor toward production and reproduction of life in the creative process of nation building under the conditions of Africa's vision of the world. The third dimension can come about by a rational construct and application of a system of production and industrial, technological and agricultural policies that are consistent with the social stage and national character of the society.

The socioeconomic rationality points to the direction where by democratizing education and health we democratize responsibility, freedom, justice and fairness for all in the effort of nation building composed of social deconstruction and reconstruction toward Africa's redemption. At the level of economic practice relative to Nkrumaist goals and objectives, economic rationality on the basis of nation building from within requires that education and health facilities be provided by the state in all provinces, towns and cities. The underlying decision intelligence became the health and education policy of Nkrumah's vision where other Africans were given opportunities to benefit from this grand social design of Africa's tomorrow of socio-political and economic integration. At the level of policy practice, the socio-economic rationality points to an integrated approach where the policies of education, health, technology, industry and agriculture are unified under a national plan for sustainable development and national reconstruction. Education and health backed by an African-centered ideology must be directed toward the welfare of the people through the recognition that Africa's emancipation and redemption require solutions to Africa's problems in the fields of economics, technology, culture and science.

At the level of production-consumption practice, Nkrumah's decision intelligence points to a social direction where results of production are for the improvements of the welfare of the people but not simply for individual profit. The wisdom of this rational synthesis is that economic development of a nation is brought about through the peoples' effort and creativity. The effort must be organized on the basis of the African tradition of the communal principle where each is for all and all is for each in unity that reflects African humanism. Besides democratization of education and health and the creation of corresponding facilities, macroeconomic rationality compelled Nkrumah to organize the workers and the youth so that economic development should proceed from within the nation where internal factors would be the basis for change and external factors would be the conditions that point to direction of change (see [60b]). This approach is supported by an economic rationale that development and nation building are labor processes that rest on the population of a nation (see [44]).

This organization of workers and youth must be composed of skill training, work-ethics development and complemented with ideological orientation of good citizenship, nation building and love for Africa. The ideological orientation is particularly important since the entrenched colonial collective and individual mentality of the nation after decolonization must be replaced with an African-centered ideology that is culturally consistent with African way of life in other to point to a correct direction of use of education and skills in the service of the nation and in support of Ghana's African policy, rather than the use of education and skills to support the colonial machinery of exploitation and oppression as happened in the period of colonization and colonialism.

The national demands of skilled workers with good work ethics, citizens with African consciousness and the external conditions of imperialists led Nkrumah to follow a rational policy of development of organization of a portion of the Ghana laborforce into the Workers Brigade where the workers were trained in discipline at all levels, responsibility to self and the community and good citizenship with the African Personality and African consciousness [60b] [114] [138c]. On this policy objective Nkrumah states "They [the workers] are being given the elements of skill which will enable them to find employment in agriculture and industry" [105, p.126]. This kind of organization of workers was rationally appropriate for a country where about ninety percent of the population was locked in under-self-employment on agriculture without the experience and discipline of having to work for anybody.

The need for sustainable socioeconomic development requires creating conditions that allow the youth to be ideologically connected to the working masses. It is easy to change the ideological habits of the society by starting with the youth. To this end Nkrumah established the Young Pioneers as a youth movement

> …which is designed to give them training in citizenship within a society which will be tooted in co-operation and not acquisitive competition. For this end Africa needs a new type of citizen, a dedicated, modest, honest and informed man. A man who submerges self in services to the nation and mankind. A man who abhors greed and detests vanity. A new type of man whose humility is his strength and whose integrity is his greatness. [105, p. 130].

The logic of the socio-ideological deconstruction and reconstruction after decolonization is that the members of the Workers Brigade and Young Pioneer Movement must be imbued with African-centered ideology and personality to allow them to think in terms of African nationalism in the use of their education, knowledge and skills. In other words, to change the frame of reference that allows the use of education, skills and knowledge that the Africans possess. Instead of using knowledge and skills to service the colonial machinery and the interest of the imperial predators they were now put to the service of the nation and nation building. The rational path for organizing the workers and the youth in Nkrumah's model of Africa's emancipation and redemption was motivated by the internal and external conditions of African history. As Nkrumah observed, "Our cruel colonial past and the present-day intrigues of neocolonialism have hammered home the conviction that Africa can no longer trust in anybody but herself and her resource" [105, p. 127]. This Nkrumah statement is fundamental in examining Africa's socioeconomic reconstruction, technological development and the casting of relevant institutional configuration in support of Africa's policy process. The Nkrumaist model of Africa's complete emancipation is constructed on the basis of self-reliance, internal transformation and continental unity. Our domestic state policies must closely follow our African policy for integration and unity and that we must take advantage of the beauty of our diversity and strength must come from our unity. The solutions to Africa's internal and external problems can be found on the African continent and in African unity. No other choice is available to us looking at the strategies of the imperial predators and their insatiable appetite for more and more resource and global dominance without consideration of the interest of other countries in the fringe as we have explained in Chapter 6 of this book.

8

REFLECTIONS, CONCLUSIONS AND COMMENTS

A critical analysis of Nkrumah's goals and objectives and his vision of Africa suggest strongly a well thought out program for Africa's political, economic and cultural emancipation. This is the foundation of the Nkrumaist model for Africa's complete emancipation. The goals and objectives are composed of a grand goal and a supporting system of hierarchical objectives which constitutes the vehicle to reach the grand goal. The grand goal is political and economic freedom completely anchored in African traditions and African way of life that is based on the cultural tapestry of the African people. The achievement of this goal is the ultimate emancipation of Africa and her children through African integration and unity.

The supporting system of objectives may be divided into subsystems of short-term objectives, medium-term objectives and long-term objectives. The goal and objectives are to be achieved through the application of positive actions on both political and economic fronts. The positive actions are then divided into tactical and strategic ones that correspond to the objectives. In setting out these objectives, Nkrumah was completely aware of the idea that freedom must be based on strong material foundation as well as encapsulated in the people's culture. The construction of the system of objectives and the program of positive actions must acquire this cultural and material content as well as taking into account Africa's rich diversity. Within the decision framework, Nkrumah understood clearly the intrinsic meaning of the struggle of a people to be free. He states:

> Progress does not come by itself, neither desire nor time can alone ensure progress. Progress is not a gift, but a victory. To make progress, man [or woman] has to work, strive and toil,

tame the elements, combat the environment, recast institutions, subdue circumstances, and at all times be ideologically alert and awake [110, p. 113].

The goal and objectives of Nkrumah's program for complete Africa's emancipation and how they relate to one another and the overall vision are presented abstractly and schematically in Figure 8.1.

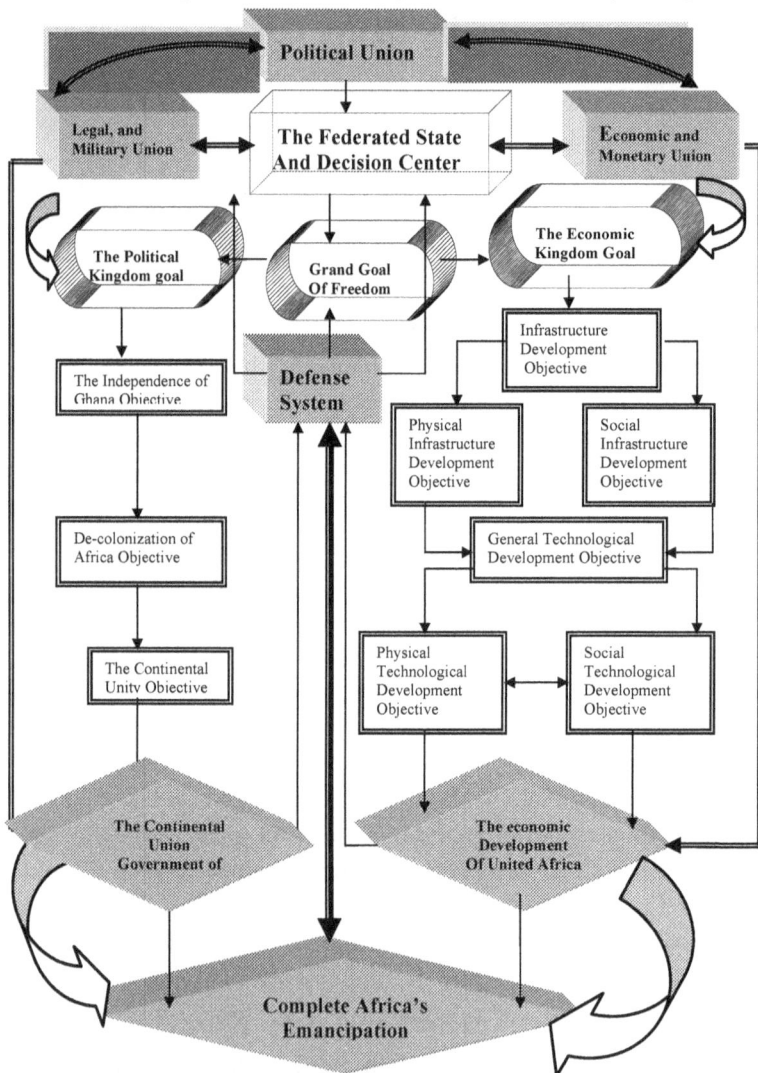

Figure 8.1 A Simple Diagrammatic Representation of the Goals and Objectives in Nkrumah's Program for Africa's Emancipation at All Fronts

The grand goal of Nkrumah's program is the complete Africa's emancipation. The structural process for attaining this grand goal works through conceptually interdependent and inter-supportive strategies for attaining the goals of political and economic kingdoms. The goal of the political kingdom is to establish first African states that are politically decolonized from the oppressive colonial machines of the Europeans, and then construct a unity of African states that will lead to a Continental Union Government of Africa.

We have already touched directly or indirectly on most of these goals and objectives and how they define the path to Africa's freedom and restoration of African traditions and redemption. However, a word or two on them will be helpful and useful in order to fully appreciate their relative importance, operative unity and the power of the structure of the overall program. A full discussion will require, at least, three volumes on political, legal and economic theories that correspond to the political, legal and economic structures of the African Union. These theories must belong to the class of prescriptive theories rather than the class of explanatory theories. They must suggest the path of creation of new structures that are significantly different from those of colonial imposition and divorced from the conditions where the African political, economic and legal structures are simple extensions and appendages of the imperial systems. In this respect we must keep in mind that from the viewpoint of prescriptive science the required theories are guides to decisions and actions. The theories must provide us with the logical frameworks for designing the political, legal and economic structures that are consistent with Africa's unification, federal democracy, good governance and social progress.

8.1   The Political Theory and African Unification

The political theory will be used to present a cognitive map that will provide guidance for a fair distribution of decision-making power between the state governments and federal government, and between the governing bodies of the state localities and the state governments. Additionally, it will provide guidance for the development of relevant political institutions, the channels through which the citizens can participate in the political life of the newly federated nation and efficient political management of all African affairs among others. In other words the political theory is to show how the full democratization of the political structure can be effected on the basis of

African traditions and interest taking account of the strength and beauty of our natural diversity.

The political theory should define the path through which political unity can be achieved and managed. It must point to the direction of creating conditions of efficient establishment of stable structure of intra-African political relationships in terms of state sociopolitical behavior and how such state political relationships can bring about a continental government where the central decision-making power is vested in the federated state. In the theoretical construct, we must keep in mind that political institutions constitute the organic key to unlock the gates of integration and unity at the levels of economics and law. The political theory that establishes the organic edifice for designing the framework for Africa's applied political structure at the micro and macro levels calls for considerable creative effort, logical capacity, historical understanding and complete rejection of preconceptions and social prejudices that usually constrains socio-political integration. We can take some lessons from the problems of the European integration process but not follow their path. The sustainable solutions to Africa's problems require Africa's creativity and independent thinking without subjecting ourselves to deceptive technical help from the imperial predators who are the major sources of socio-political tensions in our continent.

8.2 The Legal Theory and African Unification

The legal theory will provide a logical system that will serve as a guide for institutional and personal practice of freedom, justice and fairness on the basis of African humanism and tradition. It will also guide the creation of relevant legal institutions that will define the parameters for intra- and inter-state economic and political practices as well as establishing the framework and instruments for enforcement. It will guide the development of a framework for establishing rules, regulations and the manner in which the political, legal and economic structures can be altered in accordance with Africa's permanent interest. In other words, the legal theory will point to a framework for democratization of freedom and justice in human decision practices in all aspects of African life. The legal theory to be developed as part of our integration process must recognize the three legacies of Eastern Islamic and Euro-Christian elements of Africa and African traditions that Nkrumah pointed out. The legal theory developed must synthesize these elements into a stable unity and in a way that meets the ideological conditions of African personality, and African nationalism and efficient governance as well as the clustering principles of humanism that constitute the foundation of African philosophical and cognitive traditions as elemental backbones of the African essence.

In this process of legal theorizing, it is necessary to understand the critical relationships among statutes, by-laws, social practice and tradition. Here the legal theory must accommodate as well as reconcile the behavioral conditions of the three African legacies in a manner that retains the essential elements of African traditions and personality. The legal theory must for all practical purposes deal with the concept of law and its relevance to socio-cultural integration, social cohesion and stability at all levels. It must also deal with the concepts of liberty, justice, responsibility, enforcement and punishment by harmonizing state differences and their impacts on the individual and the collective. The goal of the theoretical construct is to provide a legal order that is consistent with African experiences, tradition, and statecraft to support the development of the political, economic and legal decision structures. Here a broad socio-philosophical approach in an integrated manner to the construct of the legal theory will promote proper understanding of the essential elements of the legal conceptual system that is appropriate to Africa's conditions for unification. Conceptually, the implied legal conditions of the three legacies must be analyzed and synthesized in a manner that promotes and preserves African nationalism, personality and humanism.

8.3 Economic Theory and African Unification

The economic theory, on the other hand, will consist of a system of interconnected ideas and logic that will constitute a cognitive *modus operandi* for creating relevant economic institutions and managing and developing the economic structure in terms of allocation, production and distribution on the basis of efficiency and just order that is compatible with African traditions. It will also provide guidance for developing the appropriate, necessary and sufficient conditions for supporting the political, legal and economic structures that are the foundations of the grand goal and the overall organization of the African social construct. The economic theory therefore should point to a framework for democratizing the economic structure in terms of decision and participation.

The case for African unity has been made. This unity must involve the three structures of the social organism. This requires that we work to integrate the political, economic and legal structures of individually decolonized countries into a mega-unit with a common grand sovereignty. The rational basis of the argument is laid down in this book. The strategies for actualizing the African Unity into a continental union must be designed and implemented. This will require dedication from all member states of the African Union where institutions of unity are created at micro and macro levels of the African emancipation process. These institutions must be African-centered in a way that reflects Africa's ingenuity, wisdom, strength, courage, hope, freedom and justice. The case for African unity is also made by Green and Seidman by stating that:

> The need for radical economic changes in the structure of production and international economic relations, combined with the near-impossibility of attaining them within economic units as small as the present states, forms the basic economic case for African political unity. Economic unity would enhance the possibility of achieving rapid continental growth in four major respects. ....Third, an economic unit encompassing all free African states would be able to exert significant bargaining power on the world market. A unified African economy would be considerably larger than even the largest foreign concern [64b, p.346].

This statement is in support of Nkrumah's intrinsic position that:

> The forces that unite us are intrinsic and greater than the superimposed influences that keep us apart. These are the forces that we must enlist and cement for the sake of the trusting millions who look to us, their leaders, to take them out of the poverty, ignorance and disorder left by colonialism into an ordered unity in which freedom and amity can flourish amidst plenty [105, p. 221].

The African leaders must take the need for African unity as a serious and urgent matter that requires immediate political action if they are to avoid intensification of poverty, hopelessness and neocolonial slavery. The political and intellectual leaders in the individually decolonized territories must agree on the fundamental desire on the basis of collective freedom, justice and fairness that continental economic unity supported by politico-legal unity is imperative. This must be supported by creating appropriate institutions of policy coordination on the level of economics, politics, law and diplomacy. The integration process toward unity will require the establishment of optimal monetary and trading system at the level of the continent. Similarly, at the level of the continent a legal system that is fair and just must be established by creating appropriate legal institutions that will respect individual and collective rights of the people and their activities in the unification and emancipation process. The whole process of integration toward the African Union and the required institutions demands that we work toward a permanent political union under a well-defined democracy that will support the creation of institutions of legal, economic and political structures for Africa's emancipation and social progress where the African people form the foundation of wealth and beneficiaries of socio-economic activities and endowments of Africa. Above all the ideology of African nationalism must form the basis of our decisions and action domestically and internationally.

Finally we simply conclude that only united Africa can, by her own internal forces redeem its past glory, change the terms of her global relationships, reinforce her strength and courage, and renew her hope for her emancipation and the realization of her destiny in accordance with her will toward her redemption. This was the cognitive tradition and organizational beauty of unadulterated traditions of African social formations on the basis of which the beginning of knowledge was established for social management and governance on the basis of democratic principles of "each for all and all for each". It must be noted that African unity is not simply the redemption of Africa and her past glory. African unity is a strategy to ensure Africa's tomorrow, Africa's security, Africa's progress and Africa's defense where the people are the backbone of Africa's greatness. This unity is defined on all fronts of politics, economics, law, culture and cognition. We have discussed the philosophical and ideological foundations for this unity in a companion book entitled *Polyrhythmicity* [43d].

8.4   Reflections on Sociology of African Union

A case is made in this book for speedy and complete African political, economic and legal integration if Africa is to achieve complete emancipation at all fronts of human endeavor. For the integration process to rationally proceed to create a federated state with political stability, it is necessary to visit Africa's recent history in terms of sociology of independence and the structure of organization of individual states. Our argument is that central to the creation of stable political African Union is the concept of African nationalism that must be embraced completely by all African states. The type of African nationalism required for creating a politically stable African Union is distinguished from state-specific nationalism that emerged through the decolonization process. The sequential process on the ladder of stable integration is such that the state-specific nationalism is sociologically distinguished from ethnic and tribal specific affinities.

The condition for a stable state, it is argued, is that ethnic and tribal affinities, while important to the members, must be supportive of state-specific nationalism which must in turn support ethnic and tribal affinities with fairness and justice based on accepted rules and regulations for the state formation from ethnic and tribal communities. The condition for the stability of a federated state, it is also argued, is that state-specific nationalism and African nationalism must be inter-supportive where justice, fairness and equity are the foundation stones of political, economic and legal institutions of the federation on the basis of rules and regulations governing the formation of the federated state.

The conditions of a stable political African union and its integration at all levels must be drawn from freedom, justice and order given the conditions of African nationalism. Here tribal affinity is subservient to ethnic affinity; ethnic affinity is subservient to state-specific nationalism which is subservient to African nationalism. To guarantee stability in such a relationship freedom, justice and order must operate in full force within the accepted rules and regulation in the formation of the federation. From the conditions of the creation of a stable federated state we examined the *modus operandi* of the imperial predators whose aim and objective is full spectrum domination which is easily achieved over the current territorial regime of Africa with simple instruments of aid, loans, grants and intimidation. Given the *modus operandi* of the imperial predators we present a model of African full spectrum resistance against the full spectrum imperial domination. This is the Nkrumaist model for complete Africa's emancipation where African

Unity is the organic vehicle to accomplish the emancipation through a systematic design of integration strategies Africa's future.

The theory of crony imperialism shows the complex working mechanism of the current process of neocolonialism, globalization and full spectrum dominance of imperial predators. Globalization has replace neocolonialism with a new face. Competitive imperialism has been replaced with cooperative imperialism. The techniques and methods of crude imperialism has been replaced with those of crony imperialism. Here the central goal of the imperial predators is the control of the directions of resource, technology and commodity flows for their benefits. They have no interest in democratic liberty, justice and development of other lands except those lands that can be appended to the imperal system of explotations as the history of colonialism instructs us. The organic instrument to effect the control of resource-technology-commodity flows is the asset of the system of neocolonial states with puppet governments that are created or must be manufactured by the imperial predators with all kinds of violence, terror and intimidations. Aid, grants and loans of all forms are merely attractive tricks and manufactured traps to lure weak states into the machinery for creating neocolonial states and national subservience. At this point references to Noam Chomsky, Edward N. Herman, J. Williams are very useful [29b] [70c] [71c] [151a]. The international organizations such as United Nations, World Bank, IMF and imperial development organizations are institutions of policy transmission of the imperial predators (see for example Cheryl Payer[127c] and John Perkins [128a]). The same institutions offer the members of the fringe a forum to cry for imperial love and mercy under illusions of national independence and sovereignty.

With this *modus operadi*, the stage is set for international resource-technology-commodity game between the politico-economic incumbent and the fringe where the incumbent will an awesome power that creates the rules of the resource-technology-commodity game, the process of development, underdevelopment, national politico-economic stabilities and global instabilities in governance, finance and peace. As set up, the members of the imperialist club constitute collectivelly the international politico-economic monopoly whose awesome power cannot be overcome by individual African states acting alone in the theater of resource-technology-commodity game except in unity that will create a vehicle for full spectrum resistance against the full spectrum domination of the imperialist club which is actively working to maintain the status of incumbency. An uncompromising analytical case is thus made for *Africa Must Unite* and a Continatal Union Government of Africa must result from the current *African Union*. The sociology of integration and unity presents the conditions that will maintain a stable political *African Union*.

REFERENCES

[1] Abraham, W.E., *The Mind of Africa*, London, Weidenfeld and Nicholson, 1962.

[2] Ahuma, Attoh S.R.B., *The Gold Cost Nation and National Consciousness*, in [88], pp. 161-72.

[3a] Ajala, Adekunle, *Pan-Africanism : Evolution, Progress and Prospects*, London, Andre Deutsch, 1973.

[3b] Allen, J. *et al.*, *Without Sanctuary: The Lynching Photography in America*, Santa Fe, N.M., Twen Palms Publishers, 2000.

[3c] Allen, James P., *Genesis in Egypt: The Philosophy of Ancient Egyptian Creation* Accounts (Yale Egyptological Studies, #2), New Haven, Yale University, Department of Near Eastern Languages and Civilizations, 1988.

[3d] Alston, W. and R.B. Brandt (eds.), *The Problems of Philosophy*, Boston, MA, Allyn and Bacon, 1967.

[3e] Amate, C.O.C., *Inside OAU: Pan-Africanism in Practice*, New York, St. Martin's Press, 1986.

[3f] Amen, Ra Un Nefer, *Metu Neter* Vol. 1, Bronx, New York, Khamit Co. Pub., 1977.

[4a] Amin, Samir, *Neo-Colonialism in West Africa*, New York, Monthly Review Press, 1973.

[4b] Amin, Samir, *Eurocentrism*, New York, Monthly Review Press, 1989.

[5a] Amo Afer, A.G., *The Absence of Sensation and the Faculty of Sense in the Human Mind and Their Presence in our Organic and Living Body, PhD Dissertation and other Essays 1727-1749*, Halle, Wittenberg, Jena, Martin Luther University Translation, 1968.

[5b] Ani, M., *Yurugu: An African-Centered Critique of European Cultural Thought and Behavior*, Trenton, N.J., Africa World Press, 1994.

[5c] Apostel, Leo, *African Philosophy: Myth or Reality*, Ghent, Belgium, Scientific Publishers, 1981.

[5d] Appolus, Emil (ed.), *The Resurgence of Pan-Africanism*, London, Freedman Brothers, 1974.

[5e] Aristote, N., *Politique*, Books I and II, Paris, Les Belles Lettres, 1960.

[6a] Armah, Ayi Kwei, *Two Thousand Seasons*, Oxford, Heineman, 1973.

[6b] Armah, Ayi Kwei, *Osiris Rising*, Dakar, Senegal, Africa Per Ankh Publishers, 1995.

[7] Asante, Molefi K. *et al.* (eds.), *African Culture: The Rhythms of Unity*, Trenton, New Jersey, African World Press Inc., 1990.

[8a] Asante, Molefi K., *Afrocentricity*, Trenton, New Jersey, Africa World Press, Inc., 1989.

[8b] Asante, Molefi K. *et al.* (eds.), *African Intellectual Heritage: Book of Sources*, Philadelphia, PA, Temple University Press

[9] Asante, Molefi K., *Kement, Afrocenticity and Knowledge*, Trenton, New Jersey, Africa World Press, Inc., 1990.

[10a] Asante, S.K.B., *Pan-African Protest: West Africa and the Italo-Ethiopian Crisis*, 1934-1941, Legon History Series, London, Longmans, 1977.

[10b] Ashby, M.A., *The African Origins of Civilization: Book I, Mystical Religion and Yoga Philosophy*, Miami, FL, Cruzan Mystic Books, 1995.

[10c] Ashby, M.A., *The African Origins of Civilization, Book II: African Origins of Western Civilization, Religion and Philosophy*, Miami, FL, Cruzan Mystic Books, 2001.

[10d] Ashby, M.A., *The African Origins of Civilization Book III: The African Origins of Eastern Civilization, Religion, Yoga Mysticism and Philosophy*, Miami, FL, Cruzan Mystic Books, 2001.

[10e] Ashby, M.A., *Egyptian Yoga Vol. I,: The Philosophy of Enlightenment*, Miami, FL, Cruzan Mystic Books, 1997,

[10f] Auma-Osolo, A., *Cause-Effects of Modern African Nationalism on the World Market*, University Press of America, 1983.

[10g] Axinn, Sidney, "Kant, Logic and Concept of Mankind," *Ethics*, Vol 48 (XLVIII), 1958, pp. 286-291.

[10g] Bakewell, Charles M., *Source Book in Ancient Philosophy*, New York, Charles Scribner's Sons, 1909.

[11a] Bascom, William, *African Art in Cultural Perspective: Introduction*, New York, Norton, 1973.

[11b] Bebey, Francis, *African Music: A People's Art*, Westport, CT, Lawrence Hill and Co., 1980.

[11c] Bell, Richard H., *Understanding African Philosophy: A Cross-cultural Approach to Classical and Contemporary Issues*, New York, Routledge, 2002.

[12] Ben-Jochannan, Joseph A.A., *Cultural Genocide in the Black and African Studies Curriculum*, New York, River Nile Universal Books, 1972.

[13] Ben-Jochannan, Joseph A.A., *Africa: Mother of Western Civilization*, Baltimore, MD, Black Classic Press, 1988.

[14] Ben-Jochannan, Joseph A.A. *et al.*, *African Origins of Major Western Religions*, New York, Alkebulan Books, 1970.

[15] Ben-Jochannan, Joseph A.A., *Black Man of the Nile*, Baltimore, MD, Black Classic Press, 1989.

[16] Ben-Jochannan, Joseph A.A., *We the Black Jews*, Baltimore, MD, Black Classic Press, 1983.

[17a] Ben-Jochannan, Joseph A.A., Hugh Brooks and Kempton Webb, *Africa: Land, People and Cultures of the World*, New York, W.H. Sadlier, 1971.

[17b] Bergsten, C.F. (ed.), *Global Economic Imbalances*, Special Report #4, Washington, D.C., Institute for international Economics, 1985.

[17c] Berkeley, George, *Treatise Concerning the Principles of Human Knowledge*, *Works*, Vol. I (edited by A. Fraser), Oxford, Oxford University Press, 1871-1814.

[17d] Berkeley, George, "Material Things are Experiences of Men or God" in [3c], 1967, pp. 658-668.

[18] Blyden, E.W., "African Life and Customs" in [88] pp. 78-87.

[19] Blyden, Edward W., *Christianity, Islam and the Negro Race*, Baltimore, MD, Black Classic Press, 1994.

[20a] Boahen, A. Adu, *African Perspectives on Colonialism*, Baltimore, Johns Hopkins University Press, 1987.

[20b] Bonnefoy, Yves, *Mythologies*, Vols 1-2, Chicago, University of Chicago Press, 1991.

[21] Bovill, E.W., *The Golden Trade of the Moors*, London, Oxford University Press, 1958.

[22a] Bovill, E.W., *Caravans of the Old Sahara*, London, Oxford University Press, 1933.

[22b] Breasted, James H., *Ancient Records of Egypt*, Vols. 1-5, Chicago, The University of Chicago Press, 1906-1907.

[22c] Breasted, James Henry, *Development of Religion and Thought in Ancient Egypt*, New York, Charles Scribner's Sons, 1912.

[22d] Brody, Baruch A. (ed.), *Readings in the Philosophy of Science*, Englewood Cliffs, NJ., Prentice-Hall Inc., 1970.

[22e] Browdes, Anthony T., *Exploiting the Myths, Vol. 1: Nile Valley Contribution to Civilization*, Washington, D.C., The Institute of Karmic Guidance, 1992.

[22f] Browdes, Anthony T., *Egypt on the Potomac*, Washington, D.C., IKG Publishers, 2004.

[22g] Brown, Lee (ed.), *African Philosophy: New and Traditional Perspectives*, New York, Oxford University Press, 2004.

[23] Budge, Willis E.A., *Osiris and the Egyptian Resurrection*, Vols. 1 and 2, New York, Dover, 1973.

[24a] Budge, Willis E.A., *The Gods of Egyptians*, Vols. 1 and 2, New York, Dover, 1969.

[24b] Budge, Willis E.A., *Amulets and Talismans*, New Hyde Park, University Books, 1961.

[24c] Budge, Willis E.A., *The Bandlet of Righteousness, an Ethiopian Book of the Dead*, London, Luzac and Co., 1929.

[25] Budge, Willis E.A., *The Egyptian Book of the Dead*, New York, Dover, 1967.

[26a] Budge, Willis E.A., *The Papyrus of Ani*, Vols. 1, 2 and 3, New York, G. P. Putman's sons, 1913.

[26b] Budge, Willis E.A., *The Negative Confession*, New York, Bell Publishing Co., 1960.

[26c] Budge, Willis, *The Egyptian Sudan*. Vols I and II, London, Kegan, Trench & Co., 1907.

[27] Cabral, A., *Return to the Source*, New York, Monthly Review Press, 1973.

[28] Cameron, J., *The African Revolution*, New York, Random House, 1961.

[29a] Chinweizu, *The West and the Rest of Us: White Predators, Black Slaves and the African Elite*, New York, Vintage Books, 1975.

[29b] Chomsky, Noam, *Pirates and Emperors: International Terrorism in the Real World*, New York, Claremont Research Publication, 1986.

[29c] Chomsky, Noam, *Profit Over People*, New York, Seven Stories Press, 1999.

[29d] Chomsky, Noam and E. S. Herman, *The Washington Connection and Third World Fascism*, New york, South End Press, 1979.

[29e] Clark, Gordon Haddon, *Thales to Dewey: a History of Philosophy*, Boston, MA, Houghton Mifflin, 1957.

[30] Clark, Rundle R.T., *Myth and Symbol in Ancient Egypt*, New York, Thames and Hudson, 1978.

[31a] Clarke, John H., *Notes on African World Revolution: Africa at the Crossroads*, Trenton, N.J. African World Press, 1991.

[31b] Clarke, John H., *Marcus Garvey and the Vision of Africa*, New York, Random House, 1974.

[31c] Cowan, L.G., *The Dilemmas of African Independence*, New York, Warker and Co., 1964.

[31d] Cromwell, Adelaide M. (ed.), *Dynamics of the African Afro-American Connection: From Dependency to Self-Reliance*, Washington, D.C., Howard University Press, 1987.

[32] Cruse, Harold, *The Crisis of the Negro Intellectual : A History and Analysis of the Failure of Black Leadership*, New York, Quill Press, 1967.

[33a] Danquah, J.B., *Friendship and Empire*, London, Fabian Colonial Bureau, 1949.

[33b] Danquah J.B., *The Akan Doctrine of God: A Fragment of Gold Coast Ethics and Religion*, London, Frank Cass and Co., 1968.

[34] Danquah, J.B., *Ancestors, Heroes and God*, Kibi, Ghana, George Boakie Pub. Co., 1938.

[35a] Davidson, Basil, *The Lost Cities of Africa*, Boston, Little, Brown & Co., 1959.

[35b] Davis, Kortright, *Emancipation Still Comin': Explorations in Caribbean Emancipatory Theology*, New York, Orbis, 1990.

[35c] Dawson, Christopher, *The Making of Europe, Part 1: The Foundations*, New York, The World Pub. Co., 1956.

[35d] De Buck, Adriaan and Alan H. Gardiner (eds.), *The Egyptian Coffin Texts*, Vols. 1-7, Chicago, University of Chicago Press, 1935-1961.

[35f] Descartes, René, *The Philosophical Works of Descartes*, Cambridge, Cambridge University Press, 1931.

[35e] Descartes, René, "Man as Two Substances" in [3c], 1962, pp. 386-402.

[35f] Descartes, René, *Meditations on First Philosophy*, New York, Boobs-Merrill and Co, 1960.

[36] Diop, Cheikh A., *The African Origins of Civilization: Myth or Reality*, Brooklyn, New York, Lawrence Hill, 1974.

[37] Diop, Cheikh A., *The Cultural Unity of Black Africa*, Chicago, Third World Press, 1978

[38] Diop, Cheikh A., *Pre-colonial Black Africa*, Brooklyn, New York, Lawrence Hill, 1987.

[39] Diop, Cheikh A., *Civilization or Barbarism*, Brooklyn, New York, Lawrence Hill, 1991.

[40] Diop, Cheikh A., *Black Africa: The Economic and Cultural Base for a Federated State*, Brooklyn, New York, Lawrence Hill, 197.

[41a] Doane, Thomas W., *Bible Myths and Their Parallels in Other Religions*, New Hyde Park, New York, University Book, 1971.

[41b] Dodson, H. *et al.*, *Jubilee: The Emergence of African-American Culture*, Schomburg Center for Research in Black Culture, New York, New York Public Library, 2002.

[42] Dompere, Kofi K., "On Epistemology and Decision-Choice Rationality" in R. Trapple (ed.), *Cybernetics and System Research*, New York, North Holland, 1982, pp. 219-228.

[43a] Dompere, Kofi K., *Africentricity and African Nationalism*, Langley Park, MD, IAAS Publishers, 1992.

[43b] Dompere, Kofi K., *Cost-Benefit Analysis and the Theory of Fuzzy Decisions: Identification and Measurement Theory* (Series: Studies in Fuzziness and Soft Computing, Vol. 158), Berling, Heidelberg, Springer Verlag, 2004.

[43c] Dompere, Kofi K., *Cost-Benefit Analysis and the Theory of Fuzzy Decisions: Fuzzy Value Theory* (Series: Studies in Fuzziness and Soft Computing, Vol.160), Berling, Heidelberg, Springer Verlag, 2004.

[43d] Dompere, Kofi K., *Polyrhythmicity: Foundations of African Philosophy*, London, Adonis-Abbey Pub., 2006.

[44] Dompere, Kofi K. and M. Ejaz, *Epistemics of Development Economics: Toward a Methodological Critique and Unity*, Westport, CT, Greenwood Press, 1995.

[45a] Douglass, Frederick, "Fourth of July Oration," in [8b], pp. 637-640.

[45b] Dray, W.H., "Historical Understanding as Re-thinking," in [22d], pp. 167-179.

[45c] DuBois, W.E.B., *The Souls of Black Folk*, New York, Feiwcell World Library, 1961 (see also [135b]).

[46] DuBois, W.E.B., *Dust of Dawn: An Essay Toward an Autobiography of a Race Concept*, New York, Harcourt, Brace, 1968

[47] DuBois, W.E.B., *The World and Africa*, New York, International Publishers, 1987.

[48] DuBois, W.E.B., *On Sociology and Black Community*, Chicago, The University of Chicago Press, 1978.

[49a] DuBois, W.E.B., *W.E.B. DuBois Speaks: Speeches and Addresses 1890-1919*, New York, Pathfinder, 1970.

[49b] DuBois, W.E.B., *The Education of Black People; Ten Critiques, 1906-1960* (Ed. H. Aptherker), New York, Monthly Review Press, 1975.

[50] Duchein, R.N., *The Pan-African Manifesto*, Accra, Guinea Press Ltd., 1957.

[51a] Emerson, Rupert, *From Empire to Nation*, Boston, MA, Beacon Press, 1963.

[51b] Engels, Frederick, *Dialectics of Nature*, New York, International Pub., 1940.

[52a] Esedebe, P.O., *Pan-Africanism: The Idea and the Movement 1963-1976*, Washington, D.C., Howard University Press, 1982.

[52b] Ewing, A.C., "A Reaffirmation of Dualism" in [3c], pp. 454-461.

[53a] Fagg, William B., *Nigerian Images, The Splendor of African Sculpture*, New York, Praeger, 1963.

[53b] Fanon, Frantz, *The Wretched of the Earth*, New York, Grove Press Inc., 1963.

[54] Fanon, Frantz, *Toward the African Revolution*, New York, Grove Press Inc., 1964.

[55] Fanon, Frantz, *Black Skin, White Masks*, New York, Dover Press Inc., 1967.

[56a] Faulkner, R.C., *The Ancient Egyptian Coffin Texts*, Warminster, England, Aris and Philips, 1973.

[56b] Faulkner, R.C., *The Ancient Egyptian Pyramid Texts*, Oxford, Clarendon, 1969.

[56c] Fedoseyer, P.N. *et al.*, *Philosophy in USSR: Problems of Dialectical Materialism*, Moscow, Progress Pub., 1977

[56d] Felder, C.H., *Troubling Biblical Waters: Race. Class and Family*, New York, Orbis Press, 1989.

[57a] Foote, George W. and W.P. Bell (eds.), *The Bible Handbook for Freethinkers and Inquiring Christians*, London, The Pioneer Press, 1921.

[57b] Frankford, Henri, *The Intellectual Adventure of Ancient Man*, Chicago, University of Chicago Press, 1957.

[57c]   Frankford, Henri, *Ancient Egyptian Religion: An Interpretation*, New York, Columbia University Press, 1948.

[57d] Fraser, Douglas (ed.), *African Art as Philosophy*, New York, Interbook, 1974.

[57e] Frazer, James G., *The Golden Bough; a Study in Magic and Religion*, Vols. 1 – 13, London, Macmillan, 1911-1936.

[58a] Frobenius, Leo, *The Voice of Africa*, Vols. 1 and 2, London, Hutchinson and Company, 1913.

[58b] Gabre-Medhim, "The Origin of the Trinity in Art and Religion," in [17b], pp. 99-120.

[58c] Gadamer, Hans Georg, *The Beginning of Knowledge* (Translated by Rod Coltman), New York, Continuum, 2001.

[59] Garvey, Marcus, *The Philosophy and Opinions of Marcus Garvey*, Dover, MA, The Majority Press, 1986.

[60a] Geiss, I., *The Pan-African Movement*, London, Methuen Press, 1974.

[60b]   Ghana Ministry of Information and Broadcasting, *Nkrumsh,s Subversion in Africa*, Accra, Ghana, Government Printing Press, 1966.

[60c] Gillings, Richard J., *Mathematics in the Times of the Pharaohs*, London, M.I.T. Press, 1972.

[61] Glover, Ablade E. (ed.), *Adinkra Symbolism*, Accra, Liberty Press Ltd., 1971.

 [62a] Glover, Ablade E., *Linguist Staff Symbolism*, Accra, Liberty Press Ltd., 1971.

 [62b] Glover, Ablade E., *Stools Symbolism*, Accra, Liberty Press, 1971.

[63]   Goma, L. K. H., *The Hard Road to the Transformation of Africa*, Aggrey-Fraser Guggisberg Memorial Lecture 1991, University of Ghana, Legon-Accra, Communication Studies Press, 1991.

[64a] Graves, Robert and Raphael Patai, *Hebrew Myths: The Book of Genesis*, New York, Doubleday and Company, 1964.

[64b] Green, R.H. *et al.*, *Unity or Poverty: the Economics of Pan-Africanism*, Baltimore, MD, Penguin Books, 1968.

[65a] Griaule, M., *Conversations with Ogotemmele*, London, Oxford University Press, 1969.

[65b] Groves, Charles P., *Planting of Christianity in Africa*, Vols.1-4, London, Lutterworth Press, 1948-1958.

[66] Guyer, David, *Ghana and the Ivory Coast*, New York, An Explotion Press, 1970.

[67a] Gyekye, K., *An Essay on African Philosophical Thought: The Akan Conceptual Schemes*, New York, Cambridge University Press, 1987.

[67b] Gyekye, Kwame, *Tradition and Modernity: Philosophical Reflections on African Experience*, New York, Oxford University Press, 1997.

[68a] Hargreaves, J. D., *Prelude to the Partition of West Africa*, London, Macmillan, 1963.

[68b] Harris, Joseph E. (ed.), *Global Dimensions of the African Diaspora*, Washington, D.C., Howard University Press, 1982.

[69a] Hayford, Casely J.E., "African Nationality," in [88], pp. 203-219.

[69b] Hegel, George, *Collected Works*, Berlin, Duncher und Humblot, 1832 – 1845 [also *Science of Logic*, translated by W. H. Johnston and L. G. Struther , London, 1951].

[69c] Hempel, Carl G. and P. Oppenheim, "Studies in the Logic of Explanation," in [22d], pp. 8 – 27.

[69d] Herman, Edward N. and N. Chomsky, *Manufacturing Consent*, New York, Pantheon Books, 1988.

[69e] Hess, R., "Travels of Benjamin of Tudela," *Journal of African History*, Vol. 6, 1965, p. 17 (also in [13] p. 5).

[70a] Hill, Cromwell A., and Martin Kilson (eds.), *Apropos of Africa: Sentiments of Negro American Leaders on Africa From 1800 to the 1950*, London, Frank Cass and Co., 1969.

[70b] Hillard, Asa G. (eds.), *The Teachings of Ptahhotop: The Oldest Book in the World*, Atlanta, Blackwood, 1987.

[70c] Hirschman, A. O., *National Power and the Structure of Foreign Trade*, Berkeley, University of California Press, 1945

[71a] Hochschild, Adam, *King Leopold's Ghost,* New York, Houghton Mifflin Co., 1998.

[71b] Hodgkin, Thomas, "National Movements in West Africa", *The Highway,* February, 1952, pp. 169-175.

[71c] Hoskins, L Halford (ed.) *Aiding Underdeveloped Areas Abroad, The Annals,* Vol. 268, March 1950.

[71d] Hountondji, Paulin J., *African Philosophy: Myth and Reality,* Bloomington, Indiana, Indiana University Press, 1983.

[72a] Hufbauer, G.C. *et al., Economic Sanctions in Support of Foreign Policy Goals,* Washington, D.C., Institute for international Economics, 1983.

[72b] Hughes, L. and M. Meltzer, *A Pictorial History of the Negro (African American),* New York, Crown, 1963.

[72c] Ilyenkov, E.V., *Dialectical Logic: Essays on its History and Theory,* Moscow, Progress Pub. 1977.

[73] Jahn, Janheinz, *Muntu, The New African Culture* (Trans. Marjorie Grene), New York, Grove, 1961.

[74] James, C.L.R., "Kwame Nkrumah: Founder of African Emancipation", *Black World,* Vol. XXI (9), July, 1972.

[75] James, George G.M., *Stolen Legacy,* Newport News, Virginia, United Brothers Communication System, 1989.

[76a] Jeffreys, M.D.W., " The Negro Enigma," *West African Review,* September, 1951.

[76b] Johnson, De Graft J.C., *African Glory,* New York, Praeger, 1955.

[77a] July, R.W., *The Origins of Modern African Thought,* London, Faber, 1967.

[77b] Kant, Immanuel, *On History,* New York, Bobb-Merrill and Co. Inc, 1963.

[78] Karenga, N., *Kwanzaa: Origin, Concepts, Practices,* Los Angeles, Kawaida Publishers, 1988.

[79a] Karenga, N., *The African American Holiday of Kwanzaa,* Los Angeles, University of Sancore Press, 1988.

[79b] Kaunda, K., "Ideology and Humanism", *Pan-African Journal*, Vol.1 (1) 1968, pp. 5-6.

[79c] Kaunda, K., *Humanism in Africa*, London, Longmans, 1966.

[80] Keita, L., " African Philosophical Systems: A Rational Reconstruction," *The Philosophical Forum*, Vol. 9 (23) Winter-Spring, 1977.

[81] Keita, L., " Two Philosophies of African History: Hegel and Diop," *Présence Africaine*, No. 91, Third Quarter, 1974.

[82] Keita, L. " La Philosophie Africaine Contemporaine à la Recherche d'une Méthode," *Diogène*, No. 130, Avril-Juin, 1985.

[83a] Keltie, J.S., *The Partition of Africa*, London, E. Stanford Press, 1893.

[83b] Kenyatta, Jomo, *Harambee!: The Prime Minister of Kenya's Speeches 1963-1964*, New York, Oxford University Press, 1964.

[83c] Kenyatta, Jomo, *Facing Mount Kenya*, New York, Vintage Books, 1965.

[84a] Knight, Richard P., *The Symbolic Language of Ancient Art and Mythology*, New York, J.W. Bouton, 1876.

[84b] Kohn, H., *African Nationalism in the Twentieth Century*, Princeton, New Jersey, Van Nostrand, 1965.

[85] Krafona, Kwesi (ed.), *Organization of African Unity: Essays in Honour of Kwame Nkrumah*, London, Afroword Publishing Co., 1988..

[86] Langley, J. Ayodele, *Pan-Africanism and Nationalism in West Africa 1900-1945: A study in Ideology and Social Classes*, Oxford, Clarendon Press, 1973.

[87] Langley, J.A., "Garveyism and African Nationalism," *Race*, Vol. 11 (2), pp. 157-172.

[88] Langley, Ayo J. (ed.), *Ideologies of Liberation in Black Africa:1856-1970*, London, Rex Collings, 1979.

[89] Legum, C., *Pan-Africanism*, New York, Praeger Pub., 1962.

[90a] Lynch, H.R., *Edward Wilmot Blyden: Pan-Negro Patriot*, London, Oxford University Press, 1967.

[90b] MacEwan, A., *International Economic Instability and U.S. Imperial Decline*, New York, Monthly Review Press, 1990.

[91a] Mandela, Nelson, *The Struggle for My Life*, New York, Pathfinder Press, 1986.

[91b] Martin, Tony, *The Pan-African Connection: From Slavery to Garvey and Beyond,* Dover, MA, The Majority Press, 1983.

[91c] March, J. C., "Bounded Rationality, Ambiguity and Engineering of Choice," *The Bell Journal of Economics*, Vol. 9 (2), 1978

[91d] Mark Cohen, S. *et al.* (eds.), *Readings in Ancient Greek Philosophy: From Thales to Aristotle*, Indianapolis, Indiana, Hackett, 2000.

[92a] Marx, Karl, *Contribution to the Critique of Political Economy*, Chicago, Charles H. Kerr and Co. 1904.

[92b] Marx, Karl, *Economic and Philosophic Manuscripts of 1884,* Moscow, Progress Pub., 1967.

[92c] Marx, Karl, *The Poverty of Philosophy*, New York, International Publishers, 1971.

[93a] Massey, Gerald, *Ancient Egypt: The Light of the World*, Baltimore, MD, Black Classic Press, 1992.

[93b] Massey, Gerald, *A Book of the Beginnings*, Vols. 1-2, London, William and Norgate, 1881.

[93c] Massey, Gerald, *Pyramid Text*, Vols. 1-4, New York, Longmans Green, 1952.

[93d] Massey, Gerald, *The Natural Genesis*, Vols. 1 and 2, Baltimore, MD, Black Classic Press, 1998 (First published 1883).

[93e] Mathews, Wendell, *Basic Symbols and Terms of the Church*, New York, Fortress Press, 1971.

[94] Mazrui, Ali A.A., *Nationalism and New States in Africa from About 1935*, Nairobi, Kenya, Heinemann, 1984

[95] Mazrui, Ali A.A., *toward a Pax Africana*, Chicago, The University of Chicago Press, 1967.

[96] Mbiti, J.S., *African Religions and Philosophy*, New York, Anchor, 1970.

[97] M'buyinga, E., *Pan-Africanism or Neo-Colonialism: The Bankruptcy of the O.A.U.*, London, Zed Press, 1975

[98a] McCray, W.A., *The Black Presence in the Bible*, vols. 1 and 2, Black Light Fellowship, 1990.

[98b] Mendoza, M.G. et al. (eds), *Trade Rules in the Making: Challenges in Regional and Multilateral Negotiations*, Washington, D.C., Brookings Institutions Press, 1999.

[98c] Meyerowitz, Eva L.R., *The Divine Kingship in Ghana and Ancient Egypt*, London, Faber and Faber, 1960.

[98d] Moody, R.A., *Life After Life*, New York, Bantam, 1976.

[99a] Murapa, R., "Nkrumah and Beyond: Osagyefo, Pan-Africanist Leader," *Black World*, Vol. XXI (9), July, 1972.

[99b] Niane, D.T., *Sundiata: An Epic of Old Mali in Transactions*, G. D. Pickett (ed.), London, Longmans, 1965

[99c] Nketia, J.H., *Ethnomusicology in Ghana*, Legon, Ghana, Ghana University Press, 1969.

[100] Nkrumah, Kwame, *Toward Colonial Freedom*, London, Heinemann, 1962 (First Published 1946).

[101] Nkrumah, Kwame, *Ghana, The Autobiography of Kwame Nkrumah*, London, Thomas Nelson and Sons Ltd., 1957.

[102] Nkrumah, Kwame, Speech at the Conference of Independent African States, Accra, April 15, 1958.

[103] Nkrumah, Kwame, *I Speak of Freedom*, London, PANAF Press, 1965.

[104] Nkrumah, Kwame, Speech at the Closing Session of Casablanca Conference, Casablanca, January 7, 1961.

[105] Nkrumah, Kwame, *Africa Must Unite*, New York, International Publishers, 1963.

[106] Nkrumah, Kwame, *Consciencism*, London, Heinemann, 1964.

[107] Nkrumah, Kwame, *Neo-Colonialis: The Last Stage of Imperialism*, New York, International Publishers, 1965.

[108] Nkrumah, Kwame, Speech at the Fourth Afro-Asian Solidarity Conference, Winneba, Ghana, May 10, 1965.

[109] Nkrumah, Kwame, Challenge of the Congo, London, PANAF Press, 1967.

[110] Nkrumah, Kwame, *Axioms*, New York, International Publishers, 1967.

[111] Nkrumah, Kwame, Dark Days of Ghana, London, PA-NAF Press, 1968.

[112] Nkrumah, Kwame, *Handbook of Revolutionary Warfare*, London, PANAF Press, 1968.

[113] Nkrumah, Kwame, *Class Struggle in Africa*, London, PANAF Press, 1970.

[114] Nkrumah, Kwame, *Revolutionary Path*, London, PANAF Press, 1973.

[115] Nkrumah, Kwame, *Rhodesian File*, London, PANAF Press, 1976.

[116]   Nkrumah, Kwame, "Principles of African Studies," Address Delivered at the Time of Official Opening of the Institute for African Studies, University of Ghana, Legon,   *Voice of Africa*, Vol. 3, (3) December, 1963.

[117]   Nsanze, Terence, "In Search of an African Ideology," *Pan-African Journal*, Vol.1 (1), 1968, pp. 27-30.

[118a] Nyerere, Julius K., *Freedom and Unity (Uhuru Na Umoja)*, Nairobi, Oxford University Press, 1966.

[118b]   Nyerere, Julius K., *Freedom and Socialism (Uhuru Na Ujamaa)*, Nairobi, Oxford University Press, 1968.

[119]   Odinga, Oginga, Not Yet Uhuru, New York, Hill and Wang, 1967.

[120]   Ofori-Ansah, Kwaku P., *Symbols of Adinkra Cloth*, Washington, D.C., 1999.

[121]   Ofosu-Appiah, L.H., *Encyclopaedia Africana* Vols. 1 and 2, New York, Reference Publication, Inc., 1977.

[122]   Okwonko, R. L., " The Garvey Movement in British West Africa," *Journal of African History*, Vol. 21, 1980, pp. 105-117.

[123] Olugboji, D., *The United States of Africa and Realpolitik*, Lagos, Nigeria, CMS Press, 1959.

[124a] Omari, Peter T., *Kwame Nkrumah: The Anatomy of African Dictatorship*, New York, Africana Publishers, 1970.

[124b] Organization of African Unity, Lagos Plan of Action for the Economic Development of Africa, 1980 – 2000, Geneva, International Institute for Labour Studies, 1981

[125a] Owusu-Ansah, J.V., *New Versions of the Traditional Motifs*, Kumasi, Ghana, Degraft Graphics and Publications, 1992.

[125b] Ovason, David, *The Secret Architecture of Our National Capital,* New York, HarperCollins, 2000.

[126] Padmore, George, *Pan-Africanism or Communism*, London, Dennis Dobson, 1956.

[127a] Padmore, George, *Africa: Britain's Third Empire*, London, Dennis Dobson, 1949.

[127b] Paterson, Thomas G. (ed.), *Major Problems in American Foreign Policy: Documents and Essays*, Lexington, MA, Heath and Co., 1978.

[127c] Payer, Cheryl, *The Debt Trap: The International Monetary Fund and the Third World*, New York, Monthly Review Press, 1974.

[127d] Perham, M., "Psychology of African Nationalism," *Optima*, Vol. 10, 1960, pp. 27-36.

[128a] Perkins, John, *Confessions of Economic Hit Man*, San Francisco, Berrett-Koehler Pub. Inc., 2004.

[128b] Peters, Jonathan A., *A Dance of Masks: Senghor, Achebe, Soyinka*, Washington, D.C., Three Continents Press, 1978.

[128c] Petrie, William M.F., *The Pyramids and Temples of Gizeh*, London, Field and Tuer, 1885.

[128d] Rattray, Robert S., *Religion and Art in Ashanti*, New York, AMS Press, 1979.

[129a] Resnick, Idrian N., "The University and Development in Africa," *Pan-African Journal*, Vol. 1 (1), 1968, pp. 30-34.

[129b] Robeson, P., "Power of Negro Action," in [8b], pp. 522-532.

[129c] Robinson, E.A.G. (ed.), *Economic Consequences of the Size of Nations*, New York, Macmillan, 1963.

[129d] Rodney, Walter, *How Europe Underdeveloped Africa*, London, Bogle-L'Ouvertune Pub., 1972.

[129e] Roger, Joel A., *Africa's Gift to America: The Afro-American in the Making and Saving of the United States*, New York, J.A. Rogers Publications, 1959.

[130a] Rotberg, R.I., *The Rise of Nationalism in Central Africa: The Making of Malawi and Zambia, 1873-1964*, Cambridge, MA, Harvard University Press, 1965.

[130b] Sampson, G.P. (ed.), *The Role of the World Trade Organization in Global Governance*, New York, United Nations University Press, 2001.

[130c] Seligman, Charles G., *Egypt and Negro Africa: A Study in Divine Kingship*, London, George Routledge and Sons, 1934.

[130d] Seme, Pixley Isaka, "The Regeneration of Africa," in [88], pp. 261-265.

[130e] Serequeberhan, Tsenay, *The Hermeneutics of African Philosophy: Horizon and Discourse*, New York, Routledge, 1994.

[131a] Shorter, A., *African Christian Theology—Adaptation or Incarnation*, New York, Orbis, 1977.

[131b] Shorter, Aylward, W. ., *African Culture and Christian Church: An Introduction to Social and Pastoral Anthropology*, New York, Orbis Books, 1974.

[132] Sithole, N., *African Nationalism*, New York, Oxford University Press, 1969.

[133] Smertin, Y., *Kwame Nkrumah*, New York, International Publishers, 1987.

[134a] Smith, A., *The Geopolitics of Information, How Western Culture Dominates the World*, New York, Oxford University Press, 1980.

[134b] Snowden Jr., Frank M., *Blacks in Antiquity: Ethiopians in the Greco-Roman Experience*, Cambridge, MA, The Belknap Press of Harvard University Press, 1970.

[134c] Steindorff, G. and K.C. Seele, *When Egypt Ruled the East*, Chicago, Chicago University Press, 1957.

[135a] Sundkler, B.G.M., *Bantu Prophets in South Africa*, London, Oxford University Press, 1961.

[135b] Sundquist Eric J. (ed), The Oxford W.E.B. DuBois Reader, New York, Oxford University Press, 1996.

[136] Tambo, Oliver, *Preparing for Power: Oliver Tambo Speaks*, New York, George Braziller Inc., 1988.

[137] Tekyi, K., "Racial Unity," in [88] pp. 402-404.

[138a] Temples, Father Placide, *Bantu Philosophy*, Paris, Présence Africaine, 1959.

[138b] Tennemann, Wilhelm G., *A Manual of the History of Philosophy*, London, H. G. Bohn, 1852.

[138c] Tetteh, M.N., *The Ghana Young Pioneer Movement*, The Institute of African Studies, University of Ghana, Tema, Optimum Design and Publishing Service 1985.

[138d] The Editors, "One Afrikan-Centric Continental Afrikan Government Now", *The Afrikan Truth Magazine* Vol. 1 (2) 1995.

[138e] *The Lost Books of the Bible and Forgotten Book of Eden*, New York, The World Pub. Co., 1963.

[139] *The Spark* Editor, *Some Essential Features of Nkrumaism*, London, PANAF Press, 1975.

[140a] *The Torah: The Five Books of Moses*, Philadelphia, The Jewish Publication of America, 1962.

[140b] Thompson, V. Bakpetu, *Africa and Unity*, London, Longman, 1969.

[141] Thompson, W. S., *Ghana's Foreign Policy 1957-1966*, Princeton, New Jersey, Princeton University Press, 1969.

[142a] Toure, A. Sekou, *Africa on the Move*, London, PANAF Press, 1977.

[142b] United States National Security Council, *Memorandum 200 Study: Implications of World Wide Population Growth for U.S. Security and Overseas Interest*, December 10, 1974, Classified by   h.c. Blaney III, Declassified July 3, 1989, Executive Order 12358.

[142c] United States of America, Department of States, *Foreign Relations of the United States, Vol. XXIV: 190,* Africa, 1964-1968.

[143a] Van Sertima, I., *African Presence in Early Europe,* New Brunswick, New Jersey, Transaction, 1986.

[143b] Van Sertima, I., *They Came Before Columbus: The African Presence in Ancient America,* New York, Random House, 1977.

[144a] Van Sertima, I. (ed.), *Great African Thinkers, Vol. 1, Cheikh Anta Diop,* New Brunswick, New Jersey, Transaction, 1987.

[144b] Van Sertima, I. (ed.), *Blacks in Science,* New Brunswick, N.J., Transaction Publishers, 1998.

[145a] Wallerstein, I., *Africa: The Politics of Unity,* New York, Random House, 1967.

[145b] Wallerstein, I., *Africa: The Politics of Independence,* New York, Random House, 1961.

[146] Walters, Ronald W., "The Afrocentic Concept at Howard University", *New Directions,* Fall, 1990.

[147] Walters, Ronald W., *Pan Africanism in the African Diaspora: An Analysis of Modern Afrocentric Political Movements,* Detroit, Michigan, Wayne State University Press, 1997.

[148a] Watson, R. L., *The Slave Question: Liberty and Property in South Africa,* Hanover, New England, University of New England Press, 1990.

[148b] Weber, Alfred, *History of Philosophy,* New York, Scribner's Sons, 1896.

[149] Welsing, Cress F., *The Isis Papers: The Keys to the Colors,* Chicago, Third World Press, 1991.

[150a] Whitman, Daniel, "The Dual Soul and Double in Africa and West," *Chrysalis: Aspects of African Spirit,* Vol. 3 (1) Spring, 1988, pp. 22-27.

[150b] Williams, Chancellor, *The Destruction of Black Civilization: Great Issues of Race From 4500BC- 2000AD,* Detroit, Harlo Press, 1974

[151a] Williamson, J., *The Lending Policies of the International Monetary Fund,* Washington, D.C., Institute for International Economics, 1982.

[151b]   Wilson, H. S. (ed.), *Origins of West African Nationalism*, London, Macmillan, 1969.

[151c] Witt, R. E., *Isis in the Graeco-Roman World*, Ithaca, N.Y., Cornell University Press, 1971

[152] Woodson, Carter G., *Mis-Education of the Negro*, Washington, D.C., The Associated Publication, 1933.

[153a] Woodson, Carter G., *The African Background*, Washington, D.C., The Associated Press, 1936.

[153b]   World Health Organization, *Interrelationships between Health Programs and Socio-economic Development*, Public Health Paper #49, Geneva, WHO, 1973.

[154] Wright, Richard A. (ed.), *African Philosophy: An Introduction*, New York, University Press of America, 1984

[155] Yesufu, T.M. (ed.), *Creating the African University: Emerging Issues of the 1970s*, Ibadan, Oxford University Press, 1973.

[156] Zartman, William I., *International Relations in the New Africa*, Englewood Cliffs, New Jersey, Prentice-Hall, 1966.

[157]   Zeller, Edward, *Outline of the History of Greek Philosophy*, London, Longmans, Green and Co., 1914.

[158]   Zeller, Edward, *A History of Greek Philosophy From the Earliest Period to the Time of Socrates*, Vols 1 – 2, London, Longmans, Green and Co., 1881.

NAME INDEX

SUBJECT INDEX

N

O

OAS, 128-129
OAU, 62, 97, 105, 200,
OECD, 13, 140, 138
OECD Countries, 137
Oneness, 41-42
Opprisive ideology, 52
Optimal control, 167
Optimal mix,116
Organizational skills, 89-91

P

Pan-African agenda, 2, 168-173
Pan-African foundations, 20
Pan-African imperative, 173, 186-187
Pan-African institutions, 186
Pan-African way, 195
Pan-Africanism, 2-5, 16, 20, 22, 65, 168
Pan-Africanist agenda, 2,168
Pan-Africanist model, 168
Pan-African movement,173
Panama, 78, 138
Parcipitory democracy, 172
Paradigms of thinking, 153
Partition of Africa, 11
Path of slavery, 176
Perceptions, 43-50
Permanent interest, 203
Pharaoh's palace, 28
Pharaonic pristhood system, 9
Phenotypic African, 82
Philippines, 138
Philosophical thought, 191
Pinochet of Chile, 131
Policy game, 122
Policy of preemption, 165
Policy of regimebchange, 165

Policy transmission, 120-124, 167-168
Political decolonization, 69
Political destabilization, 164
Political freedom,169-175
Political fundamentalism, 188
Political hegemony, 198
Political kingdom, 135-136, 169, 175, 185-189, 213
Political oligopolies, 133-146,
Political progress, 32
Political rationality, 205-206
Political structure, 122-129, 170-180,204-210
Political theory, 213-214
Political union, 36, 175, 176, 182, 201, 217
Politico-economic order, 112
Polo Ground , 173
Polyrhythmicity, 2, 30, 108, 149, 156, 199
Polyrhythmics, 30, 156
Population distribution, 114-116
Portuguese, 8, 74
Portugal, 8, 10
Portuguese colonialism, 8
Positive action imperative, 169-174
Post-idependence African
    nationalism, 19-20
Predators, 111-158
Predatory-prey duality, 117
Predatory-prey dynamics game, 115-129,
Predatory-prey process 117-128,
Predatory-prey space, 119
Preferences, 43-49
Pre-idependence African
    nationalism, 19-20
Prescriptive science, 213
Prescriptive theories, 213
Principle of :
    African nationalism, 193
    African personality, 20-23

Q

R

S

T

Y

Z

Ordering this book and other books by Adonis & Abbey Publishers

Wholesale inquiries in the UK and Europe:
Gardners Books Ltd
+44 1323 521777: email: custcare@gardners.com

Wholesale enquiries in USA and Canada
Ingram Book Company (ordering)
+1 800 937 8000 website: www.ingrambookgroup.com

*Online Retail Distribution: All leading online book sellers including www.amazon.co.uk, www.amazon.com, www.barnesandnoble.com

*Shop Retail: Ask any good bookshop or contact our office:
http//:www.Adonis-abbey.com
Phone: +44 (0) 2077 938893

www.ingramcontent.com/pod-product-compliance
Lightning Source LLC
Chambersburg PA
CBHW020342270326
41926CB00007B/283